Transnational Corporations and Economic Development

To Daniel Van Den Bulcke

Transnational Corporations and Economic Development

From Internationalization to Globalization

Edited by

Ludo Cuyvers

and

Filip De Beule

First published in 2005 by
PALGRAVE MACMILLAN
Houndmills, Basingstoke, Hampshire RG21 6XS and
175 Fifth Avenue, New York, N.Y. 10010
Companies and representatives throughout the world.

PALGRAVE MACMILLAN is the global academic imprint of the Palgrave
Macmillan division of St. Martin's Press, LLC and of Palgrave Macmillan Ltd.
Macmillan® is a registered trademark in the United States, United Kingdom
and other countries. Palgrave is a registered trademark in the European
Union and other countries.

ISBN-13: 978–14039–4783–3
ISBN-10: 1–4039–4783–X

This book is printed on paper suitable for recycling and made from fully
managed and sustained forest sources.

A catalogue record for this book is available from the British Library.

Library of Congress Cataloging-in-Publication Data
    Transnational corporations and economic development: from
internationalization to globalization / edited by Ludo Cuyvers and
Filip De Beule.
        p. cm.
    Includes bibliographical references and index.
        ISBN 1–4039–4783–X
        1. International business enterprises. 2. Investments, Foreign.
3. Globalization – Economic aspects. 4. Economic development. 5. International
business enterprises – Developing countries. 6. Investments, Foreign –
Developing countries. 7. Globalization – Economic aspects – Developing
countries. 8. Developing countries – Economic conditions. I. Cuyvers, L.
II. De Beule, Filip, 1970–
HD2755.5.T67919 2005
338.8'8—dc22   2004066397

10 9 8 7 6 5 4 3 2 1
14 13 12 11 10 09 08 07 06 05
Printed and bound in Great Britain by
Antony Rowe Ltd, Chippenham and Eastbourne

Contents

v

List of Tables and Figures

Tables

Figures

List of Abbreviations

AIB	Academy of International Business
CACM	Central American Common Market
CARICOM	Caribbean Community
DITE	Division of Investment Technology and Enterprise Development
EIBA	European International Business Academy
FAO	Food and Agriculture Organization
FCC	Former Communist Countries
FDI	Foreign Direct Investment
FIE	Foreign Invested Enterprise
GATT	General Agreement on Tariffs and Trade
GEP	Group of Eminent Persons
HPAE	High Performing Asian Economies
ICSID	International Centre for the Settlement of Investment Disputes
ILO	International Labour Organization
LDC	Less Developed Country
M&A	Merger and Acquisition
MBO	Management Buy-Out
MERCOSUR	Southern Cone Common Market
NAFTA	North American Free Trade Area
NGO	Non Governmental Organization
NIEO	New International Economic Order
NIC	Newly Industrialized Country
OECD	Organisation for Economic Co-operation and Development
OEM	Original Equipment Manufacturing
R&D	Research and Development
TNC	Transnational Corporation
TNCMD	Transnational Corporations and Management Division
UN	United Nations
UNCTAD	United Nations Conference on Trade and Development
UNCTC	United Nations Centre on Transnational Corporations
UN–DESA	United Nations–Department of Economic and Social Affairs
UNDP	United Nations Development Programme
UNESCO	United Nations Educational Scientific and Cultural Organization.
UNESOC	United Nations Department of Economic and Social Affairs
UNIDO	United Nations Industrial Development Organization

UNIHP	United Nations Intellectual History Project
UNITAR	United Nations Institute for Training and Research
UNRISD	United Nations Research Institute for Social Development
WHO	World Health Organization
WIPO	World Intellectual Property Organization
WTO	World Trade Organization

Preface

This edited research volume serves two purposes. First, the volume investigates the specific role of transnational corporations in the process of economic development. It thereby draws on a long history of academic research and also shows new ways forward. Second, the book honours Professor Daniel Van Den Bulcke on the occasion of his retirement from the Institute of Development Policy and Management at the University of Antwerp, where he worked for more than twenty years. It recognizes his outstanding academic work on transnational corporations, the reason for their existence, the way they function and their role in development.

The chapters in this volume were presented in two different locations, first in Antwerp (Belgium) and also in Ljubljana (Slovenia). The Institute of Development Policy and Management organized a colloquium on the occasion of Professor Van Den Bulcke's retirement on 3 December 2004, while on 6 December, during a special session of the 30th Annual Conference of the European International Business Academy, a second set of essays was presented in honour of Danny Van Den Bulcke as Professor Emeritus. The editors are grateful to the authors who have contributed to the successful completion of this project.

The subtitle of this volume 'From Internationalization to Globalization' is very appropriate as it somehow reflects the stages in the longstanding academic career in the international business field of Daniel (Danny) Van Den Bulcke. Along the lines of the Scandinavian internationalization model his activities started from a local or national interest in international economics and international business and gradually moved into activities abroad, first in some neighbouring countries and later in faraway continents. And as Danny Van Den Bulcke has always been very versatile this internationalization process is evident, not only in his research record, but also in his teaching career and his active participation in academic networking with colleagues and doctoral students from all over the world. Although other aspects of his career might be highlighted, this introduction will be limited to the three aforementioned dimensions.

Research

After a fellowship of six months in Canada as Laureate of the Prize of the Belgian Minister of Foreign Trade and MA studies at the University of Toronto, Danny Van Den Bulcke was asked by Professor Vlerick at the Ghent University to carry out a major research project about 'Foreign Enterprises in the Belgian Manufacturing Industry'. The project was sponsored by the

Belgian Agency of Productivity, an offspring of the Marshall Plan. The study was published in 1971, regretfully only in Dutch and French, and was one of the first thorough researches about the impact of foreign enterprises on a national economy (Van Den Bulcke, 1971). Later on he used the extensive database set up for this project to analyse the newly 'discovered' phenomenon of the transnational corporation (TNC) for his doctoral thesis (Van Den Bulcke, 1974).

When he moved to the University of Limburg in 1972, he continued his research activities at Ghent University and carried out a new major empirical research project that was not only limited to inward FDI in the Belgian manufacturing sector, but also included services and outward FDI.

Danny Van Den Bulcke was one of the very first researchers to tackle new emerging issues in international business–often at the request of international organizations and national institutions–such as disinvestment (European Centre for the Study and Information on Multinationals), employment aspects (International Labour Organization), restructuring (Belgian Ministry of Economics) decision-making (Institute of the Enterprise), regional headquarters (Ministry of Brussels Affairs), coordination centres (Federation of the Coordination Centres), American direct investment in Belgium (American Chamber of Commerce).

When he moved full time to the University of Antwerp in 1985, Danny Van Den Bulcke's research interests spread also in their geographic scope. In a study about the 'Globalization of the Belgian Economy', the so-called Asian connection received most attention because by that time he had found another challenge, namely the study of the Chinese economy. Together with his collaborators he wrote extensively about European direct investment in China, Chinese outward FDI, state-owned enterprises and corporate restructuring, and clusters. During this whole period he maintained his interest in FDI in Belgium, especially American investments, and the activities of MNEs in Europe

Teaching

When Danny Van Den Bulcke got started in his academic career, the subject matter of international business did not yet exist in Belgium and most other European countries. The first courses he was asked to teach at Ghent University dealt with European economic integration and international aspects of economic development. It was only after he left Ghent University and was appointed at the University of Limburg that he was able to launch a special course about issues of FDI and TNCs. During the second half of the 1970s and the first half of the 1980s he was one of the few professors in the Benelux who had been following up on such matters. Consequently he was asked to kick-start such courses in other universities. At one particular time he taught at seven different institutions and universities in Belgium and the Netherlands in three different languages. Although he had taken on some of those courses on the condition that someone would replace him after two or three years he actually taught for more than ten years at the College of Europe in Bruges, and ICHEC in Brussels. During his long career he taught at no less than ten Belgian institutes and universities, including the Universities of Leuven, Ghent, Brussels and of course Antwerp, which at that time consisted of three separate universities.

At the University of Antwerp he was based at the Institute of Development Policy and Management (IDPM) from 1982. He was President of the IDPM from 1996 through 2001. He taught courses on international management, international business and development at five different institutes and/or faculties, including the Faculty of Applied Economics, the Institute of Transport and Maritime Management (ITMMA) and the University of Antwerp Management School (UAMS).

Like his research, his teaching followed the gradual learning route of the Scandinavian internationalization model and spread from Belgium to, first the Netherlands, where during the 1980s he lectured at five Dutch universities, including Tilburg University and Maastricht University. He was also active in Poland. His first intercontinental teaching assignment took place in Indonesia in 1986 (University of Padjadjaran) and would extend later to the Philippines, Thailand, Vietnam, Cambodia, Laos and India. Together with his colleague Ludo Cuyvers, he was responsible for institutional support of 5 universities in South East Asia for the development of the business curriculum and research as part of the development programmes of the Flemish Interuniversity Council.

At the beginning of the 1990s Danny Van Den Bulcke also taught for several years an international management course at the China Europe Management Institute in Beijing, the predecessor of the China Europe International Business School in Shanghai, and later on at the Institute of European Studies in Macau. He was also responsible for institutional development of the Xian Institute of Finance and Economics and also lectured there. His contribution to the educational development of Chinese universities won him the Sanqin Prize of Shaanxi Province in China and the Friendship Prize awarded by the Chinese Ministry of Foreign Experts in 2000.

Other activities

As a student Danny Van Den Bulcke was involved in AIESEC (Association Internationale des Etudiants en Sciences Economiques et Commerciales), an international student organization that provided traineeships for students in companies abroad. He was president of the local Committee of AIESEC and member of the Board of the Belgian National committee. It was in this capacity that he participated in his first international conference in Marseilles, where he was a member of the committee that decided the applications of the universities to become part of AIESEC.

In 1974, together with a number of colleagues from other Belgian universities, he founded the 'International Trade–Invest Institute' (ITI). He was president of ITI from 1981 to 1984. The objective of ITI was to establish more cooperation between academics active in international trade and practitioners both from business and the government by organizing seminars and colloquia. It was on his insistence that issues about FDI and the transfer of technology were incorporated in the mission of ITI.

From the end of the 1970s most of Danny Van Den Bulcke's energy went on two international academic organizations, that is the European International Business Academy (EIBA) and the Academy of International Business (AIB). He was national representative for Belgium for EIBA from 1979 to 2004 and President from 1985 to 1987 and elected Chairman for 2003–6. In AIB he was chapter chair of the Western European Region from 1987 to 2000 and vice president during 2000–2. During his term as AIB vice president he succeeded in bringing India under the AIB umbrella and was instrumental in creating the conditions for getting China into the organisation. Both academic associations recognized Danny Van Den Bulcke's contributions by electing him as a Fellow (AIB in 1992, EIBA in 2003).

A major imprint of Danny Van Den Bulcke's mark is the doctoral tutorials he organized for EIBA from 1987 until 2004. During that period, together with other faculty members, he gave advice and suggestions to about 200 PhD students from all over the world. At the Belgian level he was scientific director of the Intercollegiate Centre of Management Science (ICM) from 1988 to 1993 that awarded doctoral scholarships to promising Belgian students in management. He was a member of doctoral committees in Belgium, the Netherlands, the United Kingdom, Sweden and Australia and member of the Faculty of the Danish Summer Research Institute which was also organized on behalf of PhD students at the beginning of the 1990s. This contribution to the establishment of countless careers cannot be overestimated.

The editors and authors are proud to dedicate this book to Professor Daniel Van Den Bulcke. Fortunately, it is not time to take the 'baton' from him. But it is time to further profit from his advice to improve our knowledge on the study of transnational corporations. As always, we hope he will be present at doctoral tutorials, and at EIBA and AIB Conferences. meanwhile, we may contact him by mail. Even being at those faraway places he frequently travels to, he will respond to provide a wise and well focussed advice. With his very peculiar sense of humour, of course!

LUDO CUYVERS
FILIP DE BEULE

Notes on the Contributors

Peter J. Buckley is Professor of International Business, Director of the Centre for International Business (CIBUL), University of Leeds (UK), and Director of the Institute for Research on Contemporary China. He is a Fellow of the Academy of International Business (AIB), British Academy of Management (BAM) and the Royal Society of Arts (RSA).

John Cantwell is Professor of International Business at Rutgers University (USA), and Professor of International Economics at the University of Reading (UK). He is a former President of EIBA, and is Secretary of the EIBA Fellows.

Ludo Cuyvers is Professor of International Economics at the University of Antwerp (Belgium). He is Chairman of the Department of International Economics, International Management and Diplomacy at the Faculty of Applied Economics and Director of the Centre on ASEAN Studies at the University of Antwerp, and President of the European Institute for Asian Studies.

Daniëlle Cloodt is a doctoral candidate at the Department of Organization and Strategy, Faculty of Economics and Business Administration, at Maastricht University (Netherlands).

Filip De Beule is Assistant Professor at the Institute of Development Policy and Management at the University of Antwerp (Belgium). He is Secretary of the Centre for International Management and Development at the University of Antwerp (CIMDA) and Belgian representative of the European International Business Academy.

James R. Dewald is a Research Associate at the Faculty of Management, University of Calgary (Canada). He has been the CEO of a number of Calgary-based companies and directs the company Stormpilots, an executive coaching and strategic consulting practice.

Philippe De Lombaerde is Research Fellow at the United Nations University–Comparative Regional Integration Studies (UNU–CRIS), Bruges (Belgium), and Associate Professor at the Faculty of Economics, Universidad Nacional de Colombia, Bogotá.

Michel Dumont is Assistant Professor of International Economics at the University of Antwerp (Belgium).

Juan J. Durán is Professor of Business Economics and Finance and Director of the Centro Internacional Carlos V at the Universidad Autónoma de Madrid (Spain). He is a Fellow and former President of EIBA.

John H. Dunning is Emeritus Professor of International Business at the University of Reading (UK), and State of New Jersey Professor of International Business at Rutgers University (USA).

Katherina Glac is a doctoral student at the Wharton School of the University of Pennsylvania (USA).

Erika B. Pedraza Guevara is Analyst at the Departamento Nacional de Planeación Bogotá and Lecturer at the Pontificia Universidad Javeriana, Bogotá (Columbia).

John Hagedoorn is Professor of International Business and Strategy at the Department of Organization and Strategy, Faculty of Economics and Business Administration, at Maastricht University (Netherlands).

Sylvain Plasschaert is Emeritus Professor at the the University of Antwerp and Katolieke Universiteit Leuven (Belgium).

Vitor C. Simões is Professor at the Instituto Superior de Economia e Gestão (ISEG), Universidade Técnica de Lisboa (Portugal). He is a former President of the European International Business Academy (EIBA).

Alain Verbeke is an Associate Fellow at Templeton College, University of Oxford (UK), and holds the McCaig Research Chair in Management at the Haskayne School of Business, University of Calgary (Canada). He is also associated with the Solvay Business School, Vrije Universiteit Brussel (Belgium).

Haiyan Zhang is Research Assistant at the University of Antwerp Management School (UAMS). He is Director of the Euro China Centre at UAMS (Belgium).

1
Transnational Corporations and Economic Development: An Introduction

Ludo Cuyvers and Filip De Beule

This volume, which is dedicated to Prof. Daniel Van Den Bulcke on the occasion of his retirement, contains chapters from scholars on subjects which can all be placed under the heading of international business, transnational corporations (TNCs), developing countries, and economic development. These are also the four pillars that have fascinated Danny Van Den Bulcke for most of his academic career. Although each of these subjects has been studied for many decades and has attracted much attention, there has been a changing perception and stance towards international business and transnational corporations, in particular, and their role in development over the years.

The presence and activities of transnational corporations in general and their role in development and in the developing world, in particular, have been the subject of much controversy. The first serious discussions about the effects of foreign direct investment (FDI) on host countries date back to the late 1950s, when neo-classical economists started to analyse the implications of capital movements in standard models of international trade. Treating foreign direct investment simply as a capital flow between countries, it was shown that foreign investment and trade could be substitutes for each other and that both were welfare-improving. The liberal attitude towards FDI during the immediate postwar period was consistent with this theoretical understanding.

The unreservedly positive picture of the impact of FDI on host-country welfare changed dramatically by the end of the 1960s. Academic literature began to emphasize the connection between market imperfections and foreign investment, with a focus on market structure issues. In line with Hymer (1960), foreign direct investment was often seen as a result of oligopolistic home-country markets, and it was feared that FDI would spread the market imperfections of those industrialized countries to the rest of the world. The earlier discussions about the potential gains from the inflow of foreign capital in terms of tax revenues, economies of scale and external economies gave way to analyses of transfer pricing, uneven development and dependency in

1

general. The scepticism was often based on negative experiences in the late 1960s and early 1970s, with some blatant examples of incorrect behaviour by particular companies, for example inappropriate influence of political decisions, exploitative wages and poor social conditions. As such, until the beginning of the 1980s the general approach to transnational corporations and developing host countries reflected considerable suspicion and reservation.

By the 1980s, there was a general warming of attitudes to FDI not just in the development literature but also on the part of the national governments traditionally strongly hostile to TNCs. There are several explanations for this change of mind. In general terms, there has been a change in terms of government policy, international business theory and company behaviour. First, thanks to the progression in the theory of international production, there was a better understanding and appreciation of the nature and advantages of TNCs in host countries. The connection between market imperfections and the activities and effects of TNCs were better understood and appreciated. TNCs could benefit developing countries because market imperfections generally are more widespread in developing countries than in industrialized countries. In particular, markets for intermediate products such as technology, capital and supporting services are not functioning in many developing countries.

Second, the experience of developing countries – with some exceptionally successful countries drawing heavily on FDI and many regimes restrictive to TNCs doing fairly poorly – led to serious rethinking of their role. Specifically, the failure of import substitution in Latin America and Africa, and autarchic development policies in Mao's China; the apparent success of the more outward-oriented Asian tigers; and the debt crisis of the early 1980s, led to a change in attitudes of governments towards transnationals. The general change in focus was that foreign direct investment was perceived as being an important determinant of economic growth in developing countries.

Due to an increasing globalization of economic activity and the integration of international production and cross-border markets by TNCs, it is also becoming increasingly difficult – if not impossible – for a country to exempt itself from this process. Given this considerable and growing importance of international production to the world economy, the influence of TNCs on the economic future of a country can be huge. Besides, the key ingredients of contemporary economic growth such as created assets – for example technology, human capital, learning experience and organizational competence – are not only becoming more mobile across national boundaries, but are also increasingly housed in transnational organizations and systems.

More generally, there was a renewed faith of most countries in the workings of the market economy, as demonstrated, for example, by the wholesale privatization of state-owned enterprises and the deregulation and liberalization of markets. While these events are being most vividly played out in Central and Eastern Europe and in China, the need to remove structural market distortions has also been acknowledged in many other parts of the world. Host developing countries also improved their capabilities to deal with TNCs. The more advanced ones showed the ability to absorb leading-edge technologies transferred by TNCs, and to even attract R&D facilities. TNCs themselves changed their patterns of behaviour, and many new sources of FDI emerged, reducing the threat of domination by a handful of giant enterprises. The debt crisis – and more recently the Asian financial crisis – also showed that FDI was more stable in difficult periods than other forms of capital inflows, such as bank loans and portfolio investments.

Also, the criteria for judging the success of FDI by host governments have changed over the years in a way which has made for a less confrontational and a more cooperative stance between host countries and foreign investors. More particularly, the emphasis in evaluating inbound TNCs over the past two decades has switched from the direct contributions of foreign affiliates to economic development, to their wider impact on the upgrading of the competitiveness of host-countries' indigenous capabilities and the promotion of their dynamic comparative advantages.

Third, the events outlined above have also affected the attitudes, organizational structures and behaviour of business corporations. Companies have found it increasingly necessary to capture new markets to finance the escalating costs of research and development and marketing activities, both of which are considered essential for preserving or advancing the competitiveness of firms. Firms have been no less pressured to reduce costs and improve the quality of raw materials and components. As a growing number of countries are building their own pools of skilled labour and technological capacity, foreign investors are finding it more and more desirable to diversify geographically their information gathering and learning capabilities.

Finally, in the increasingly more complex global environment, TNCs are being forced to pay more attention to achieving the right balance between the forces making for the global integration of their activities and those requiring them to be more oriented and sensitive to localized supply capabilities, consumer tastes and needs, and new concerns such as ecology and ethical behaviour. This systemic view of TNCs implies very different governance structures than those implemented by traditional foreign investors. Rather than acting as an owner of a number of fairly autonomous, or stand alone, foreign affiliates, each of which is expected to earn the maximum economic rent on the resources invested in it, the systemic TNC aims at managing its portfolio of spatially diffused human and physical assets as a holistic production, financial and marketing system.

In sum, global economic events, particularly those driven by technological advances, and the realignment of economic systems and policies, have fundamentally altered the perception of governments of host countries of how FDI can contribute towards their economic and social goals. These same events have also caused a reappraisal by firms of why and how and, indeed, where they need to engage in international transactions.

Since the late 1990s, scholarly interest in globalization and development has been growing exponentially. This volume picks up on this growing interest, particularly in topics, such as the role of innovation and R&D, clustering, divestment, terrorism and strategy. These topics have gone through an internationalization process themselves to the extent that most issues are no longer thought of on a country-by-country basis but increasingly on a global scale, although some regional patterns persist, which might be due to political, economic or historical reasons, such as regional integration in Europe, North America or Asia. Much recent work thereby disregards former research on the subject. A volume that covers not just the current state of the art, but also tackles its dynamic history, is therefore long overdue. It will also benefit the growing number of young researchers that have not lived this history. However, the volume does not just dwell in the past, but deals with up-to-date topics using the current body of research.

In the following chapter John Dunning reviews and criticizes the attitudes and deliberations of, and actions taken by, the United Nations and its various constituent agencies over the last forty years, with respect to the role of transnational corporations in economic development and international relations. During this period, the world has witnessed a number of exciting and far-reaching changes in the global, political and economic scene, and in the objectives and priorities of its constituent institutions and organizations. These, as Dunning argues, have markedly affected the significance of both TNC-related activity and of foreign direct investment – the main modality by which TNCs engage in such activity – and also of the perceptions by developing countries of the formers' contribution to their economic and social goals. The evolving relationship between TNCs and the rest of society – be it national or global – over the past four decades has emphasized two things above all. Firstly, it has strongly reflected the economic, social and technological context in which the interface has been fashioned. Such a context, which also includes the values of the main stakeholders in the wealth-creating process, is partly exogenous and partly endogenous to the players themselves. Secondly, one should also point to the role of incentive structures and enforcement mechanisms in influencing how changes in the external economic environment may affect the role of TNCs and their contribution on national economic goals, an aspect which has been underplayed by both scholars and practitioners, including the UN. Such institutions which range from formal rules and regulations to informal norms, conventions, moral suasion and social mores, embrace both top-down sanctions and incentives to bottom-up spontaneous ideas and actions on individual and corporate stakeholders. It is the network of private and public institutions – the institutional matrix of societies – which, along with the resources, capabilities and markets possessed or accessed by them, will determine both the objectives of their constituents, and the way they are advanced. Underpinning and influencing these institutions are values, which, in turn, reflect the belief systems of the individuals and organizations implementing them. John Dunning points out that the way in which the multiple stakeholders in the national and global economy prepare or adapt their institutions and enforcement mechanisms to external technological and economic events will, in the end, determine how and in what way TNC activity can best serve the interests of the people in the world. He believes it is incumbent on the UN to give more attention to examining the institutions and belief systems underpinning and influencing the actions of TNCs or of governments. As the social and economic aspects of TNC-related activities are too intertwined to be considered independently, a holistic and integrated institutional approach is needed, and centralized modern governance has to be integrated with more decentralized modes.

In Chapter 3, Vitor Simões endeavours to show that international disinvestment analysis requires, on the one hand, the clarification and 'fine-tuning' of the concept of disinvestment and, on the other, the convergence of a set of explanatory factors, often intertwined. He is doing both. The suggested framework also has implications for host-country economic policy. With regard to explanatory factors, it is convincingly argued that four dimensions are relevant. While each dimension may be seen in isolation, their interrelationships should be analysed, which may take different patterns for each specific disinvestment case. The analytical tools of sectoral and territorial context are seen as of paramount importance to understand disinvestments.

Simões suggests a co-evolution between local economic conditions and subsidiaries' characteristics and competences, and he points out that the subsidiary is not an innocent player or a pawn that passively suffers the consequences of decisions taken at headquarters level; sectoral vicissitudes or host-country policy changes and consequently subsidiary strategy, competences, dynamics and initiative cannot be omitted when studying disinvestment processes. Under the condition that its negative social effects are well-managed and that it goes together with economic restructuring and upgrading in the host country, disinvestments may even have a positive side. It is, however, the key responsibility of the policy-makers in the host countries to prevent disinvestments and to promote the relevance of the foreign subsidiaries for the TNC network.

In the fourth chapter, Sylvain Plasschaert investigates company profit taxation in the European Union as a key incentive in the promotion of foreign direct investment. Although the 25 member states of the European Union are engaged in an evolving sequence of further economic integration, in the field of corporate taxation several national tax obstacles still impede the smooth operation of a level playing field. The European Treaties mandate no harmonization in the field of direct taxation. Plasschaert critically evaluates the rationales that are behind the proposals for comprehensive or 'holistic' formats of company taxation in the EU, and also comments on the issue of which types of TNCs should be eligible to holistic schemes.

The author argues that the adoption of a fiscal group concept, even if limited to the definition of the taxable base and not extending to the tax rate, would achieve a significant reduction in compliance costs not only for TNCs but also for the national tax administrations. Moreover, such adoption would bring company profit taxation in line with the ever-increasing pan-European ambitions of firms in EU-member countries.

Chapter 5 by Alain Verbeke and James R. Dewald is entitled 'Managerial Responses to Borderless Risk'. The authors point out that with globalization, many risks that TNCs and internationally operating businesses are confronted with have also become global. In an innovative way, they analyse the impact of the Al-Qaeda September 11 attacks on the United States, and the subsequent changes in public policy, from the perspective of the international business manager. From this angle, these events mark the shift from a world of geographically well-defined risk towards a world of borderless risk. A new framework is developed and presented which can be helpful to the international manager to consider future strategies for resource protection within a new world of borderless risk. Verbeke and Dewald developed their conceptual framework in close collaboration and thorough discussion with four well-known top managers of large TNCs, with headquarters in Canada. They conclude that managerial attention needs to be devoted to the development of new firm-specific assets in a variety of resource areas. Senior managers in TNCs should engage in formal assessments of the risks faced by each of the resource areas such as raw materials and intermediate products, finished products, fixed assets, information, human resources and external relations, in particular government and community-based relations, human-resources management and protection of finished products.

Chapter 6 by John Cantwell and Katherina Glac is concerned with locational clustering and its relevance for economic development. Their analysis starts with the observation that while overall the integration of activity between countries has become closer, there is an increasing concentration of some specialized knowledge-based functions within selected sub-national regions. These factors, taken together, have contributed to a revival of the interest in location as a major topic in the international business literature, because both TNCs and host regions have recognized the importance of location as a potential source of competitive advantage that helps to ensure development and growth. The authors offer an overview of the work in this area to date, outlining the interactions between location characteristics and TNC strategy and activity, as well as the underlying forces that shape these interactions, with specific emphasis on the developmental effects.

They point out that the globalization process not only brought a greater dispersion of certain kinds of economic activity, but also that 'sticky places within such slippery space' (Markusen, 1996) are emerging especially with respect to knowledge-intensive activities. These developments evidently make the location decision increasingly important, which has led in turn to a rising awareness by TNCs of locational advantages as a competitiveness enhancing and sustaining factor. Therefore, the understanding of the processes and phenomena involved in a variety of locational types has become fundamental. This is even more important if it is realized that the interplay between TNC activity and the development of a host economy is complex and does not always result in a virtuous cycle, thus preventing the use of one-size-fits-all recommendations and approaches. Cantwell and Glac argue that a careful analysis of the individual characteristics of a place, its history, its resource availabilities and capabilities is crucial if the host-country authorities and policy-makers want the locational benefits and dynamics to lead to economic development. However, even then there is no guarantee for success.

Chapter 7 by Daniëlle Cloodt and John Hagedoorn presents an analysis of major historical trends and sectoral patterns in international R&D partnering between independent companies from 1971 to 2000, through formal agreements (for example contractual agreements and joint ventures). The ongoing process of globalization has increased global competition and enlarged the complexity of technology, together with the risks and costs of innovation. This in turn has exercised a strong impact on the growth of these international inter-firm R&D partnerships, particularly in technology-intensive industries. The authors focus on differences between the developed economies, newly industrialized countries, less-developed countries, and in particular the East European former communist countries. The opening of the markets of the latter group has evidently expanded the scope for international partnerships to China, Eastern Europe and the former Soviet Union. Using the MERIT-CATI database, Cloodt and Hagedoorn study patterns in R&D partnerships in several industries, in different regions of the world over the above-mentioned period of time. They find that international R&D partnerships are dominated by companies from the developed economies, particularly from the USA. Companies from OECD countries participate in nearly 99 per cent of all the international R&D partnerships, and more than 90 per cent of these partnerships are within the OECD. They also find that some 85 per cent of the recently established international partnerships are of a contractual nature, so that today the former dominant position of joint ventures in inter-firm R&D agreements is almost completely lost.

Chapter 8 by Ludo Cuyvers and Michel Dumont looks into the determinants of the East Asian economic growth performance. Unlike the still much-debated issue of the role of liberalization versus government intervention, there is somewhat more unanimity in the profession as to the role of international technology transfer and spillovers. The obvious question is then, why the East and Southeast Asian economies, in contrast with so many other developing countries, benefited from these spillovers. The authors point to institutional factors and policy instruments that enhance the absorptive capacity of firms (for example investment in education and human capital).

In the empirical part of the chapter, Cuyvers and Dumont use a global vector error-correction model, which takes intra-regional dependence between the countries considered into account. Their results suggest that exports have led economic growth in Hong Kong, Indonesia, South Korea and Malaysia with only a significant positive feedback of growth on exports for Hong Kong. On the other hand, imports had a positive impact on growth in the Asian tiger countries Hong Kong and South Korea but a significant negative effect on growth in Indonesia and Malaysia. The authors are inclined to look at the latter finding as indicating the impact of 'export enclaves', that is foreign-owned plants producing more for exports than for the domestic market; because of lacking backward linkages, the production in these enclaves contributes little to domestic technological development and economic growth. Another important finding is that regional economic growth had a significant long-term effect on domestic growth, which lends support to the 'flying-geese' theory of economic development. This theory states that the industrialization process was transmitted from Japan to the backyard Asian tiger economies, and in a later stage to the 'next tier' newly industrializing countries (NICs) (which the authors call 'pussycat countries'). Although this transmission process is said to be triggered by FDI, the authors are unable to test this, due to lacking data.

In Chapter 9, Haiyan Zhang investigates how FDI contributed to the development of the electronics industry in China. The author analyses aggregated firm-level data to emphasize the agglomeration economies in the Chinese electronics industry on the one hand, and to assess the effects of FDI on the geographical agglomeration of Chinese electronics industries on the other hand. From the statistical and geographical mapping analysis, Zhang draws several conclusions. First of all, agglomeration has significantly contributed to labour productivity and industrial growth, especially in the regions of China where there is a strong concentration of FDI, thus confirming the finding of previous studies on the impact of industrial clusters on productivity. Yet, Zhang points out that the positive impact of industrial clusters on the productivity and regional growth of the electronics industry in China seems closely related to FDI, which has improved the productivity, either through the higher productivity of foreign plants, or through strategic original equipment manufacturing (OEM) in foreign joint ventures which improves productivity of its manufacturing operations in order to reduce costs.

Secondly, the agglomeration trends in China's electronics industry are positively related to the regional competitiveness in the international market, which is measured by the export ratio of its industry. The results show that the regions with stronger agglomeration tend to have higher export ratios, meaning that China's electronics manufacturing clusters are highly integrated into global production networks, especially in the coastal regions where foreign subsidiaries and domestic subcontracting firms are clustered in export processing zones for low-cost outsourcing manufacturing.

Thirdly, the findings of Zhang's research show that both the agglomeration and FDI are negatively related to local competition. This is clearly in contrast with the findings of the existing literature, which assumed that agglomeration as well as FDI tends to favour local competition and that the high competitive pressure in a cluster and the associated push to innovate provide the dynamic advantage of the cluster.

Finally, it is shown that the concentration of FDI and the geographical agglomeration are positively related to the innovation capability of the industry. Internationally integrated networks within the firm may lead to an improvement of innovation capacity both of the TNC and of the host location. Inter-firm networks, established between TNC subsidiaries and local firms may, in addition, amplify the advantages of geographical agglomeration in some particular lines of technological development, reinforcing the existing sectoral pattern of technological specialization of local systems. Therefore the innovative activity tends to cluster due to knowledge spillovers.

Chapter 10 by Philippe De Lombaerde and Erika Pedraza Guevara is devoted to FDI productivity spillovers in the Andean region. The authors start from the observation from the empirical literature that observed spillover effects of foreign direct investment on the activity and efficiency of domestic firms experienced a major qualitative step forward thanks to the availability and recent incorporation of firm-level data, were often not as expected. The authors present new results on productivity spillovers using Colombian manufacturing firm-level panel data for the 1995–2000 period. They test (1) whether foreign ownership is associated with an increase in productivity at the plant level, and (2) whether foreign ownership in an industrial sector affects the productivity of domestically owned firms in the same industry. Their results show no or very weak (and not significant) spillover effects. If positive effects on the productivity of domestic firms are found at all, they are apparently completely absorbed by the most productive domestic firms.

As privatizations have widened the scope of TNCs regarding geographical range and target sectors, such as energy, communications, transport and basic industries, by bringing about closer international integration of highly regulated industries and, particularly, by directing FDI towards less-developed countries, Juan Duran sets himself the task in Chapter 11 of addressing the potential of privatizations for the internationalization of companies. He examines the impact of privatizations on FDI. Duran outlines new scenarios that emerged over the last two decades, and describes the relationship between privatizations and corporate internationalization. Against this background, large Spanish public operators in telecommunications, electricity, fuel, gas, air transport and banking were privatized from the late 1980s and became TNCs themselves by acquiring other privatized businesses in host countries, especially in Latin America. The impact that the privatizations have had on the level of economic development according to the investment development path are also discussed.

Finally, in Chapter 12, Peter Buckley and Filip De Beule examine the past, present and future direction of research in international business and suggest ways forward. These include the various aspects of globalization, geography and location, international mergers and acquisitions, restructuring and new international institutions. This research agenda clearly appears to be fully in line with much of the research that Daniel Van Den Bulcke has contributed to during his academic career, both as an individual and as a team member.

2
The United Nations and Transnational Corporations: A Personal Assessment

*John H. Dunning**

Introduction

This chapter reviews and critiques the attitudes and deliberations of, and actions taken by, the United Nations and its various constituent agencies over the last forty years or so, with respect to the role of transnational corporations (TNCs)[1] in economic development and international relations. This period has seen a number of exciting and far-reaching changes in the global, political and economic scenarios, and in the objectives and priorities of its constituent institutions and organizations. These, as I shall seek to show, have markedly affected the significance of both TNC-related activity and of foreign direct investment (FDI) – the main modality by which such corporations engage in such activity – and also of the perceptions by developing countries of the formers' contribution to their economic and social goals.

This, of course, is a vast and complex subject, and a history of the interface between the UN and TNCs and their foreign affiliates is currently being prepared.[2] This chapter presents a more personal view of one who has worked closely with the UN and several of its agencies since the late 1960s. I should, however, first observe that over the last two decades Danny Van Den Bulcke has closely followed the activities of the United Nations with regard to TNCs. Indeed, in 1979, he co-authored an article about TNCs and World Development with K. Sahlgren, the first Director of the UN Centre on Transnational Corporations. In 1982 Danny was asked to write a number of reports about Belgian transnationals with investments in developing countries. Each year, he also presents the World Investment Report at an international press conference in Brussels on behalf of UNCTAD.

The chapter takes a chronological perspective. In the next section I trace the gradual disillusionment of many host countries, and particularly developing countries, in the late 1960s and 1970s, about the contribution of inbound direct investment to their economic needs and social objectives. Most noticeably, there was a growing perception among ex-colonial economies that they were exchanging one form of metropolitan imperialism for another (Gray, 1972).

This was followed, in the mid and later 1980s, by a switch to a more positive stance by the UN and most of its agencies towards TNCs. This largely reflected the renaissance of market-oriented approaches to macro-economic management, the collapse of communism in Central and Eastern Europe, and the opening up of China to all forms of international commerce. The third phase dates from the early 1990s to the present day, and mirrors the impact of globalization and advances in communications and transport technologies both on the character and significance of international business activity, and on its impact on national and international economic goals – and particularly on such issues as the alleviation of poverty, the pursuit of social justice, regional economic integration, national competitiveness, cross-border mergers and acquisitions (M&As), the environment, and the burgeoning of the Chinese and Indian economies.

In each of these three phases I have observed – and sometimes been part of – the deliberations of the staff and consultants of the UN and its agencies[3] about how best TNCs and their global networks might be used to promote the various economic and social objectives of both home and host countries; and, in particular, how national governments, and increasingly over the years supranational entities, might appropriately adjust their domestic and international policies as a result of these developments.

The 1960s to the mid-1970s: from enthusiasm about TNCs to scepticism

My first association with the UN dates back to 1968 when I was asked to prepare a report for UNCTAD on the extent and pattern of UK direct investment in less-developed countries (LDCs). This was followed, six years later, by a request, again by UNCTAD, to undertake one of the first field surveys into the trade and balance of payments effects of the activities of British TNCs in developing countries in 1972.[4]

This latter project for UNCTAD coincided with two others. One was by Ray Vernon on the (alleged) restrictive practices of US TNCs, which operated affiliates in LDCs, and their impact on trade, industrial concentration and local suppliers (UNCTAD, 1970). The other was a major empirical investigation – again sponsored by UNCTAD – by Paul Streeten, Lionel Needleman and Sanjaya Lall, on the income and balance of payments effects of inbound direct investment on five developing countries (UNCTAD, 1973; Streeten and Lall, 1977).

Indeed, it was UNCTAD, and to a lesser extent UNIDO, UNITAR and the ILO, that were the UN agencies initially the most active in identifying the unique characteristics of TNCs, and their contribution to economic development. In the 1960s, FDI was generally welcomed as a tool for restructuring and upgrading the indigenous resources and capabilities of recipient countries. Most noteworthy, in 1964 UNCTAD I adopted five sets of recommendations with respect to inbound FDI, and two of these are particularly worth reiterating. The first was directed to capital exporting countries that were urged to 'take all appropriate steps to encourage the flow of private investments to developing countries' (UNCTAD, 1964: 49). Examples included tax exemptions or reductions and giving investment guarantees to private investors. The second was addressed to capital importing countries who were encouraged to take 'all appropriate steps to provide favourable conditions for direct private investment including the setting up of investment bureaux and investment advisory services' (UNCTAD, 1964: 49–50).

The other three sets of recommendations were in a similar vein. In the mid-1960s there was little sign of an adversarial relationship between national governments and TNCs on any financial obligations or performance requirements expected of the latter by the former – or, indeed, any suggestion that the strategies of foreign investors might not accord with the economic and social objectives of host developing countries. This positive (if somewhat sanguine) approach was further endorsed in 1968 in a report by the UN Department of Economic and Social Affairs (UN, 1968). After stressing the current 'inadequate' level of inward FDI 'in terms of what most developing countries which are interested in developing their private sector need and want' (p. 1) the report then sought to identify various ways that developing countries could better market their domestic attractions to foreign TNCs. These included more active and systematic investment-promotion schemes, the upgrading of domestic resources and capabilities (to facilitate joint ventures), and the provision of assurances to foreign investors against non-business risks, for example expropriations and limitations on capital repatriation, and the provision of appropriate tax incentives (UN, 1968: 13–28).

Disillusionment and confrontation

Between the late 1960s and the mid-1970s, however, the 'sweetness and light' of the 1960s had largely disappeared, and a much more critical stance by developing countries towards FDI had emerged and accelerated.

There were several reasons for this. First the learning experience of several developing countries about the effects of FDI in the 1960s suggested that, not only was its beneficial impact very unevenly spread, but that the large and powerful TNCs, particularly in resource-based sectors, were (perceived to be) gaining more than their equitable share of the benefits of their foreign value-adding activities. Second, there was accumulating evidence that some TNCs were engaging in unacceptable business practices, such as transfer-pricing manipulation and export restrictions (UNCTAD, 1972). Third, some developing countries, which had recently gained political autonomy, saw any suspicion of a dominant share of local output by metropolitan TNCs as a form of economic imperialism, and as a possible threat to their newly found sovereignty; India was a prime example of such a country. Fourth, on these and other issues (for example to do with employment and training, transfer of technology, research and development (R&D), the environment, local linkages, and so on), an increasing body of scholarly work was suggesting the goals and strategies of foreign TNCs towards their foreign affiliates was not always coincidental with those of the countries host to these affiliates.

The late 1960s and early 1970s saw a plethora of studies – mostly undertaken by UNCTAD and academia – on some of the downsides of the operational practices of TNCs. Foremost among these – and as mentioned above – were the questionable TNC strategies with respect to intellectual property rights, allocation of export markets[5] and cross-border intra-firm transactions. While most of these concerns were voiced by, or on behalf of, developing countries, there was no less disquiet in some developed countries. It was, for example, Jacques Servan Schreiber, a French scholar and journalist who first questioned the wisdom of allowing US TNCs unrestricted participation in Europe's technologically advanced sectors (Servan Schreiber, 1968); while in Canada, Australia and New Zealand – countries in which foreign TNCs often controlled more than one-half of the output of their resource and manufacturing sectors – the conventional wisdom of the benefits of inbound FDI, as earlier identified by scholars such as Ed Safarian (1966), Donald Brash (1969), R.S. Deane (1970) – was being increasingly questioned.[6] It was under the influence of studies such as these that Danny Van Den Bulcke (1971) also carried out a major survey about TNCs in Belgium. In other developed countries, notably the UK and the USA, the focus of interest was more on the impact of outward FDI on domestic employment and the balance of payments (Reddaway *et al.*, 1968; Hawkins, 1972; Hufbauer and Adler, 1968). In Asia, Japan was perhaps the most protectionist developed country of all, as, for most of the 1960s and 1970s, it virtually denied the opportunity to foreign investors to help reconstruct its industrial infrastructure and upgrade its technological capacity.[7]

Enter the USA!

But, perhaps, of all of the attitudes by developed countries which were to exert the most profound influence on the future work of the UN on FDI and TNCs, the most critical was that expressed by the USA – allegedly (at the time) the most market-oriented country in the world. By 1967, US TNCs accounted for over one-half of the stock of outbound FDI (Dunning, 1993). In the 1960s, scholars, particularly those teaching in American business schools, were actively exploring the implications of US outbound FDI for the US economy. One of the first volumes setting out the results of this research was entitled *US Private and Government Investment Abroad*. It was published in 1962, and edited by Raymond Mikesell. In this study, several of the critical issues, later to be highlighted in the public arena, were examined by scholars such as Douglass North, Jack Behrman and Paul Simpson.

In 1969, the US Department of State's Bureau of Intelligence and Research and the Policy Planning Council convened a conference in Washington DC to discuss some of the policy issues emerging from the growing importance of the TNCs in the world economy. It was attended by the leading academics of the day, notably Ray Vernon and Charles Kindleberger, business executives and

US government officials. The conference both recognized the growing importance of FDI as a means of cross-border capital and technology transfer, and as a generator of, or substitute for, trade. It also accepted the USA's responsibility to assist developing countries in their development process. It identified many of the costs and benefits of outbound FDI, later evaluated in more detail in the academic literature (Dunning, 1993; Caves, 1996; UN, v.d.). It also enunciated the various tensions which might arise between TNCs and the governments which were host to their affiliates.[8] However, perhaps the key recommendation of the conference was for the establishment of a multilateral mechanism to reconcile and, where possible, harmonize national economic regulations and policies towards FDI and TNCs.[9] This, indeed, was the starting point for a bevy of new institutions initiated by firms, governments and supranational entities in the 1970s and 1980s. These were to range from guidelines and codes of conduct to binding bilateral and multinational investment agreements.[10]

In the same year, the US government set up a federally funded investment insurance agency (the Overseas Private Investment Agency) to help promote more private enterprise in those developing countries friendly to free-market policies.

Yet, the real lightning rod to an enhanced UN involvement on TNC-related issues in the 1970s was a combination of the Watergate scandal and a series of allegations with respect to the malpractices of a number of large and influential US TNCs, identified *inter alia* by the US Securities and Exchange Commission. Such allegations culminated in the interference by some US corporations in the political affairs of developing countries. This prompted the setting up of the Church Committee to investigate the role of US TNCs, and the interface between their global objectives and strategies and American foreign policy; and, in the latter part of 1970, more specifically, to an examination of all the documents relating to ITT's operations in Chile. It also led to the enactment of the Foreign Corrupt Practices Act (1976), the purpose of which was to minimize corporate malfeasance, bribery, corruption and other kinds of unethical behaviour.

The group of eminent persons

The results of the Church enquiry and its hearings, which lasted three years, were contained in no less than 17 volumes.[11] Together with the recommendations of the Securities and Exchange Commission, the disquiet increasingly expressed by many developed and developing governments about the less-desirable aspects of TNC activity, and a growing volume of scholarly research on the global reach and power of large US and European TNCs, sparked a new initiative by the UN. In 1972, the Economic and Social Council (ECOSOC), on the recommendation of Phillipe de Seynes – an Under-Secretary General and backed by several delegations to the UN, including that of the Chilean government – requested the Secretary General to set up a Group of Eminent Persons (GEP) to advise the Council on the present role of TNCs in economic development and their impact on international relations.

In its deliberations, the group, which consisted of 20 individuals[12] drawn from academia, business and politics, was guided by a report prepared by the Department of Economic and Social Affairs (DESA) under the direction of the economist Jacob Mozak. In this project, Mozak drew heavily on the advice and writings of scholars at Harvard and Pennsylvania Universities.[13] Among its proposals – subsequently endorsed by the GEP – was the setting up of a permanent UN commission on TNCs (supported by a secretariat) to collect data and undertake research on these activities and give advice to host (developing) countries of how they might best promote their economic and social goals.

This is not the place to detail or comment on the proceedings and findings of the GEP; these have been dealt with elsewhere[14] and a critique of them will appear in the volume which Tagi Sagafi-Nejad is preparing for the UN Intellectual History project (UNIHP).[15] The points we wish to emphasize here are three. The first is that as a result of the GEP's work, a huge amount of information on TNCs, and the opinions and views of those most knowledgeable about their strategies and likely impact on the economies in which they operated, came to light.[16] The second is that from 1974 onwards, the Commission and the Centre on Transnational Corporations (UNCTC) became the focal entity of the UN for its work on TNCs; although, in trade and development matters, UNCTAD continued to undertake research and offer policy advice, as did (and still does) the International Labour Office (ILO) on employment and labour issues, the World Health Organization (WHO) on health issues, and the Food and Agriculture Organization (FAO) on food and agricultural issues.

The third observation is that, from the start, it was envisaged by the UN that the new organizational entities concerned with the activities of TNCs would be an integral part of the *New International Order* and the *Charter for Economic Rights and Duties* initiated by the UN General Assembly in the 1970s; and, more generally, to support the North/South agenda which exercised the minds of so many UN agencies at this time.[17] *Inter alia*, this was because such organizations and their underlying values and belief systems were becoming an increasingly significant force in shaping economic activity and patterns of development throughout the world; and of cross-border intra and inter-organizational relations.

In 1975, in addition to the work of the Commission and Centre on Transnationals, various other initiatives on FDI-related issues were implemented by the UN and its agencies. In May of that year, the UNCTC set out a three-pronged approach which was intended to ensure TNC strategy and behaviour was kept in line with the interests of developing countries. This included the drawing up of a code of conduct relating to the rights and duties of investing and recipient countries and of TNCs; the setting down of terms and conditions in respect of the entry, operations and exit of TNCs and their subsidiaries; and the requirement that adequate information and publicity should be given in respect of both government regulations and corporate goals and performance. In its July 1975 session, ECOSOC recommended the establishment of liaison and support units in each of the UN's five regional commissions to assist the work of the Commission on TNCs. In the Fall of that year, UNDP offered the first of a series of training courses for government officials from developing countries on TNC-related issues. These embraced such items as the costs and benefits of FDI, taxation, negotiation techniques and criteria by which TNC-related projects might be judged. At the same time, UNCTAD continued to work on restrictive business practices, as did ILO on employment-related matters and UNIDO on entrepreneurship and technological development.

The Commission and the UNCTC

After my own participation in the GEP, I became a frequent consultant to UNCTC serving, in turn, three Assistant Secretary Generals – viz. Klaus Sahlgren, Sydney Dell and Peter Hansen. During the later 1970s and 1980s, the work of the Commission and the Centre focused on four main areas. The first was the assembling of a databank on the extent, geographical origin and spread, and sectoral characteristics of TNCs and of FDI. In this, the Centre was aided by some earlier work by John Stopford, Klaus Haberich, Bob Pearce, John Cantwell and myself. Drawing on *Fortune* data, a series of studies analysing the growth and internationalization of the world's leading industrial enterprises were published by Dunning and Pearce (1969, 1975, 1981, 1985). In 1980, a Directory which profiled each of the 500 largest industrial TNCs was published by Macmillan (Stopford, Dunning and Haberich, 1980); while, in 1987, a statistical analysis of the extent, pattern and ownership of both inward and outward FDI for some 80 countries was also published by Macmillan (Dunning and Cantwell, 1987).

Over the last 20 years or so, the UNCTC – and later UNCTAD[18] – has considerably broadened and refined its statistical base on the economic and legal characteristics of TNCs and FDI; and, today, the Division of Investment, Technology and Enterprise Development (DITE) (at UNCTAD) is widely accepted as the most authoritative world source of such data – albeit that most of these are obtained directly from national governments and/or individual corporations.

Second, UNCTC (and UNCTAD still does today) undertook and/or commissioned substantive research studies into all aspects of TNC activity, and their impact on economic and social development. Throughout the period it was based in the USA, UNCTC produced two major surveys of the characteristics and significance of TNC activity (UN, 1978, 1983) and no less than 55 specialized reports on particular FDI-related issues, for example trade and the balance of payments, technology transfer, trans-border data flows, transfer pricing, linkages and negotiating procedures, and on particular sectors, for example automobiles, pharmaceuticals, petroleum, agricultural machinery, food, beverages, tourism and accounting standards. It also played a critical part in the hearings on the role of TNCs in South Africa; in the

WHO's studies on the role of TNCs in fostering the sale of tobacco products and the marketing of breast-milk substitutes; and UNITAR's training and research programmes on the character of technology transfer by TNCs, and its impact on economic development.[19]

As the years passed, I sensed that there was a very gradual shift in the attitudes of both the Commission and the UNCTC towards TNCs, and the part they might, should, play in promoting global and national economic objectives. Certainly by the mid-1980s there was a less aggressive or adversarial approach towards assessing the benefits of inbound FDI, and some of the reasons for this will be given later. However, as far as the staff of the UNCTC and its advisors were concerned, I personally welcomed not only a better appreciation of the unique characteristics of TNCs,[20] but also a realization that to get the best out of them and/or their affiliates, and to fully exploit the access to global markets and supply chains they offered, it might be necessary for the national administrations of host countries to reconfigure their own policies and strategies – both at a macro and microeconomic level.

Third – and this to my mind was the UNCTC's most distinctive contribution to our understanding about the interface between the economic strategies of the TNCs and the national and social regimes in which they were embedded – was the advice it offered to developing country governments on the ways and means of attracting the *right* amount and kind of inbound FDI, and in ensuring that it upgraded their indigenous resources, capabilities and institutions in the most efficient and socially acceptable way. A large number of training sessions were held for government officials, and visits and seminars were organized by UNCTC to individual developing countries to discuss matters pertinent to their own particular interests. In these tasks, a large number of external legal, economic and business consultants were used. But, once again, I would stress that in the 1970s at least, the UNCTC – though less so than some of their advisers! – saw its brief as (a) providing national governments with information about TNCs and their likely impact on economic and social welfare; and (b) advising the former on negotiation, bargaining and evaluatory procedures, and not on whether or how inbound FDI might require a reorientation of their own domestic economic policies.

Fourth, and in pursuance of the recommendation of the GEP and the UN's endorsement of its findings in 1975 (earlier described), the UNCTC almost immediately started work in devising a comprehensive code of conduct for TNCs. It was clear that, at this time, any proposal to extend the work of GATT to incorporate rules on FDI was likely to be a non-starter; and that any attempt to influence the practices and behaviour of TNCs had to be implemented through a set of agreed guidelines or codes.[21] However, while such an idea was in tune with the economic philosophy of the 1970s and early 1980s – indeed the OECD *Guidelines for TNCs* were first adopted in 1976 – negotiations about the UN-initiated code were abandoned some 16 years after these had started. For not only had the attitudes of governments towards the activities of TNCs become less confrontational, the international focus of attention and concern had widened from that of bilateral TNC/ nation-state interaction to the impact of the activities of international firms on global economic and social welfare, and how best the international community and its constituent organizations (including the UN, the World Bank and the GATT (later the WTO)) might play their part in ensuring *all* stakeholders in the global economy actively promoted that goal.

The mid-1980s to date

A changing mood

During the last two decades, and particularly since 1991 – the first year of the publication of UNCTAD's annual flagship *World Investment Report*[22] – I have observed a marked realignment of the attitudes and policy recommendations of the UN and its constituent agencies towards TNCs and FDI. Much (though not all) of the adversarial stance, and the perception that the bargaining procedures between TNCs and host (particularly host-developing) countries were part of a zero-sum game, has been replaced by a more accommodatory approach and the recognition that, in the right circumstances, both host countries and TNCs might benefit from the latter's investment in the former. Such a change was perhaps most clearly articulated in the UNCTC's assessment of progress on the code of conduct in 1990. In referring to the interface between TNCs and nation states, the report asserted that the key issue was no longer 'whether to regulate business but how to structure cooperative national approaches that facilitate rather than inhibit international transactions' (UNCTC, 1990: 16/17) and again, in anticipation of the likely future demise of negotiations on the Code, 'the major challenge is to structure a collective international approach to managing the systemic costs and benefits of a global economy driven by transnational business corporations' (p. 17).

Finally, with reference to the new environmental agenda and the emergence of the knowledge-based economy, the report averred that 'these developments need coordinate definitions and regulatory processes which facilitate rather than impede business transactions' (*ibid.*: 16/17).

As I saw it at the time, this was the beginning of a fundamental recast of the concerns and actions of the UN and (most of) its agencies with respect to the (net) benefits of cross-border business activity; a recast which many economists and business analysts (including myself) had been urging for some time. It was a decisive change of position in three respects. The first was that words such as 'regulation and control' (as applied to the role of host governments) were increasingly supplanted (or at least supplemented) by those of 'facilitation and empowerment'. The second was that the frame of reference in evaluating the impact of TNC activity was widened to embrace global or regional, as well as national, economic and social considerations. The third was that governments were now starting to realize that the suitability of their own economic policies rested, in part at least, on circumstances beyond their control.

It is possible to identify several reasons for this change of emphasis that began to emerge in the debating chambers of the UN and in its publications in the late 1980s, and that accelerated and widened in the 1990s.

The first, and undoubtedly the most significant, was a series of events and actions associated with the advent and maturing of the (contemporary) global economy – what elsewhere we have referred to as 20/21 globalization (Dunning, 2004). These were sparked off, initially in the 1980s, by the renaissance of pro-market policies of several national governments – especially in the USA and the UK – and later, in the 1990s, the repercussions of the fall of the Berlin Wall and the emergence of China as a major player on the world economic stage. Throughout this period, barriers to international trade and investment in goods and services, assets, and the cross-border movement of information, ideas and people tumbled. As a result, new locational opportunities were opened up both to TNCs and to the countries seeking to upgrade their indigenous resources, capabilities and institutions, and their access to global markets.

Second, these years also saw the reconfiguration of the development strategies of most developing countries, from those based on economic autonomy and import substitution to those more outward-looking in their orientation. At first, the latter trade and industrial strategies were confined to East Asian countries, but in the later 1990s they were now being increasingly adopted by many Latin American states, India, and a few African countries.

Third, coincident and partly driving these changes, were a number of dramatic technological advances – and especially the advent of new forms of transport and communications technology such as e-commerce. These latter had two effects. First they facilitated the cross-border transfer of all kinds of information and knowledge. Second, because *inter alia* of the rising costs of, and need for, complementary technologies in the innovation and production of a wide range of goods and services they led – and sometimes necessitated – new cross-border forms of alliances and networks among firms, which were so much a feature of the mergers and acquisitions (M&A) boom of the 1990s.[23]

Fourth, the growing consensus of scholarly research was pointing to (a) the potential benefits of globalization and TNC activity in upgrading the indigenous resources and capabilities of both home and host countries, (b) the identification of the kind of actions which national governments and supranational entities (including the UN) needed to pursue if these advantages were to be fully realized and sustained at minimum cost, and (c) the role which TNCs might, or might not, play in advancing the social objectives of the countries in which they operate.

Fifth, the growing competition between both developed and developing countries for foreign resources and capabilities and markets, and the perceived need to protect or upgrade their global competitiveness has led their firms and governments to actively seek out the unique assets of TNCs and/or their foreign partners. In contrast to the 1970s, when countries imposed extensive restrictions on the scope and behaviour of TNCs, the 1990s saw an increasing number of incentives, bilateral investment agreements, a liberalization (deregulation) of performance requirements and other impediments to FDI, and a strengthening of the role of investment promotion agencies.

Sixth – and partly as a consequence of these other developments – the UN and its agencies, and especially UNCTAD, widened its earlier brief of providing governments with information and advice on the benefits and costs of inbound FDI, to suggesting ways and means of how best they might take the appropriate action so that such investment might best upgrade the indigenous human resources, created assets and capabilities and institutions under their jurisdiction. In my own consultancy work for the UN, I observed that TNCs were increasingly being seen as first-best co-partners with indigenous firms, and as a means of promoting the host country's dynamic comparative advantage rather than being reluctantly accepted as a second-best alternative to locally managed and controlled economic development.

This change of heart was especially seen in the case of the more advanced (middle-income) developing countries, which were themselves becoming significant outward investors (UN, v.d.). Indeed, in the 1990s the guidance most frequently sought from UNCTAD by governments of countries such as Korea, Taiwan, Singapore, Malaysia, Thailand, Brazil and China was not how inbound FDI might best be regulated or guided so as to fit in with their own domestic economic policies, but rather on how they could create or enhance their indigenous resources and capabilities so that their own firms might become effective global players.

Attention was then being increasingly addressed to policies to improve the overall institutional and economic environment not only for foreign direct investors, but for domestically owned companies in the international arena. This, indeed, is one of the challenges of globalization, and it contrasts markedly with a policy designed to maximize the contribution of all forms of TNC activity to development within a given national policy framework.

Seventh, although the idea of an enforceable UN-initiated code of conduct for TNCs was abandoned in the early 1990s, in its place saw the emergence of a new institutional and enforcement mechanism, namely the *Global Compact*. We will elaborate on this later in the chapter. However, the point we wish to emphasize here is that this initiative (by the Secretary General of the UN) is different from the earlier Code in two ways. First, it is a covenantal rather than a more formal institutional arrangement; and second, in its focus, content and implementation, it embraces not only TNCs and governments but other constituents of capitalism, notably non-governmental organizations

(NGOs). Indeed, the UN is now at the forefront in promoting both a consensus and multifaceted approach to globalization and TNC activity. In doing so it recognizes and seeks to encourage not only the distinctive contribution of the individual constituents of capitalism, but also the benefits arising from collective responsibility.

Impact on the UN

What then has been the impact of these changes on the UN's attitude and approach to TNCs? To what extent has the UN been reactive, and to what extent proactive, in influencing our knowledge and understanding about the interface between TNCs and the actions taken by governments and supranational agencies?

Since the incorporation of most of the programme of work on TNCs, initiated by the UNCTC in New York, into the UNCTAD system in Geneva, it has become rather more focused. Though the contemporary Division on Investment Technology and Enterprise (DITE)[24] still arranges seminars and workshops, offers guidance on capacity-building, undertakes training seminars, works actively on international investment instruments, arranges a variety of fact-finding and advisory missions to developing countries, initiates dialogues between TNCs, national governments and civil society groups, and makes important input into the wider work of the UN (for example with respect to environmental issues and its sister organizations in Geneva, viz. the ILO, WTO and UNRISD), it is, perhaps, best-known and respected through the publication of its annual *World Investment Reports* (originally modelled on the *World Development Reports* of the World Bank), its regularly updated *World Investment Directories*,[25] and a series of advisory and issue-based studies on foreign investment policy and investment promotion instruments.[26]

It is in these publications that perhaps one is given the best glimpse of the scope of interest, evolving ideology and technical competence of UNCTAD. Having been closely associated with the preparation of each of the WIRs, I can testify both to the proactive contribution of the staff and consultants at UNCTAD under the creative and dedicated leadership of Karl Sauvant; and also to the way in which UNCTAD has accessed and absorbed the huge literature on TNCs which has burgeoned over the last 13 years.[27] However, I believe that both UNCTAD (and indeed the other UN agencies including the World Bank and IMF,[28] would be the first to acknowledge the debt they owe to academic scholars throughout the world. In the 2003 WIR, for example, the assistance of 80 consultants was acknowledged (p. iv), while over 300 books, articles and reports are referenced at the back of the report.

The evolving (and unique) role and contribution of UNCTAD

How in my judgement has the UN and its various agencies responded to the changes just described? What is its and their current role? And what have been its (and their) most significant contributions to our understanding about TNCs and their impact on the extent and form of economic development?[29]

The first role of the UN – and the DITE at UNCTAD in particular – has been to provide a *creative vision* of how the evolving pattern and structure of FDI and TNC activity might best be harnessed to promote economic development; and, coupled with this vision, an identification of and *commitment* to explore the respective merits of the critical policy options of the day. At UNCTAD, Karl Sauvant, who has been intimately involved in the preparation of the 14 WIRs so far published, deserves the fullest possible credit. He has ensured that each of the annual publications has addressed issues of decisive importance to the global economy and to developing countries, as and when they have arisen in the 1990s. In their data gathering, research deliberations and policy recommendations, Dr Sauvant and his colleagues have sought to promote a *consensual* approach between the interested parties, and in so doing have eschewed *confrontation* for *concord* and *coaction*.

The second role is that the UN (and UNCTAD and ILO in particular) has (have) been the leading *catalyst* in the world for work on the political economy of TNC activity. Though other international agencies, for example the World Bank and OECD, and many universities and research institutions have done important work, none has managed to assemble or draw upon the research of such a powerful group of consultants and researchers as has UNCTAD. There are few eminent scholars working on the interface between TNCs, governments and the international economic system who have not participated in the preparation of one or other of the WIRs.[30] The results of this *collaboration* and the *coordination* of widely diffused intellectual inputs by the UNCTAD team have been demonstrated in the scope of the coverage, in the quality of analysis, and the diagnosis of each of the WIRs, and also of the many papers issued on specialized topics – most of which have been commissioned from academic scholars.

Over the last three decades, the UN has also been an important catalyst for an important disseminator of scholarly thinking on TNC-related issues. In the mid-1980s the UNCTC organized three training courses for university teachers from developing countries in the Asian and Pacific region, which dealt respectively with the development role of TNCs in economics development, business strategy and law. In the early 1990s the UNCTC's successor in New York, namely the Transnational Corporations and Management Division (TNCMD) of the Department of Economic and Social Development, commissioned a 20-volume library on (what were perceived by the editors to be) the most influential scholarly articles and chapters in books on a wide range of TNC-related topics.[31] I had the privilege of being the general editor of the library, and the volumes were published during 1993 and 1994 (Dunning, 1993–94).[32]

How then have these newly evolving roles of the UN and its agencies advanced our understanding about TNCs, their impact on development and their interface with national governments? Let me first focus on some of the contributions of the UNCTAD team, and then later of the UN itself and some of its other agencies. I have already alluded to the fact that, prior to the closure of the UNCTC and the removal of part of its staff to Geneva, UNCTAD only peripherally and intermittently concerned itself with TNC-related issues. Since the early 1990s, however, and the emergence of the knowledge-based global economy, such issues have become increasingly central to the trade, economic restructuring and development debate. Somewhat reluctantly at first, UNCTAD has now fully incorporated FDI into its core portfolio of interests and, more particularly as a result of the (partial) renaissance of the earlier philosophy of UNCTAD I towards the interface between TNCs (and their affiliates), the policies and strategies of developing countries. Today one of the flagship divisions of UNCTAD is that of the DITE within which, as we have said, all work on TNCs is coordinated.

With hindsight, I believe that the role and stature of the UN, and UNCTAD in particular, has been considerably strengthened by the work on TNCs in Geneva. Certainly the annual WIRs are one of the most widely read and highly regarded documents published by the UN. Of the varied TNC-related *contributions* made by UNCTAD, I would single out two of particular importance:

1   The first is to advance our knowledge and appreciation of the nature and changing role of TNC-related activity in the global economy. Over the past 15 years or so, successive WIRs have contained not only an increasing amount of unique and valuable data on the extent to which and ways in which TNCs and their subsidiaries have impacted on a whole range of economic and social issues of concern to both developed and developing countries; but they also have provided a careful analysis and critical interpretation of their motivation and strategies, and how these have affected, and been affected by, events in the global economy.[33]

In doing so, the DITE team at UNCTAD has not only drawn upon received theories of TNC activity,[34] but, with respect to particular situations such as the emergence of China as a major player in the global economy, the explosive growth of mergers and acquisitions in the 1990s, the burgeoning of cross-border networks and agreements, and the spread of integrated international production systems, has made its own modifications and extensions to such theories.

Moreover, as the 1990s have progressed, the DITE team has done its work in a scholarly and carefully balanced way. It has recognized, but not bowed to extreme views about the nature and character of TNCs – be they expressed by the most fervent supporters or fiercest critics. Partly as a result of its objective reporting and analysis, it has gained the respect of all the major constituents interested in global business operations, viz. the stakeholders of TNCs, NGOs, governments, academic scholars and supranational entities.

In addition, the regular revision, extension and updating of TNC-related statistics, including some novel statistical measures of the extent and significance of such activities and how important FDI is to individual countries, has enhanced the stature of UNCTAD to that of *the* major supplier and interpreter of TNC data, and how these relate to other indices of global economic development.

2 The second – and perhaps an even more – distinctive contribution of UNCTAD has been in respect of the institutions of, and policy formation by, national and regional governments, and the influence it has exerted on the thinking of supranational agencies (notably the WTO and the World Bank). Most of the WIRs, for example, contain carefully considered appraisals of the options open to national authorities in coping with the impact of TNC activity on virtually every aspect of economic and social life. Particularly impressive have been the thorough, and often quite original treatment given to the issue of international investment agreements[35] and rule-making at all geographical levels.

Once again, the attitudes, statements and writings of the DITE in the year 2004, are much more a reflection of those expressed by UNCTAD 40 years earlier, than those of the turbulent 1970s and 1980s. Today, the emphasis is how the globalizing world economy and the technological trends associated with it, affects the perceived desirability for both inbound and outbound TNC activity by nation states; and, in the light of the latters' economic and social needs and priorities, what strategies should their governments pursue to ensure that (a) the right kind of FDI is attracted at the right price, and (b) what must be done to promote and utilize such investment in the most cost-effective and socially acceptable way.

Now clearly each country is, to a certain extent at least, unique in its economic and social goals, and in the availability and quality of its resources, capabilities and institutions as means of achieving these goals. Each country must identify and promote its own particular dynamic comparative advantage and development path. At the same time, to benefit from a global economic system and from TNC activity, which is, perhaps, the most cogent expression of such a system, requires the implementation of certain common attitudes and policies towards both TNCs and domestic firms. Foremost among these is an entrepreneurial culture, *inter alia* with respect to technological change; and an emphasis on continual upgrading of human capabilities, for example as shown in its education and training policies, and the priority it affords to innovatory activities.

In its various documents, and in its advice to national governments, UNCTAD has been fully cognizant of the need to properly balance the needs and aspirations of the people in countries host and home to TNC activity, with those of the TNCs themselves and the demands of liberalized markets.

Yet, as globalization has accelerated and deepened, UNCTAD has increasingly directed its attention to the appropriate role of supranational entities, some of which have come under severe criticism in the last decade.[36] Most of this attention has related to specific issues arising from the value-added activities of TNCs (for example in respect of competition, linkages, investment agreements) which, in UNCTAD's view, are best treated from a supranational viewpoint. More than perhaps any other UN agency UNCTAD has sought to emphasize the need for common or harmonized international actions to ensure that the actions taken by national governments – for example with respect to taxation, investment incentives, dumping, export subsidies and so on – do not lead to a fruitless bidding war or other unintended consequences. Here, as particularly shown in the WIR for 2003, the careful and detailed analysis of the interface between bilateral and multinational investment agreements and (the freedom to initiate) national economic policies, UNCTAD has played a critical brokerage and advisory role.

If there is one aspect of UNCTAD's most recent work I would like to see strengthened, it is in respect of the interface between the incentive structures of institutions and that of global capitalism, as it is now evolving, and the impact of that interface on the character and impact of TNC-related activity and the response of governments to it. I would be the first to accept that issues such as corporate citizenship, changing belief systems, ethical perceptions, social mores and incentive structures are very difficult areas for the DITE to tackle. Yet since the events of 11 September 2001, an increasing volume of monographs is addressing such issues,[37] and I think it highly appropriate and desirable that UNCTAD should give more attention to them.[38]

The global compact and a new mandate to TNCs

This brings me to the initiatives of the UN in this area. In particular I shall outline those of the Secretary General in setting up a Global Compact at the World Economic Forum at Davos in 1999, and also a recent statement issued by the ECOSOC on the norms of behaviour expected of TNCs as regards the former initiative. While in some respects the Compact is a natural successor to the Code of Conduct, as it is addressed primarily to corporations (and *de facto* to TNCs), it encompasses a much wider range of social and ethical issues. It is also more ambitious in its intent. It is very much a creature of its time in that it is a search for a covenantal and conciliatory avenue to promoting responsible global capitalism rather than for a more contractual approach. This being so, it is deliberately informal and open-ended. It is a novel experiment in private and public partnership. Its radius is multifaceted in that it embraces all of the major constituents of global capitalism – viz. TNCs, national governments, and a wide variety of special interest groups are involved. Its enforcement mechanisms are, however, largely of a self-regulatory nature. Its success is likely to rest heavily on the quality of the trust, honesty, forbearance and goodwill of the parties to the Compact.

This is not the place to discuss the components and the consequences of the Global Compact in any detail.[39] Essentially its intent is to provide a framework of reference and dialogue to stimulate best corporate practices around a set of universally shared values. The Compact consists of nine principles based upon three core universal sets of values – the protection of international human rights, the ILO's declaration on decent labour standards, and the Rio Declaration (1992) on the Environment and Development.[40] These are set out in Appendix 2 to this chapter.

As already indicated, the Global Compact is an innovatory experiment in multi-stakeholder cooperation and problem-solving in helping to make globalization more socially inclusive and democratically responsible, while advancing cross-border corporate citizenship. Since its inception in 1999, the number of countries in which the Compact has been rooted has grown to more than 50, while the number of participating companies has risen to over 1,000, over half of which are from developing countries (UN, 2003). By the end of 2002, more than 20 civil society organizations (NGOs) – including ATNC International, the International Confederation of Free Trade Unions and the World Resources Institute – were engaged at a global level while most of the leading UN agencies, notably UNESCO, the ILO, UNDP and UNIDO, and 21 universities were closely involved. The network of the Compact also extends to a variety of academic institutions and business associations.[41]

I believe the Global Compact should best be regarded as a catalyst and a template for the promotion of global standards, or norms of behaviour of each of the stakeholders in the contemporary world economy. By itself it is not sufficient to ensure responsible global capitalism or good corporate citizenship. It needs a *bottom-up* or *groundswell* of support by the millions of consumers, workers and investors. Neither is it a substitute for (nor should it indeed compromise the need for, or authority of) more-formal institutions and enforcement mechanisms, for example constitutions, legal sanctions, the police and the judiciary (Zamit, 2004).[42] But it does aver that, in the long run, without the virtues which cannot be legally enforced, and which in the end define *sustainable* human relationships, the downsides of globalization cannot be adequately overcome, and the hopes and aspirations of its major participants are unlikely to be achieved (Bhagwati, 2004).

One further initiative by the UN, or more specifically by the Department of Economic and Social Affairs (UN-DESA) is, I think, worthy of note; and this is because, for no other reason, the UN – as a public institution – is now urging the private sector (in this case the TNCs) to take on board more responsibility in enhancing at least some of the values and goals of the international (public) community.

In a recent draft proposal, the UN has reemphasized the role of TNCs in furthering one of the critical objectives of the *Global Compact*, viz. to uphold and enhance human rights. To quote directly from the document, the authors write:

Recognising that, even though states have the primary responsibility to ensure respect for, protect abuses of and promote human rights, transnational corporations and other business enterprises, as organs of society have the obligation to promote and secure the human rights set forth in the Universal Declaration of Human Rights. (UN 2003b: 1) and again:

> Transnational corporations and other business enterprises shall respect civil, cultural, economic, political and social rights and contribute to their realisation, in particular the rights to development, adequate food and drinking water, the higher attainable standard of physical and mental health; adequate housing, education, freedom of thought, conscience and religion; and freedom of opinion and expression, and refrain from actions which obstruct the realisation of these rights. (*ibid.*: 2)

Are these, one wonders, just so many words or a pious hope? Are they a new/or truncated version of the earlier aborted code of conduct proposed by the UNCTC? Or are they a further example of an emerging and genuine desire to upgrade the responsibilities and authority of private actors in a domain previously the exclusive reserve of national or international public authorities? (Kobrin, 2004).

Other initiatives

Two other UN-related initiatives in this area deserve brief mention, the International Labour Office (ILO) and the United Nations Research Institute for Social Development (UNRISD).

• **The ILO.** In its 279th Session (in November 2000) the governing body of the International Labour Office issued a revised version of the Tripartite Declaration of Principles Concerning Transnational Corporations and Social Policy, first issued in 1977 (ILO, 1977). The earlier document was something of a landmark in that for the first time, universal guidelines to TNCs relating to the conditions of work and life were added to those of employment, training and industrial relations.[43] The current Declaration widens the social content of the 1977 agreement to take account of the changes in the global economy and the role of TNCs since then. *Inter alia* it pays more attention to voluntary initiatives in corporate social responsibility, and broadening the participation and knowledge on labour-related matters through ILO networks.

A no-less important initiative was the setting-up, in February 2002, by the (then) newly appointed Director General, Juan Somavia, of a World Commission to study the Social Dimension of Globalization. In doing so it flagged its interest in a more value-oriented and institutional approach to its terms of reference.

The Commission is currently made up of 26 politicians, academics, business people and leaders of society. More especially it is addressing six main issues: (i) identifying policies that can best promote responsible globalization, (ii) how its benefits can be made more inclusive, (iii) how the advantages of cross-border integration can be reconciled with (and indeed advanced) by the diversity of cultures throughout the globe, (iv) how transparency and accountability in the public and private spheres can be advanced, (v) how best may a dialogue between the main stakeholders in globalization be advanced; and (vi) what might be the shape of a more cogent and coherent rules-based framework which promotes responsible and sustainable global capitalism.

- **The UNRISD.** The other, and perhaps less well-known, initiative is that of United Nations Research Institute for Social Development (UNRISD) which, over the last decade, in particular,[44] has produced a series of research reports on the role of TNCs in social development, and how best might both formal and informal institutional and enforcement mechanisms help promote socially responsible business in developing countries. Indeed, in several respects, UNRISD has been a pioneer UN organ in analysing the potential and limits of a range of institutional arrangements for fostering both transnational corporate responsibility and that of other stakeholders in the global economy – including NGOs, supranational entities and various cross-border trade unions – in establishing and sustaining an effective global regulatory system to complement more voluntary initiatives such as the Global Compact of the UN, and the incentives and constraints of the global marketplace.[45]

Conclusions

In my opinion, the UN, and its various agencies, have contributed more to our understanding about TNCs and FDI and their impact on economic development than any other supranational entities. Certainly the publications of UNCTAD on FDI are more frequently cited by academic scholars than that of any other international organization. The annual WIRs, in particular, have gained considerable prestige and authority in the business community and among trade and investment departments of national governments.[46] Most noticeably the DITE has greatly advanced our appreciation of the implications of TNC activity for national economic policies, and for the deliberations and actions of supranational agencies.

Over the last 40 years, the attitude of the UN towards the contribution of TNCs to economic development has fluctuated. So, indeed, has its role as an advisory and capacity-building organization changing the goals, behaviour and power of both TNCs and host developing countries, and the findings of scholarly research. From a welcoming stance towards TNCs in the 1960s, through a period of confrontation in the 1970s and 1980s, to a cautious alliance, but a general acknowledgement of the value of responsible FDI in promoting national economic and social goals in a global economy in the 1990s, the wheel of attitudes and recommended actions by the UN has turned full circle.

However, in the early 2000s there are some additional unique features. First, as is perhaps best illustrated by the Global Compact, it is now recognized that if TNCs are to fulfil their purpose as wealth-creators, not only must this

be achieved through the optimization of TNC/national government relations, but by the involvement of *all* constituents in the global economy.
In particular, the collective action of consumers, workers and investors, and
that of particular parts of civil society and supranational entities, notably the
WTO and the World Bank, is likely to play a more active role in the future.

In my judgement, the evolving relationship between TNCs and the rest of
society – be it national or global – over the past forty years has emphasized
two things above all others. First it has strongly reflected the economic,
social and technological context in which the interface has been fashioned.
Such a context, which also includes the values of the main stakeholders in
the wealth-creating process, is partly exogenous and partly endogenous to
the players themselves. Second, and this aspect has been underplayed by
both scholars and practitioners – including the UN – is the role of incentive
structures and enforcement mechanisms in influencing how changes in the
external economic environment may affect the role of TNCs and their contribution on national economic goals. Such institutions which range from
formal rules and regulations to informal norms, conventions, moral suasion
and social mores, embrace both *top-down* sanctions and incentives to *bottom-up*
spontaneous ideas and actions on individual and corporate stakeholders.[47]
It is the network of private and public institutions – the institutional matrix
of societies – which, along with the resources, capabilities and markets possessed or accessed by them, will determine both the objectives of their constituents and the way they are advanced. Underpinning and influencing
these institutions are values which, in turn, reflect the belief systems of the
individuals and organizations implementing them.

It is the way in which the multiple stakeholders in the national and global
economy prepare or adapt their institutions and enforcement mechanisms to
external technological and economic events which will, in the end, determine
the extent to which, and the ways in which, TNC activity can best serve the
interests of the world's people. I believe it is incumbent on the UN – perhaps
more than any other international organization – to give more attention to
examining the institutions and belief systems underpinning and influencing
the actions of TNCs or of governments. Moreover, it needs to do so in a global
economy typified by change, volatility and uncertainty, and one in which the
character and structure of the human environment is playing an increasingly
important role in fashioning economic success and societal transformation.
The Global Compact, and the setting up of a World Commission on the Social
Dimension by the ILO are starting points, but a value-based approach to TNCs
and globalization needs to inculcate every aspect of the work of the UN. The
social and economic aspects of TNC-related activities are too intertwined to be
considered independently. A holistic and integrated institutional approach
is needed. In particular, voluntary (bottom-up) and enforceable (top-down)
initiatives need to be coordinated. Centralized modern governance needs to
be integrated with more decentralized modes.

Appendix 1:   World Investment Reports (1991–2004)

1991   *The Triad in Foreign Direct Investment*, 108 p.
1992   *Transnational Corporations as Engines of Growth*, 356 p.
1993   *Transnational Corporations and Integrated International Production*, 290 p.
1994   *Transnational Corporations, Employment and the Workplace*, 482 p.
1995   *Transnational Corporations and Competitiveness*, 491 p.
1996   *Investment, Trade and International Policy Arrangements*, 332 p.
1997   *Transnational Corporations, Market Structure and Competition Policy*, 384 p.
1998   *Trends and Determinants*, 432 p.
1999   *Foreign Direct Investment and the Challenge of Development*, 543 p.
2000   *Cross-border Mergers and Acquisitions and Development*, 368 p.
2001   *Promoting Linkages*, 356 p.
2002   *Transnational Corporations and Export Competitiveness*, 384 p.
2003   *FDI Policies for Development: National and International Perspectives*, 303 p.
2004   *The Shift towards Services*, 468p.

Appendix 2:   The UN's Global Compact's nine principles

The Global Compact's principles in the areas of human rights, labour and the environment enjoy universal consensus being derived from:

- The Universal Declaration of Human Rights;
- The International Labour Organization's Declaration on Fundamental Principles and Rights at Work; and
- The Rio Declaration on the Environment and Development.

The nine principles are:

Human Rights

Principle 1: Businesses are asked to support and respect the protection of international human rights within their sphere of influence; and

Principle 2: Make sure their own corporations are not complicit in human rights abuses.

Labour

Principle 3: Businesses are asked to uphold the freedom of association and the effective recognition of the right to collective bargaining;

Principle 4: The elimination of all forms of forced and compulsory labour;

Principle 5: The effective abolition of child labour; and

Principle 6: The elimination of discrimination in respect of employment and occupation.

Environment

Principle 7: Businesses are asked to support a precautionary approach to environmental challenges;

Principle 8: Undertake initiatives to promote greater environmental responsibility; and

Principle 9: Encourage the development and diffusion of environmentally friendly technologies.

Notes

* I am grateful to Professor Peter Gray for helpful comments on an earlier draft of this essay.

1   Transnational Corporations is the preferred nomenclature of the UN for multinational enterprises. We do not differentiate between these two terms. Both refer to enterprises or corporations that engage in foreign direct investment and own or control value-adding activities outside their home countries.

2   By Tagi-Sagafi-Nejad (under John Dunning's general guidance) as part of the Intellectual History of the UN project (UNIHP) led by Richard Jolly, Louis Emmerij and Tom Weiss (for details see Emmerij, Jolly and Weiss, 2001).

3   There are a large number of specialized UN agencies that, directly, or indirectly, are interested in the scope and impact of TNC-related activity. These include UNCTAD, ILO, UNRISD, FAO, UNITAR and WHO. For the purposes of this chapter, we will only deal with the first three of these agencies.

4   *Inter alia* the survey incorporated details of the market structure, exports, imports, subcontracting activities, intra-firm trade and the strategy of some 100 manufacturing affiliates of UK firms. This report was never published by UNCTAD, though some of its findings were used by UNCTAD in its later reports (see Dunning, 1974).

5   As for example summarized by UN (1973, 1974a, 1978, 1983) and later by Dunning (1993) and Caves (1996).

6   See especially the Watkins Committee's report (Watkins, 1968) which *inter alia* recommended greater surveillance and control of foreign-owned firms in Canada. It, and a later Gray Report (1972), asserted that the basic aim of Canadian policy should be to achieve 'healthy national independence while maximising the economic benefits of inward FDI'. For views, around this time, from other developed and developing countries see Litvak and Maule (1970).

7   This is not to say Japan did not heavily borrow or acquire European and US technological capacity, but it did so by other means (e.g. licensing and reverse engineering).

8   US scholars such as Jack Behrman, John Fayerweather, Richard Robinson and Ray Vernon were very active in the 1960s and early 1970s in analysing the reasons for these tensions, and what might be done to minimize or overcome them. These scholars, some of whom had earlier served in the US government, or government agencies, were very influential in the framing of US policy towards the outbound activities of TNCs at the time. For a more detailed assessment of US international business–government relations between 1960 and 1975 see Boddewyn (2004).

9   Later set out in some detail by Kindleberger and Goldberg (1970).

10   For recent reviews of these institutions see an excellent series of reports by UNCTAD, UN (1999a and b, and v.d.; see 2003 edition).

11   See United States Congress, Senate Committee on Foreign Relations, Sub Committee on Multinational Corporations (1973–76).

12   Ten from developing countries, ten from developed and centrally planned countries. Each acted in his private capacity.

13   Notably Ray Vernon and his team at Harvard, and Howard Perlmutter and his colleagues at the Wharton School (see UN, 1973).

14   See particularly UN (1974).

15   Sagafi-Negad.

16   For example, in its two years of existence, the GEP took testimony about different aspects of TNC-related activities from 47 witnesses. These included academic scholars, business executives, government ministers, and representatives of trade unions, consumer groups and specialized research and activist organizations.

17 See for example De Seynes (1976). The concept of the New International Economic Order (NIEO) was discussed at the 6th Special Session of the General Assembly of the UN in 1974; and the resolution which instituted a new system based on economic social equity was adopted on 1 May. Later that year, many of the provisions of the NIEO were embodied in the *Charter for Economic Rights and Duties* which aimed at the establishment of the new economic order. Among the contents of the Charter were special sections dealing with foreign investment, the transfer of technology and environmental protection (UN, 1974). Finally mention should be made of a UN resolution documenting the right of nation states for the sovereignty over their natural resources (UN, 1974b). This was to act as a template for TNC/government negotiations in resource-rich developing countries.

18 The UNCTC was located in New York until 1990. It was then disbanded, but several of its staff then moved to Geneva, when work on TNCs and FDI continued in the Transnational Corporations and Management Division of UNCTAD.

19 In addition its joint units with the regional economic commissions in Africa, the Asia and Pacific, Europe and Western Asian produced other reports relating to TNC activities in their own regions. For examples, see various editions of the UNCTC's CTC reports (v.d.).

20 In the early years of its existence, only a very few of the senior personnel of the UNCTC – notably Sydney Dell – and those who had worked with the GEP, notably N.T. Wang, Gustave Feissel and Sotirios Mousouris, were well-acquainted with the literature on and/or workings of TNCs. Indeed for most of the following decade, the Centre relied a great deal on outside (and especially academic) consultants for research advice and policy guidance.

21 At the same time, OECD countries had also liberalized their policies towards TNCs (see Dunning 1993: 570/1).

22 Published annually by the UN since 1991. See UN (v.d.).

23 Between 1990 and 2000 the value of cross-border M&As was equivalent to 65% of the total foreign direct flows of these years (UN, v.d., 2001 edition).

24 Since 1993 the Division has gone through various changes of name.

25 Giving statistical data on FDI and TNC activity, and a description of the legal framework for TNCs in more than 120 countries. (There are six regional volumes to this series covering Asia and the Pacific, Central and Eastern Europe, Developed Countries, Latin America and the Caribbean, Africa and West Asia.)

26 Between 1992 and 2003, over 50 studies, 12 investment reviews and 10 issue-based reports have been published. *Inter alia* the studies comprise discussions on the social responsibility of TNCs, management consultancy, trade linkages, debt–equity swaps, employment, national treatment, illicit treatment and transfer pricing.

27 As identified, for example, in Rugman and Brewer (2001).

28 Technically both the Bank and the IMF are part of the UN system, but in this chapter we have focused solely on the UN and the organizations which bear its name.

29 At this point the reader might like to be reminded of the function of UNCTAD in respect of TNCs and FDI. To quote from the WIR report (p. ii) in 2003 'UNCTAD seeks to further understanding of the nature of transnational corporations and their contribution to development and to create an enabling environment for international investment and enterprise development. UNCTAD's work is carried out through intergovernmental deliberations, technical assistance activities, seminars, workshops and conferences'. For a review of UNCTAD's work on foreign direct investment and TNCs between 1964 and 2004 see Fredriksson and Zimny (2004).

30 Of these Samuel Asante, Arghyrios Fatouros, Sanjaya Lall, Robert Lipsey, Charles Albert Michalet, John Stopford and myself have been among the most active.

31   Dealing with such issues as TNC theory, history, strategy, organization, natural resources, trade and the balance of payments, services, human-resource management, innovation, modes of government–TNC relations and modes of TNC involvement, technology, industrial structure, and transfer pricing.

32   A volume bringing together introductory chapters of each volume was published in 1990 (UN, 1996).

33   For a list of the topics dealt with in the annual WIRs from 1991 to 2003 see Appendix 1 to this chapter.

34   As for example summarized in Dunning (1993), Caves (1996).

35   By mid-2003 UNCTAD had published 23 papers on different aspects of the international regulatory framework underpinning FDI and TNC activity.

36   See especially Stiglitz (2002).

37   See e.g. Dunning (2003), Monbiot (2003) and Greiber (2003).

38   Exceptions include some of the issue papers and WIR (1996 and 2003). In Annex A (p. 308/18 of WIR 2003), there is a full list of the main international institutions between 1948 and 2003 relating to FDI and TNC activity.

39   An excellent recent account is given by the UN (2003a). See also Kell and Ruggie (1999) and Tesner (2000).

40   See Appendix 2 to this chapter.

41   As listed in UN (2003).

42   In her recent book, Ann Zammit argues the need for the UN and its agencies to devise a new strategy and policy framework towards economic development. In particular she emphasizes the urgency of bolstering the efforts of developing countries to draw up their poverty-reduction strategies, and to determine the critical mass of coordinated investments (including FDIs) needed to generate positive externalities and a virtuous circle of growth. Included in such a strategy would be a demand for a more clear-cut and identifiable commitment to corporate social responsibility by foreign TNCs – particularly in the area of labour and environmental standards (Zammit, 2004).

43   Although there had been various international labour conventions on several of these issues over the past four decades or more (ILO, 2002).

44   The origin of UNRISD, however, dates back over 40 years. For a review of its history and views on such questions as social policy and well-being, civil society and governments, gender and development, technology, business and society, see UNRISD (2004). For a recent exposition of UNRISD's approach to corporate social responsibility and economic development see Utting (2000).

45   Including the collective actions of consumers, investors and workers as they may affect the actions and behaviour of corporations.

46   Between 1994 and 2003, the WIRs were cited 512 times in the Social Science Citation Index. Only three international business scholars have a higher number of citations than this.

47   For more details of the institutional approach to economic growth and development see North (1999), Ozawa (2003), Gray (2004) and Dunning (2004).

References

Bhagwati, J. (2004) *In Defense of Globalization*. Oxford: Oxford University Press.

Boddewyn, J. (2004) *Early Literature (1960–75) on International Business – Government Relations: Its Twenty-first Century Relevance*. New York: Baruch College (CUNY).

Brash, D.T. (1966) *American Investment in Australian Industry*. Canberra: Australian University Press.

Caves, R.E. (1996) *Multinational Firms and Economic Analysis*. Cambridge: Cambridge University Press.

De Seynes (1976) 'Transnational Corporations in the Framework of a New International Economic Order', *The CTC Reporter*, 1(2): 15–29.

Deane, R.S. (1970) *Foreign Investment in New Zealand Manufacturing*. Wellington (UK): Sweet & Maxwell.

Dell, S. (1990) *The United Nations and International Business*. Durham, NC: Duke University Press.

Dunning, J.H. (1974) *UK Multinational Enterprises and Trade Flows of Less Developed Countries*, London, Economists Advisory Group.

Dunning, J.H. (1993) *Multinational Enterprises and the Global Economy*. Harlow, Essex: Addison Wesley.

Dunning, J.H. (ed.) (1993–94) *The United Nations Library on Transnational Corporations*, 20 vols. London and New York: Routledge.

Dunning, J.H. (ed.) (2003) *Making Globalization Good: The Moral Imperatives of Global Capitalism*. Oxford: Oxford University Press.

Dunning, J.H. (forthcoming) 'Towards a New Paradigm of Development Implications for the Determinants of International Business Activity', *Transnational Corporations*.

Dunning, J.H. and Pearce, R.D. (1969) 'The World's Largest Firms: A Statistical Profile', *Business Ratios*, 3, Winter: 1–10.

Dunning, J.H. and Pearce, R.D. (1975) *Profitability and Performance of the World's Largest Industrial Enterprises*. London: Financial Times.

Dunning, J.H. and Pearce, R.D. (1981) *The World's Largest Industrial Enterprises 1962–83*. Farnborough: Gower.

Dunning, J.H. and Pearce, R.D. (1985) *The World's Largest Industrial Enterprises 1962–83*. Farnborough: Gower.

Dunning, J.H. and Cantwell, J. (eds) (1987) *The IRM Directory of International Investment and Production Statistics*. Basingstoke: Palgrave Macmillan.

Emmerij, L., Jolly, R. and Weiss, T.G. (2001) *Ahead of the Curve: UN Ideas and Global Challenges*. Bloomington: Indiana University Press.

Fredriksson, T. and Zimny, Z. (2004) 'Foreign Direct Investment and Transnational Corporations in UNCTAD, *Beyond Conventional Wisdom in Development Policy: An Intellectual History of UNCTAD 1964–2004*. UN: New York and Geneva, pp. 127–40.

Gray Report (1972) *Foreign Direct Investment in Canada*, Ottawa: Government of Canada.

Gray, H.P. (1972) *The Economics of Business Investment Abroad*. London and Basingstoke: Palgrave Macmillan.

Gray, H.P. (2004) 'Assessing the Need for Controls over Inward Direct Investment in Developing Countries', *Global Economy Journal*, Fall.

Gray, H.P. (1972) *Foreign Direct Investment in Canada*. Ottawa: Government of Canada.

Greiber, W. (2003) *The Soul of Capitalism. Opening Paths to a Moral Economy*. New York: Simon & Schuster.

Hawkins, R.G. (1972) *Job Displacement and Multinational Firms. A Methodological Review*, Occasional Paper no. 3. Washington, DC: Center for Multinational Studies.

Hufbauer, G.C. and Adler, M. (1968) *US Manufacturing Investment and the Balance of Payments*. Tax Policy Research Studies, no. 1. Washington, DC: Treasury Department.

International Labour Office (ILO) (1977 and 2001) *Tripartite Declaration of Principles Concerning Multinational Enterprises and Social Policy*. Geneva: ILO (204th and 279th sessions).

ILO (2002) *A Guide to the Tripartite Declaration of Principles Concerning Multinational Enterprises and Social Policy*. Geneva: ILO (Multinational Enterprises Programme).

ILO (2003) *The World Commission on the Social Dimension of Globalization* (mimeo). Geneva: ILO, worldcommission@ilo.org.

Kell, G. and Ruggie, J.G. (1999) 'Global Markets and Social Legitimacy: The Case for the "Global Compact" ', *Transnational Corporations*, 8(3): 101/20.

Kidron, M. (1965) *Foreign Investments in India*. London and New York: Oxford University Press.

Kindleberger, C.P. and Goldberg, P.M. (1970) 'Towards a GATT for Investment: A Proposal for the Supervision of the International Corporation', *Law and Policy in International Business*, 2: 295–313.

Kobrin, S. (2004) *Multinational Enterprise, Public Authority and Public Responsibility. The Case of Talisman Energy and Human Rights in Sudan*. Philadelphia: The Wharton School.

Kolodner, E. (1994) *Transnational Corporations: Impediments or Catalysts of Social Development*, Geneva, UNRISD Occasional Paper, no. 5, World Summit for Social Development.

Lall, S. and Streeten, P. (1977) *Foreign Investment, Transnationals and Developing Countries*. Basingstoke: Palgrave Macmillan.

Litvak, I.A. and Maule, C.J. (eds) (1970) *Foreign Investment. The Experience of Host Countries*. London and New York: Praeger.

Mikesell, R. (ed.) (1962) *US Private and Government Investment Abroad*. Eugene, Oregon: University of Oregon Books.

Monbiot, G. (2003) *The Age of Consent*. London: Flamingo.

North, D.C. (1999) *Understanding the Process of Economic Change*. London Institute of Economic Affairs, Occasional Paper 106.

Organization for Economic Cooperation and Development (OECD) (1976) *Guidelines for Multinational Enterprises*. Paris: OECD.

Ozawa, T. (2003) 'Japan in an Institutional Quagmire: International Business to the Rescue?', *Journal of International Management*, 9: 219–35.

Reddaway, W.B., Potter, S.T. and Taylor, C.T. (1968) *The Effects of UK Direct Investment Overseas*. Cambridge: Cambridge University Press.

Robertson, D. and Pearce, R.D. (1974) 'Trade Flows of Less Developed Countries', London: Economists Advisory Group.

Rugman, A.M. and Brewer, T.L. (2001) *The Oxford Handbook of International Business*. Oxford: Oxford University Press.

Safarian, A.E. (1966) *Foreign Ownership of Canadian Industry*. Toronto: University of Toronto Press.

Sagafi-Negad, T. (with the collaboration of J.H. Dunning) (forthcoming) *The UN and Transnational Corporations. The Eye of the Hurricane: From Code to Compact*. Bloomington, IN: Indiana University Press.

Servan Schreiber, J. (1968) *The American Challenge*. London: Hamish Hamilton.

Stiglitz, J. (2002) *Globalization and its Discontents*. London: Allan Lane.

Stopford, J.M., Dunning, J.H. and Haberich, K.O. (1980) *The World Directory of Multinational Enterprises*. Basingstoke: Macmillan, now Palgrave.

Tesner, S. (with the collaboration of G. Kell) (2000) *The United Nations and Business. A Partnership Recovered*. New York: St Martin's Press.

United Nations (1968) *Foreign Investment in Developing Countries*. New York: UN Department of Economic and Social Affairs.

UN (1973) *Multinational Corporations in World Development*. New York: UN, E73.II.A.11.

UN (1974a) *The Impact of Multinational Corporations on Development and International Relations*. New York: UN, E/5500/Rev.1.

UN (1974b) *Charter of Economic Rights and Duties of States*. New York: UN General Assembling Resolution 3281(xx1x), 12 December 1974.

UN (1974c) *Permanent Sovereignty Over Natural Resources*. New York: UN, UN Document no. A/9716.

UN (1976) *Transnational Corporations and World Development*. London: International Thompson Business Press.

UN (1978) *Transnational Corporations in World Development. A Re-examination*. New York: UN, Commission on Transnational Corporations, E/C.10/38.

UN (1983) *Transnational Corporations and World Development: Third Survey*. New York: UN, E.78II.A5.

UN (v.d.1991–2003) *The World Investment Reports* (annual publications). Geneva and New York: UN.

UN (1992) *From the Common Market to EC92*. New York: UN, ST/CTC/144.

UN (v.d.1992–96) *World Investment Directory* (separate volumes for Asia and Pacific, Central and Eastern Europe Developed Countries, Latin America and the Caribbean, and Africa and West Asia). Geneva and New York: UN.

UN (1999a) *Transnational Corporations: Scope and Definition*. New York and Geneva: UNCTAD series on Issues on International Investment Agreements.

UN (1999b) *Trends in International Investment Agreements: An overview*. New York and Geneva: UNCTAD series on Issues on International Investment Agreements.

UN (2003a) *The Global Compact: Report on Progress and Activities*. New York: UN.

UN (2003b) *Draft Norms on the Responsibilities of Transnational Corporations and Other Business Enterprises with Regard to Human Rights*. New York: UN.

United Nations Conference on Trade and Development (UNCTAD) (1972) *Restrictive Business Practices*. Geneva: UNCTAD Secretariat.

UNCTAD (1973) *Main Findings of a Study of Private Foreign Investment on Selected Developing Countries*. Geneva: UNCTAD, TD/B/C/3/111.

UNCTAD (2004) *Beyond Conventional Wisdom in Development Policy – An Intellectual History of UNCTAD (1964–2004)*, Geneva: UN Section of Foreign Direct Investment.

United Nations Centre for Transnational Corporations (UNCTC) (1987–91) *CTC Reports*. New York: UNCTC.

UNCTC (1990) *The New Code Environment*. New York: UN.

United Nations Research Institute for Social Development (UNRISD) (2004) *40 Years of UNRISD Research*. Geneva: UN.

US Congress, Senate Committee on Foreign Relations, Sub Committee on Multinational Corporations (1973–76), *Multinational Corporations and United States Foreign Policy*, US Senate 93–94th Congress Hearings. Washington: US Government Printing Office.

Utting, P. (2000) *Business Responsibility for Sustainable Development*. Occasional Paper no. 2. Geneva: United Nations Research Institute for Social Development.

Van Den Bulcke, D., De Sloovere, J., Van De Walle, E. and Steel, K. (1971) Les enterprises étrangères dans l'économie belge, OBAP, Brussels.

Van Den Bulcke, D., Sahlgren, K. and Vermeire, R. (1979) Transnational Corporations and World Development, Tijdschrift voor Accountancy en Bedrijskunde, No. 1, pp. 55–69.

Watkins, M.H. (1968) *Ownership and the Structure of Canadian Industry*. Ottawa: Government of Canada.

Zammit, A. (2004) *Development at Risk: Rethinking UN–Business Partnerships*. Geneva: United Nations Research Institute for Social Development.

3
Disinvestment by Foreign-Owned Firms: Fact in Search of Framework

Vitor C. Simões

Introduction

Danny Van Den Bulcke was a pioneer in the study of 'disinvestment (or divestment or divesture) activities of ... multinational corporations' (Van Den Bulcke, 1979: 5). At a time when, after the 'golden' sixties, concerns with the 'multinationals in retreat' (Hood and Young, 1982) phenomenon were emerging in the wake of the 1973–75 economic crisis, Van Den Bulcke contributed a set of well-balanced analyses, grounded on a careful data collection, which provide a broad picture on investment and disinvestment behaviour of transnational corporations in Europe, and more specifically in Belgium (Van Den Bulcke, 1979, 1982, 1983 and 1985; Van Den Bulcke and Halsberghe, 1979; Halsberghe and Van Den Bulcke, 1978). Although since 1985 he revisited the subject only once, and from a very specific perspective – economic sanctions to South Africa's apartheid regime (Van Den Bulcke and Volkaert, 1993) – many of his thoughts are still relevant for those dealing with international disinvestment issues today. The elusive and multifaceted nature of disinvestment was underlined, thereby requiring a clear definition of the 'exact borders' of the concept in each specific exercise – it is therefore noteworthy that Van Den Bulcke (1979) narrowly defined disinvestment as well as carefully analysed the available statistical evidence. Another relevant remark concerns the different characteristics of disinvestment by transnational corporations when compared to indigenous firms: the former 'have a greater range of options' and 'closures of subsidiaries do not necessarily jeopardize the main activity of TNCs' (Van Den Bulcke, 1985: 275). This is a very relevant feature in today's global competition (Benito and Welch, 1997), where divestment is becoming an integral component of strategy (Dranikoff, Koller and Schneider, 2002; Jagersma and van Gorp, 2003). His elegant and pragmatic approach to national policies towards international disinvestments is another aspect that deserves to be revisited (Van Den Bulcke, 1979 and 1985; Van Den Bulcke and Halsberghe, 1979).

The present chapter is simultaneously a tribute to Danny Van Den Bulcke's contribution to enhance our knowledge about international disinvestment and an exercise to push further some of his ideas. I will mainly draw on two points. First, the understanding of international disinvestment as a process: as he wrote (Van Den Bulcke, 1979: 49), 'it may be easier for multinational corporations to lower their employment goals over a longer period of time'.[1] Second, the inscription of disinvestment in a wider frame where both company (and subsidiary) strategy and behaviour, and external factors interacted to influence decisions (Van Den Bulcke, 1979; Van Den Bulcke and Halsberghe, 1979 and 1984). Taking the disinvestment-as-process as a cornerstone, my objective is to develop, drawing on Van Den Bulcke's work as well as on more recent contributions, an eclectic framework for the analysis of international disinvestment.

The approach is based on two tenets. First, disinvestment is envisaged in the context of the affiliate's evolutionary path, and from this perspective disinvestment is part of the very process which may lead the affiliate to become a centre of excellence. There is a common thread of elements which influence an affiliate's autonomy level (Van Den Bulcke and Halsberghe, 1984; Taggart and Hood, 1999; Simões, Biscaya and Nevado, 2002), the creation of a centre of excellence (Holm and Pedersen, 2000; Frost, Birkinshaw and Ensign, 2002; Birkinshaw and Hood, 1998; Simões and Nevado, 2000) and disinvestment. This leads to the second aspect. As Van Den Bulcke (1979) has mentioned, to understand disinvestment processes one should focus on the interaction between company endogenous and contextual factors. The first may be seen as including the two players in the 'centralization – decentralization debate' (Van Den Bulcke, 1995: 440): the transnational corporation and the local subsidiary. Environmental and contextual factors also have two facets: sectoral characteristics, and locational features, dealing with the attractiveness of investment locations.

The chapter comprises five sections, including this introduction. The second provides a discussion of the concept of disinvestment, in order to identify different perspectives under the generic label of disinvestment. A revision of the literature on the determinants of disinvestment decisions is then undertaken, followed by the development of a new framework for analysing disinvestment. The last section summarizes the main conclusions, and puts forward a few research strands to enhance our knowledge about international disinvestment.

Disinvestment: concept and typologies

In his discussion of the concept of disinvestment, Van Den Bulcke (1979) recognizes the existence of different definitions of disinvestment, mentioning namely Torneden's (1975) definition, which associates disinvestment with a decline in ownership position in a foreign-controlled company.

He follows, however, a different approach, partly due to statistical constraints: 'withdrawals or serious curtailments of ventures which have already been started' (Van Den Bulcke, 1979: 19). With hindsight, it is remarkable that his discussion already pinpoints the two main perspectives of the disinvestment concept: the ownership, and the subsidiary activity perspectives. A brief review of extant literature better illustrates our point.

In one of the most influential papers in the management field on the issue of disinvestment, Duhaime and Grant (1984: 301) wrote 'corporate divestment can be defined as a firm's decision to dispose of a significant position of its assets'. Disinvestment, from this perspective, is associated with the dismantling of an ownership position (Vale, 2001). Other authors, namely those from the economic geography field, equate disinvestment with plant closure (Clark and Wrigley, 1997). However, manufacturing activities may come to an end while the establishment and its ownership are maintained. This case corresponds, in general terms, to what has been called the transformation of domestic market-oriented manufacturers into marketing satellites (Simões, 1992). On the other hand, ownership may change without entailing significant modifications in the current activities of the foreign subsidiary. A case in point is AutoEuropa, a former manufacturing joint venture between Ford and Volkswagen, which is now fully owned by the German partner. This discussion shows that the concept of disinvestment needs to be clarified. In such an endeavour one should have in mind that the notion of disinvestment is contingent upon the perspective adopted – namely, the TNC (Boddewyn, 1979; Benito and Welch, 1997; Jagersma and Van Gorp, 2003; Benito, 2003), the subsidiary (Griffin, 2003) or the recipient country or region (Pyke, 2003; Tomaney *et al.*, 1999; Giunta and Martinelli, 1995).

Benito (1997a, 1997b) makes a distinction between forced and deliberate disinvestment. The first corresponds to situations when foreign subsidiary ownership change is imposed upon the foreign investor (nationalization, expropriation or confiscation). The second 'is based on strategic considerations leading to the voluntary liquidation or sale' (Benito, 1997a: 366) of operations abroad. This is the kind of disinvestment in which we are interested in the purview of this chapter. One should recognize, however, that the two types of disinvestment identified by Benito are not, in reality, totally uniform. For instance, the obligation to sell a given subsidiary due to competition policy is a type of forced disinvestment very different from nationalization. In some instances, deliberate investments may be 'forced' by the behaviour of other companies; for instance, a dedicated plant to supply a key customer operation will most probably be divested should be customer discontinue such operation.

Envisaging divestment as plant closure, Watts and Stafford (1986) and Watts (1991) suggest a distinction between cessation and selective closures. The first happens when the firm is no longer in that business, either due to bankruptcy, leaving the product line concerned or outsourcing. The latter corresponds to the cases when manufacturing is transferred to, or maintained in, other plants. In the international business field, several authors also felt the need to work out distinctions between different types of disinvestment. Mata and Portugal (1997 and 2000) distinguish between divestiture, when the subsidiary pursues its activities under new ownership, and liquidation, when the subsidiary company no longer exists. In a similar vein, Hennart *et al.* (1998), studying the longevity of joint ventures by Japanese firms in the United States, draw an opposition between liquidation (that is, the subsidiary company no longer exists) and sell-offs. Two different types of disinvestment – failure and restructuring – were also considered by Mariotti and Piscitello (1997). The first corresponds to an insufficient subsidiary performance, leading the TNC to get rid of it, while the second deals mainly with the need for the TNC group to respond or anticipate competitive challenges.[2]

Based on the review undertaken, a typology of international disinvestment moves is proposed. It is based on two dimensions: (1) ownership, and (2) subsidiary activity. The ownership dimension contrasts, on the one hand, the 'traditional' perspective of disinvestment expressed in the above-mentioned definition of Duhaime and Grant (1984), and on the other the keeping of the subsidiary under TNC ownership. The activity dimension enables the continuation of current subsidiary activities to be distinguished from the downgrading or eventual discontinuation of such activities (plant closure). Figure 3.1 provides the full range of disinvestment operations as a typology.

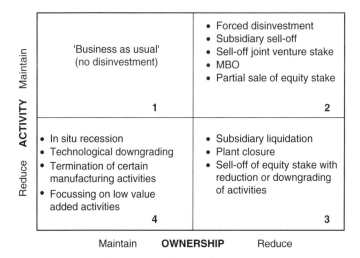

Figure 3.1 Typology of disinvestment operations

Broadly speaking, disinvestment encompasses situations included in quadrants 2, 3 and 4. This is consistent with Van Den Bulcke's (1979) discussion. The first quadrant corresponds to a situation where disinvestment does not occur: a subsidiary's activity and ownership remain unchanged. Quadrant 2 refers to cases where ownership is reduced or is totally alienated (that is, there is disinvestment from the TNC's standpoint), but the subsidiary's[3] activities do not change. If one excludes the cases of forced disinvestment, the operations under quadrant 2 broadly translate strategic reconfiguration moves by the TNC, at local, regional or global levels. In many cases they are linked with global processes of reshaping TNC assets, a feature already mentioned by Van Den Bulcke (1979: 55) when he argued that 'multinational companies are consolidating and restructuring their operations on a world level', and especially critical nowadays (Jagersma and Van Gorp, 2003; Benito, 2003; Dranikoff, Koller and Schneider, 2002). Such a strategic reconfiguration may stem from TNC competitive troubles or from subsidiary disappointing performance, but this is not necessarily the case. In some instances, 'crown jewels' may be sold to raise funds to support wider strategic reorientation moves. The 'variable geometry' of TNC assets often leads to the abandonment of some divisions or to the autonomization of subsidiaries abroad, according to worldwide competitive considerations. The alienation of a subsidiary is not, in this case, dependent on its specific performance (Benito, 2003). International mergers may also imply total or partial alienation of equity stakes. For instance, the merger of foundry activities of Renault and Fiat, creating a new company (Teksid), led to a change in ownership for all the former foundry subsidiaries of those groups, without significant changes, at least in the short term, in the scope of activities of those subsidiaries. Mergers may also be the prelude to the sell-off of businesses, although specific advantages of the subsidiaries may still be recognized and taken into account by the new owner (Griffin, 2003). An interesting example of this case is the hydromechanic division of the former Portuguese firm Sorefame, which was given the 'centre of excellence' status after Sorefame's acquisition by ABB and which still kept such a status in the context of the ABB/Alsthom joint-venture on power business (Simões and Nevado, 2000). It should be acknowledged that sell-offs may also be due to reasons specific to the subsidiary in point, as happens with many management buy-outs (MBOs) or with the sell-off of joint-venture stakes. Kogut (1991) has shown that joint ventures may be envisaged as options, the decision to keep or to sell the stakes being dependent on partners' expectations and relative interests in the development of the business.[4] In this context it is hardly surprising to find that joint-venture death happens mostly due to the sell-off of the stake held by one partner and not so much due to the liquidation of the joint-venture company (Hennart *et al.*, 1998).

The cases of subsidiary liquidation and plant closure, which are the most clear and socially sensitive examples of disinvestment, as Van Den Bulcke (1979) mentioned, are included in quadrant 3 of Figure 3.1. Often the subsidiary is liquidated (or the manufacturing establishment is closed) as a consequence of its incapacity to comply with performance requirements and/or with the technological demands of new product lines. However, if an inferior performance makes the subsidiary more vulnerable and an easy target for disinvestment operations (Van Den Bulcke, 1979; Benito, 1997a and 1997b), a selective closure may not just be the outcome of such a situation. It may also derive from other considerations such as relative plant size (Watts and Stafford, 1986), the profit generated by alternative uses of space (Clark and Wrigley, 1997), the size of the market concerned, the 'emergence' of better alternative locations (Van Den Bulcke, 1979; Hudson, 2001 and 2003; Gereffi, 2001; Jagersma and van Gorp, 2003), the continuation of the business line, or the political-economic assessment of the country as a manufacturing location.[5]

The last quadrant 4 corresponds to those cases when ownership remains unchanged, but there is a decline or a downgrading in subsidiaries' activities. It encompasses three situations which may be interrelated: in situ recession, technological downgrading, and relevance decline. In situ recession[6] amounts to a 'slimming' and 'anaemia' of the subsidiary, with a reduction of its manufacturing activity and employment. The second situation – technological downgrading – includes two distinct cases: (1) the subsidiary's specialization is gradually focused on low-technology-intensive and low-skill-demanding products; or (2) the subsidiary is not able to respond to technological challenges, losing the manufacturing of new, more sophisticated, products to other units of the transnational group, and continuing the manufacture of older products or components. Relevance decline may be envisaged as a 'slimming' of the subsidiary as a result of changes in TNC strategies to supply local markets and/or to define production locations. The subsidiary's manufacturing activities are reduced (or even discontinued), with a corresponding fall in employment (Van Den Bulcke, 1979), and it is often transformed into a mere marketing unit.

The situations indicated in quadrant 4 are often the prelude for the liquidation of the subsidiary (Freitas, 1998), and in this vein it is possible to identify a trajectory of declining TNC involvement in the subsidiary. Maintaining ownership with activity reduction is thus an intermediate step between 'business as usual' and the liquidation of the subsidiary. This is consistent with Van Den Bulcke's (1979) remark that transnational corporations may have longer periods of employment decline. In other words, the path from the first to the third quadrant often goes through the fourth.

Situations that involve reduction in ownership and/or activity are particularly relevant. Both features are important to characterize the process of declining

TNC involvement in a given country as well as to understand the fall of interest in a specific subsidiary – aspects which may lead, at the end of the day, to subsidiary liquidation, including plant closure. I must confess, however, that in the present work the main focus is on the quadrant involving reduction of activity, since these enable us to establish a nexus between disinvestment and the evolution of subsidiary competences.

Determinants of international disinvestment: literature review

General approach

The literature on the determinants of disinvestment is diversified, and includes three main strands – geography, industrial organization and strategic management – which will be briefly reviewed below.

In the field of geography the most relevant work is Watts and Stafford (1986), who present a long list of factors affecting the closure of units in multi-establishment firms. Their list is organized under four main groups, somewhat translating the authors' interests: regional factors, corporate characteristics, sectoral characteristics and key variables. These are considered to be the main explanatory factors for selective closures, including, *inter alia*, the divested unit's regional and corporate embeddedness, market access, labour market and labour skills, corporate organization, technology and environmental conditions. Although being mostly concerned with the perspectives of the region and the closed unit, they provide a large battery of elements which may be useful even for international analyses.

Entry and exit barriers are at the core of the study of disinvestment from an industrial organization standpoint. The existence of dedicated assets, the value of which is substantially reduced for alternative uses (Williamson, 1985), raises exit barriers; whilst high investments in tangible or intangible assets, envisaged as sunk costs, hamper disinvestment (Porter, 1976). It is interesting to remark that this reasoning was also recalled by geographers (Clark and Wrigley, 1995, 1997) as well as by international business scholars (Benito, 1997b, 2003; Benito and Welch, 1997). The industrial organization literature indicates that the probability of disinvestment is higher for diversified firms, and is also associated with resource leverage, company governance and, to a smaller degree, structural characteristics of markets (Haynes, Thompson and Wright, 2000).

In the strategy literature, disinvestment is chiefly related to the management, as well as to the synergies established in the building up, of a business portfolio. Broadly speaking, gains from disinvestment appear to be higher for firms which face control problems due to size or to diversity of activities. Duhaime and Grant (1984) found that divesting firms have fragile financial situations and divested units have limited assets and weak interlinkages with other company units. Following this reasoning, disinvestment decisions may be explained by the need to concentrate on corporate core businesses and by the perception of a loose strategic relationship between headquarters and the target unit (Hamilton and Chow, 1993; Dranikoff, Koller and Schneider, 2002).

The relevance of the findings mentioned above notwithstanding, it is our conviction that international disinvestment decisions raise specific challenges, and are affected by factors which were not taken into account in those general approaches. Such a specificity is due to at least four factors:

1 the restrictions faced in collecting and processing international data (Van Den Bulcke, 1979; Kobrin, 1988; McLachlan, 1992);
2 the double embeddedness of subsidiaries abroad *vis-à-vis* the TNC network and the location environment (Andersson and Forsgren, 1996; Birkinshaw and Hood, 2000; Simões *et al.*, 2002; Griffin, 2003);
3 the lower involvement of headquarters managers with foreign operations (Boddewyn, 1985); and
4 the interaction between business, functional and regional aspects imping- ing upon management modes and organizational structures (Bartlett and Ghoshal, 1989; Benito and Welch, 1997; Benito, 2003).

To sum up, international disinvestment has specific characteristics as a result of the need to balance economic, organizational and political imperatives (Prahalad and Doz, 1987).[7]

The international dimension

There seems to be a latent attraction in the international business literature to consider disinvestment as a mirror image of investment abroad. Benito and Welch (1997) envisage some disinvestment moves as 'de-international- ization' operations, displaying a reorientation or even a reversal in the inter- nationalization process. Such a 'de-internationalization', which does not necessary mean a decline in a firm's commitment to international opera- tions, would be a 'moment' of readjustment in the path leading from exports to a global strategic approach by the company concerned.

At a different level, though with a similar tone, Boddewyn (1985) argued that an international disinvestment theory could be built through a reversal of the conditions laid down in international investment theory. Taking as a reference Dunning's eclectic paradigm (Dunning, 1981, 1988), Boddewyn holds that the disinvestment from company operations abroad takes place when the company no longer: (1) has ownership advantages over host countries' companies; or (2) considers internalized exploitation of such advantages profitable; or (3) prefers to exploit those advantages outside its home country. Later, Dunning (1988) revisited and deepened Boddewyn's approach by relating it to industrial organization theory as well as to a company's expectations on the future development of its in-house competences, competition pattern and technological and marketing opportunities.

It seems, however, that Boddewyn's proposal has some drawbacks. Some of these are associated with the need to revise and adapt the eclectic paradigm to the new environment for international operations (Dunning, 1995, 2003; Cantwell and Narula, 2003). Extending Cantwell and Narula's comments on the scope and focus of ownership advantages, it may be argued that several disinvestment decisions are mainly due to the challenges of international competition from other TNCs. Furthermore, one may contend that the closure of some international operations is not contradictory with the existing ownership advantages and the interest in their internalized exploitation; it may correspond basically to a reconfiguration of locations, having in mind R&D, production, logistics and market supply and servicing considerations.

Another point is that disinvestment of a given operation is largely contingent on the history of the headquarters–subsidiary relationship (Griffin, 2003), as well as on the magnitude of specific and non-recoverable investments undertaken in the subsidiary concerned. Finally, if investments may be envisaged exclusively from the investing TNC standpoint, disinvestments always involve two actors, though with different weights – the TNC network and the subsidiary.

Since Van Den Bulcke's (1979) analysis of international disinvestments, a significant body of literature was published in the field, mostly focused on the econometric testing of sets of hypotheses concerning the influence of specific factors (Bane and Neubauer, 1981; Davidson and McFetridge, 1984; Li, 1995; Barkema, Bell and Pennings, 1996; Benito, 1997b; Larimo, 1997; Mariotti and Piscitello, 1997; Hennart, Kim and Zeng, 1998; Shin, 2000; Mata and Portugal, 2000, 2002). A summary of the major findings from this literature is presented in Table 3.1. To enable a comparison, the findings of Van Den Bulcke (1979) on disinvestment, and Van Den Bulcke and Halsberghe (1979) on employment losses, are also included, although they only provide relatively rough measures of statistical significance.

As definitions of disinvestment are not the same for all the papers considered, interpretation of results should be carefully undertaken; in some instances there is even a comparison between different disinvestment concepts in the same piece of research (Mariotti and Piscitello, 1997; Hennart, Kim and Zeng, 1998; Mata and Portugal, 2000). This is most probably the reason behind the opposite signs found for some factors in different contributions and even in the same paper – as happens, for instance with international experience and size of investing company in Mariotti and Piscitello (1997).

In spite of these problems, Table 3.1 provides interesting findings. First, with the exception of Van Den Bulcke (1979) and Mata and Portugal (2000),[8] who found a non-significant relationship, there is a widespread agreement that acquisition moves entail a higher propensity for later disinvestments.

Table 3.1 Empirical literature on divestment: a summary of the main findings

	Van Den Bulcke (1979)	Van Den Bulcke and Halsberghe (1979)[1]	Bane & Neubauer (1981)	Davidson & McFetridge (1984)	Li (1995)	Barkema, Bell & Pennigs (1996)	Benito (1997)	Larimo (1997)	Mariotti & Piscitello (1997)[2]	Hennart Kim & Zeng (1998)[3]	Shin (2000)	Mata & Portugal (2000)[4]	Mata & Portugal (2000)[5]
Political risk							ns (+)	+***	+/+*				-/-
Host-country economic growth							-***	-***	-*/-**				
Host-country manufacturing growth										-***/-***		+/+	
Cultural distance						+*	ns (+)	+					-/-
Former foreign investment												-/-	
Joint-ventures	ns (-)			+***	+***		+	+**	+/+***	+/+***		-/+	
Acquisitions	ns (-)			+***	+***		+***	+	+*/+***	+/+**			
International experience							-	-***	-				
Host-country experience				-	-*	+	+	+***		-/+			
Diversification					+***	-	-	-	+*/+**				
Size of investing company							+	+***	-***/+	-/+**			
R&D intensity of investing company			+		-***		+/-	+/-***	+***/-	-/+**			
Subsidiary industry	+[6]												
Subsidiary age	ns				+*				+**/+** +**/nd		-		
Size of subsidiary	-							-***	-***/-***	-/+		-/-	-***|
Subsidiary capital intensity		-									+*		
Ownership (%)	ns (+)												
Entry mode: Greenfield		-										-/+	-*/-**
Subsidiary human capital		-										-/-	-/-
Subsidiary export orientation													-***/-**
Subsidiary productivity													
Subsidiary growth													+***|
Minimum efficient Scale													
Economies of scale												-/+	+***|

Notes

[1] Employment change (not exactly disinvestment); [2] Failure/restructuring; [3] Liquidation/sell-off; [4] Divestment/liquidation; [5] Majority owned/fully-owned subsidiaries; [6] Food, beverages and tobacco; textiles and clothing.
+ denotes higher probability of disinvestment (however defined); n.s. denotes not significant; *** indicates significant at 1%; ** indicates significant at 5%; * indicates significant at 10%.
– denotes lower probability of disinvestment.

This is consistent with the orientations of both the industrial-organization and strategic-management literature. The second aspect concerns the influence of locational characteristics, namely political risk and cultural distance. There appears to be a consensus that political risk increases the probability of disinvestment (Larimo, 1997), while host-country economic growth reduces it. The only exception with regard to the last point is Mariotti and Piscitello (1997) where the effect of cultural distance is positive (that is, increases the probability of disinvestment), but not very strong. This last finding is consistent with the interpretation that the main influence of cultural distance takes place *ex ante*, deterring investments, especially by SMEs.[9] The third strand concerns industry factors. As may be seen in Table 3.1, most recent econometric research has disregarded industry features in explaining disinvestment, the main exceptions being Shaver (1995), not reported in the table, and Mata and Portugal (2002), who considered several 'industry environment' features as control variables. Although some of them, like concentration, industry growth and foreign presence, were found to be insignificant, economies of scale and new-firm entry rates were found to be highly significant, and increasing the probability of disinvestment by foreign-owned firms. It is interesting to remark that Van Den Bulcke (1979) had already put a strong emphasis on industry characteristics as a relevant consideration to study disinvestment decisions. Notwithstanding the difference between his work and Mata and Portugal (2002), the main message is common – the industry has to be taken into account.

The fourth finding concerns investing-country variables. There appears to be no convergence among the various pieces of research concerning the role of investing company size, but conversely it seems clear that international experience lowers the probability of disinvestment.[10] This lends support to the contention that internationalization processes involve learning phenomena, with a sharing of experiential knowledge within the TNC;[11] it may be further argued that such learning is not only dependent on time, but also on space, analogies being established between similar locations. Developing further the ideas already presented in Benito and Welch (1997), Benito (2003) argues that in the long run, subsidiaries of companies following transnational strategies would be the most vulnerable to disinvestment due to the fact that they are exposed to the vicissitudes of headquarters' 'ambitious attempts at reconciling the seemingly divergent demands of global integration versus local responsiveness' (Benito, 2003: 18).[12]

The last strand deals with subsidiary characteristics. Contrary to Van Den Bulcke (1979) and Van Den Bulcke and Halsberghe (1979), who undertook interesting exercises to grasp the influence of subsidiary behaviour on disinvestment moves, the majority of recent econometric studies tend to follow what Griffin (2003) called the headquarters perspective, overlooking subsidiary features and initiatives.[13] The only characteristics usually taken into account are age,[14] entry mode and ownership structure. Mariotti and

Piscitello (1997) and Mata and Portugal (2000, 2002), however, include information on additional subsidiary features. One of the most interesting findings by Mata and Portugal (2000, 2002) was that a subsidiary's human capital (defined as the share of university graduates in total employment) is a strong deterrent to disinvestment, through either sell-off or liquidation.

Empirical studies provide, therefore, relevant indications on the main determinants of disinvestment, often corroborating theoretical suggestions about the risks entailed by investments abroad. Particularly useful is the distinction developed by some authors between different forms of disinvestment that clearly shows that the mix of determinants is contingent upon how disinvestment is defined. The opposition between failure and restructuring, by Mariotti and Piscitello (1997), is especially instructive, namely from the international management perspective.

It appears, however, that the extant literature has shortcomings in three main areas. First, there is an almost complete absence of longitudinal perspectives, with the noteworthy exceptions of Boddewyn (1979) and Griffin (2003). Focus has been put on disinvestment determinants, overlooking the process which led to such a decision (MacLachlan, 1992). The second criticism concerns the insufficient analysis of the host-country investment climate as well as its evolution. As will be developed below, there is a co-evolution between the investment and operational conditions provided by the host country, and the characteristics of foreign subsidiaries located there, a point which also emerged in some of Van Den Bulcke's writings (namely Van Den Bulcke, 1979, 1985; and Van Den Bulcke and Halsberghe, 1979). When those conditions do not fit the locational features required by investing companies, disinvestment is more likely to take place in the vein of what was suggested by Boddewyn (1985) or Dunning (1988). This is not necessarily synonimous to low host-country economic performance; on the contrary, especially for labour-cost-reducing investments, it may be just the opposite – economic performance prevents the continuation of old, low-cost-seeking investments. The third point deals with subsidiary characteristics. Present subsidiary roles (and their evolution) are more relevant for disinvestment analysis than the subsidiary mode of establishment or age. It is striking that none of the research reviewed considered a typology of subsidiaries, although Mata and Portugal (2000) suggest that it would be helpful to do so. Therefore, in my view, the research on disinvestment needs to integrate the typologies of subsidiary roles[15] as well as the study of their temporal evolution (Taggart, 1998; Birkinshaw and Hood, 1997).[16]

Endogenous motivations and contextual factors: a new framework for studying disinvestment decisions

The comments raised above suggest that the study of disinvestment would be significantly improved if a longitudinal and process approach is taken, having in mind, in the vein of Van Den Bulcke (1979), two main groups of factors – endogenous and contextual.

Endogenous factors are those specific to the TNC network, including subsidiary characteristics and relationships with other TNC units. They may be organized along two main axes: the first concerns the strategic, managerial and international positioning and competitiveness features which shape, constrain or promote corporate investment – and disinvestment – decisions; the second deals with the features, competences, roles and initiative of the subsidiary (or subsidiaries) concerned and its integration in the TNC network – that is, what is usually called corporate embeddedness (Andersson and Forsgren, 1996). Contextual factors may also be clustered along two dimensions: sectoral and local. The sectoral dimension includes variables such as market structure, industry competitiveness patterns, and innovation trajectories. The local dimension concerns host-country (or region) investment conditions as well as territorial dynamics which may generate learning processes for the subsidiary and the whole TNC (Birkinshaw and Hood, 2000). Of course all of the four axes or dimensions mentioned above are interrelated, the subsidiary being to a large extent the locus of convergence of them all.

On the basis of this reasoning, a framework for the study of disinvestment was developed and is presented in Figure 3.2. The four dimensions suggested were already mentioned by Mariotti and Piscitello (1997); however, the present framework has three relevant differences with regard to previous work – process and longitudinal features are stronger, interrelationships between the various groups of variables are made more explicit, and a wider array of potentially relevant factors is identified.

Looking at the basic relationships displayed in Figure 3.2, two main points should be stressed. The first is the introduction of a stepwise approach in studying disinvestment; this is achieved by including the possibility of commitment decline as a preliminary step, before the more drastic decision of disinvestment either through liquidation or sell-off. This is the expression of the contention that commitment decline is often the prelude for further disinvestment moves, as Van Den Bulcke (1979) implicitly suggested. In my opinion, the motives behind sell-off are, as a rule, more ambiguous than those leading to liquidation, since they entail the attractiveness of the subsidiary to other investors. The second point deals with the relevance of the subsidiary as the locus of convergence of interactions. A subsidiary abroad has a triple embeddedness: corporate (in the TNC network), local and sectoral. The first two factors are the most important for current purposes as an expression of the subsidiary's double appurtenance – element of a transnational group and 'community' of activity (De Geus, 1997) located in a specific territory. It is possible, in this vein, to envisage the sale of an equity stake as a testimony of the subsidiary as a dynamic 'community', able to respond to change: an MBO is the highest expression of the capability and

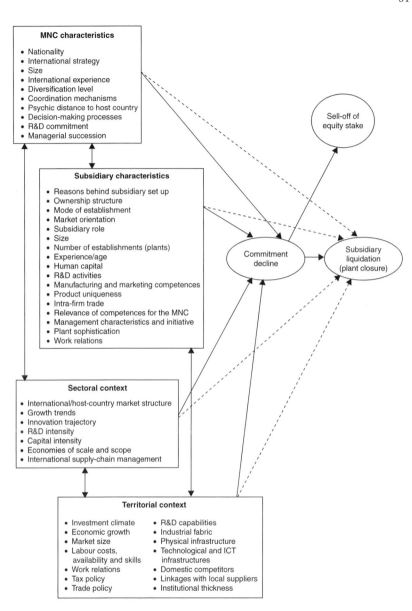

Figure 3.2   Disinvestment decision framework

involvement of such a 'community'.[17] Conversely, liquidation would correspond to the absence of persona – to use De Geus' (1997) word – or, in other terms, an incapacity of the subsidiary to survive outside the TNC environment.[18] Therefore, the idea that disinvestment may be studied in the context of subsidiary evolution gains additional support.

Figure 3.2   is largely self-explanatory, since it includes a specification of the main elements of the four dimensions suggested as well as their interrelations. Nevertheless, there are a few aspects which deserve a brief comment.

Concerning TNC characteristics, four points should be highlighted: company nationality, international strategy, coordination mechanisms, and managerial succession. TNC nationality was extensively studied in Van Den Bulcke (1979), to find that, although disinvestment by American-owned TNCs was not higher than that of EEC-based TNCs, nationality was nevertheless an important consideration in understanding subsidiary behaviour (Van Den Bulcke and Halsberghe, 1979; De Beule and Van Den Bulcke, 2001). International strategy has a decisive influence on subsidiary management and, ultimately, on the logic of disinvestment decisions (Benito, 2003). For instance, firms following multinational strategies – as defined by Bartlett and Ghoshal (1989) – will, as a rule, show a lower disinvestment propensity than those with transnational strategies; the flexibility required by transnational strategies is likely to stimulate disinvestment decisions.[19] Complementarily, the recourse to coordination mechanisms based on centralization or formalization tends to increase headquarters' decision-authority or subsidiaries' compliance with TNC rules and regulations, thereby making disinvestment decisions less problematic and conflictual at the TNC level. In contrast, socialization and the adoption of non-hierarchical organizational philosophies (Hedlund, 1986; White and Poynter, 1990) may act as a countervailing power with regard to disinvestment decisions. A final issue concerns managerial succession (Van Den Bulcke, 1979; Benito and Welch, 1997). As Van Den Bulcke (1979: 6), following Torneden (1975), wrote, 'a change of chairman, president or head of the international division often preceded a foreign disinvestment decision'.[20]

Turning now to subsidiary characteristics, three features deserve a mention: group embeddedness, local embeddedness, and subsidiary competences. The interplay among these aspects in the case of disinvestment is somewhat different than for assessing subsidiary autonomy (Van Den Bulcke and Halsberghe, 1984; Simões, Biscaya and Nevado, 2002). Group embeddedness is a critical condition to reduce disinvestment risk, as Duhaime and Grant (1984) and Koening (1988) have shown. The key element for the subsidiary to survive as such is, however, the development of interdependence relationships – neither dependence nor full autonomy. The latter situations make the subsidiary more vulnerable: the first due to the absence of 'voice' and specific weight in the TNC; the second because it promotes a 'decoupling' between subsidiary and TNC interests. Interdependence relationships are enhanced by multicentre organizational models, namely by the definition of centres of excellence (Holm and Pedersen, 2000),[21] and of course by subsidiary competence accumulation and development. In this context, a key factor is the subsidiary's capability to gain new businesses in the intra-TNC competition to capture new projects and resources (Mudambi, 1999); the lack of intra-group competitiveness will, sooner or later, endanger subsidiary survival.

Local embeddedness is also relevant as an instrument for gaining market share and having access to resources and knowledge which may be of importance not only for the subsidiary concerned, but for the TNC as a whole. It is widely recognized that international management is largely a matter of orchestrating resources and knowledge dispersed throughout a network of subsidiaries (Bartlett and Ghoshal, 1989; Cantwell, 1995; Caraça and Simões, 1995; Schmid, Schuring and Kutschker, 2002; Frost, Birkinshaw and Ensign, 2002). This is particularly relevant for subsidiaries located in countries with very dynamic or strategically relevant national systems of innovation, but it also happens in less-advanced environments where local opportunities may be exploited as a tool for the subsidiary to develop distinctive capabilities, which may be relevant for the whole TNC (Simões, Biscaya and Nevado, 2002; Simões and Nevado, 2000).

This leads to consideration of a subsidiary's role and competences. If the subsidiary is prima facie a plant, similar to others, without marketing competencies and manufacturing low value-added products, its dependence on the TNC network is usually very high. If this is the case, survival cannot be taken for granted. Unless the subsidiary is able to redefine its role through a committed initiative of activity upgrading, the very process of development of the host country, with an increase in nominal (and real) wages, endangers subsidiary survival, as Van Den Bulcke (1979) has shown for textile and clothing subsidiaries in Belgium. Manufacturing platforms and integrated manufacturers (Simões, 1992) are the kinds of subsidiaries more vulnerable to disinvestment decisions.

Looking at the sectoral context, four features deserve consideration. First, industry growth and market structure have an important bearing on disinvestment decisions, especially on what concerns the pressure for worldwide rationalization strategies. In a similar vein comes international supply-chain management, an issue that is increasingly leading to a redefinition of subsidiary roles as well as of manufacturing locations (Gereffi, 1999; Hudson, 2001). Innovation trajectories are also relevant in that low-technology-intensive, marketing-driven industries, where a divide between functional competencies exists, are more amenable to divestment. Finally, scale and scope economies were identified as relevant determinants of divestment, not only in theoretical terms (Benito, 2003), but also empirically (Mata and Portugal, 2002), for economies of scale.

A large host of factors were mentioned concerning the territorial context. A cursory look at the factors selected shows that the territory is a space of convergence and interaction of different variables, with diverse characteristics and paces of change. Furthermore, the attractiveness of a territory is not an absolute feature; rather, it is a variable which depends on evolutionary trends as well as on interterritorial competition. In other words, the influence of a given territorial context on disinvestment decisions is not independent from a TNC's assessment of alternative locations. For instance, the decision of Renault to close its plants in Portugal has to be analysed having in mind political and economic developments in Central Europe, and especially the investment opportunity in Slovenia. Even more striking is the decision of Seagate to close its plant in Ireland (where it had invested just two years earlier) and transfer manufacturing to Malaysia, after the sharp devaluation of the Malayan currency following the 1997 Asian monetary crisis.

Conclusions

The work developed above shows that international disinvestment analysis requires, on the one hand, the clarification and fine-tuning of the concept of disinvestments, and on the other the convergence of a set of explanatory factors, often intertwined. The fine-tuning of what disinvestment means demands, first of all, a distinction between subsidiary liquidation and its survival, even under different ownership. However, disinvestment often being a process and not an act, the decline of subsidiary activities may anticipate future disinvestment operations, as Van Den Bulcke (1979) remarked. This is a relevant point in at least two perspectives: the study of subsidiary life-cycles, and host-country foreign investment policies.[22]

With regard to explanatory factors, all the four dimensions pointed out above are relevant. While each dimension may be seen in isolation, it seems critical to analyse their interrelationships, which may take different patterns for each specific disinvestment case. Sectoral context is a tool to understand disinvestments, particularly in global industries where the competitive arena is the whole world and competitive shortcomings may have worldwide repercussions, as well as in industries characterized by wide-ranging changes in business cycles. Territorial context is a key element when the analysis is focused on host country, or region, welfare and on host-country foreign investment policies. The suggestion of a co-evolution between local economic conditions and subsidiaries characteristics and competences is a research path which deserves further analysis and empirical work. The relevance of TNC characteristics is obvious: at the end of the day, it is the TNC who takes the decision to reduce or downgrade activities, to sell or to liquidate the subsidiary. However, the subsidiary is the locus of convergence and intertwining of the various dimensions, as pointed out above. Therefore, the subsidiary is not an innocent pawn that passively suffers the consequences of decisions taken at headquarters level, sectoral vicissitudes or host country policy changes. It also has a role to play and some room for manoeuvre. Subsidiary strategy, competences, dynamics and initiative cannot be omitted when studying disinvestment processes.

The framework suggested in this chapter also has implications for host country economic policy, namely on what concerns foreign investment. In some instances, and provided that negative social effects stemming from disinvestment are adequately managed and countervailed, foreign disinvestment may have a positive dimension, insofar as it is a consequence of economic restructuring and the building-up of new, more sophisticated, local attractiveness factors. Van Den Bulcke's (1985: 277) contention that international corporations tend to be 'swifter and ... more thorough in carrying out rationalisation investment and in reshaping their policies' still holds. As these corporations undertake restructuring and redesign moves (Enderwick, 1989; Hamel and Prahalad, 1994; Jagersma and Van Gorp, 2003; Benito, 2003) and the patterns of investment abroad change (Ozawa, 1993), the profile of inward investment in a country also evolves as a consequence of the interplay between ownership and internalization factors, on the one hand, and location advantages on the other. This is not a fast process, but rather an evolutionary one, with key moments of punctuated change. It involves three main groups of moves: liquidation of subsidiaries or closure of plants which are no longer viable; existing subsidiaries' evolution and adaptation to new circumstances, either under the same ownership or with new forms of governance; and establishment of new subsidiary vintages, benefiting from the improved locational factors (and, on the other hand, promoting them).

With regard to policy-making, the matter is neither just to attract new investments nor mourning irreversible disinvestments (attenuating, however, their social consequences). A key factor of inward investment policy-making is to prevent disinvestments by promoting the upgrading and modernization of existing subsidiaries, in the context of co-evolutionary processes, and providing them the territorial leverage to accumulate the capacities and competences needed to enhance their relevance for the TNC network. In the cases where disinvestment is irreversible, the cooperation between companies and national authorities advocated by Van Den Bulcke (1979) may be important, not only to minimize social problems but also to find alternative solutions, enabling ownership changes without activity decline. Cooperation may even contribute to curb the opportunistic bent of some investors, reducing the scope for later conflicts.

This contribution comes in the wake of a long 'current' in which Danny Van Den Bulcke was one of the pioneers. As I have shown, many of his findings are still relevant today, particularly about the disinvestment-as-process approach, the confluence of internal and external factors behind international divestment by firms, and the policy implications. The present chapter draws on Van Den Bulcke's heritage in studying disinvestment – thereby showing my personal debt to him, not just as a friend, but also as a researcher in international business. Our knowledge about international divestment decisions and processes is still limited, and the avenues opened by Danny and other pioneers await further exploration.

Notes

1   The same perspective was followed by Boddewyn (1979) in the fellow analysis of the managerial dimension of disinvestment.
2   It is interesting to note that Van Den Bulcke (1979) already anticipated this distinction.
3   Or, to be more precise, former subsidiary in most cases.
4   See, on this topic, Chi (2000).
5   This is particularly relevant when there are regional integration processes, as is happening in Europe now.
6   In the latter case, greenfield investment led, however to a higher probability of liquidation.
7   It should be pointed out, however, that comparative research on the employment behaviour of domestic and foreign firms does not indicate significant differences between the two groups (Van Den Bulcke and Halsberghe, 1979; Van Den Bulcke, 1985; McAleese and Counahan, 1979; Simões, 1987).
8   In the latter case, greenfield investment led, however, to a higher probability of liquidation.
9   An additional interpretation is that the anticipated advantages from working in a seemingly familiar environment may be countervailed by the 'psychic-distance paradox' (O'Grady and Lane, 1996; Fenwick, Edwards and Buckley, 2003).
10 The exception is obviously the finding by Mariotti and Piscitello (1997) when disinvestment is defined as restructuring. This only happens, as a rule, for TNCs which already enjoy a relevant international experience.
11 Shaver, Mitchell and Yeung (1997) also show that, under certain conditions, companies may learn with other companies.
12 It seems to me, however, that this perspective may be a little biased by placing a higher risk on organizational difficulties to balance divergent 'imperatives' than on the competitive risk of adopting alternative approaches mainly focused on one 'imperative' only (integration versus local responsiveness).
13 To some extent this may be due to the wide use of existing databases. These concern, as a rule, investments abroad by TNCs of a given country.
14 It should be acknowledged that the results in this regard are not consistent.
15 There are several typologies of subsidiary roles which may be useful in this context: see, for instance, Taggart and McDermott (1993), Taggart (1997) and Simões (1992).
16 Although focused on corporate international strategies, Benito (2003) also raises the question of subsidiary roles (see p. 17), and may be extended in that direction.
17 See, from a similar perspective, Delany (1998) and Griffin (2003). This latter author discusses an interesting case of a subsidiary who 'survived' four divestment operations.
18 It should be noted, however, the existence of cases where the TNC liquidates the subsidiary to avoid its capabilities being used by a competitor. More generally, TNC culture and strategy also constrains subsidiary survival (Griffin, 2003).

19 This reasoning is consistent with Benito (2003). However, as pointed out above, other points of his argument are not unchallenged (see note 12 above).
20 A very interesting discussion of the impact of managerial succession on disinvestment decisions may be found in Benito and Welch (1997).
21 It should be borne in mind, however, that even subsidiaries with a centre of excellence label may be divested, especially in the context of wider strategic decisions of discontinuing some line of business; the example of ABB's hydropower subsidiary in Portugal reported by Simões and Nevado (2000) is a case in point.
22 Danny Van Den Bulcke's contribution on this issue is also noteworthy (see Van Den Bulcke, 1979, 1985; and Van Den Bulcke and Halsberghe, 1979, 1984).

References

Andersson, U. and Forsgren, M. (1996) 'Subsidiary Embeddedness and Control in the Multinational Corporation', *International Business Review*, 5(5): 487–508.
Bane, W.T. and Neubauer, F.-F. (1981) 'Diversification and the Failure of New Foreign Activities', *Strategic Management Journal*, 2: 219–33.
Barkema, H., Bell, J.H. and Pennings, J.M. (1996) 'Foreign Entry, Cultural Barriers and Learning', *Strategic Management Journal*, 15(2): 151–66.
Bartlett, C. and Ghoshal, S. (1989) *Managing Across Borders – The Transnational Solution*. Boston: Harvard Business School Press.
Benito, G. (2003) 'Divestment Seen Through the Lens of International Business Strategy', Paper presented at the International Conference on Divestment, Faculdade de Letras, University of Lisbon, Lisbon.
Benito, G.R.G. (1997a) 'Divestment of Foreign Production Operations', *Applied Economics*, 29: 1365–77.
Benito, G.R.G. (1997b) 'Why are Foreign Subsidiaries Divested? A Conceptual Framework', in I. Björkman and M. Forsgren (eds), *The Nature of the International Firm*. Copenhagen: Copenhagen Business School Press, pp. 309–34.
Benito, G.R.G. and Welch, L. (1997) 'De-Internationalization', *Management International Review*, Special Issue, 37(2): 7–26.
Birkinshaw, J. and Hood, N. (1997) 'An Empirical Study of Development Processes in Foreign Owned Subsidiaries in Canada and Scotland', *Management International Review*, 37(4): 339–64.
Birkinshaw, J. and Hood, N. (1998) *Multinational Corporate Evolution and Subsidiary Development*. London: Palgrave Macmillan.
Birkinshaw, J. and Hood, N. (2000) 'Characteristics of Foreign Subsidiaries in Industry Clusters', *Journal of International Business Studies*, 31(1): 141–54.
Boddewyn, J.J. (1979) 'Foreign Divestment: Magnitude and Factors', *Journal of International Business Studies*, 10(1): 21–7.
Boddewyn, J.J. (1985) 'Theories of Foreign Direct Investment and Divestment: A Classificatory Note', *Management International Review*, 25(1): 57–65.
Cantwell, J. (1995) 'The Globalisation of Technology; What Remains from the Product Cycle Model?', *Cambridge Journal of Economics*, 19: 155–74.
Cantwell, J. and Narula, R. (eds) (2003) *International Business and the Eclectic Paradigm*. London: Routledge.
Caraça, J.M.G. and Simões, V.C. (1995) 'The New Economy and its Implications for International Organizations', in R. Schiattarella (ed.), *New Challenges for European and International Business: Proceedings of the EIBA Annual Conference*. Urbino: Confindustria, Vol. 1, pp. 257–82.

Chi, T. (2000) 'Option to Acquire or Divest a Joint Venture', *Strategic Management Journal*, 21: 665–87.

Clark, G.L. and Wrigley, N. (1997) 'Exit, the Firm and Sunk Costs: Reconceptualizing the Corporate Geography of Divestment and Plant Closure', *Progress in Human Geography*, 21(3): 338–58.

Davidson, W.H. and McFetridge, D.G. (1984) 'Key Characteristics in the Choice of International Technology Transfer Mode', *Journal of International Business Studies*, 16: 5–21.

De Beule, F. and Van Den Bulcke, D. (2001) 'Industrial Clusters and Japanese Manufacturing Affilliates in the Belgian Small Open Economy', in Daniel Van Den Bulcke and Alain Verbeke (eds), *Globalization and the Small Open Economy*. Aldeshot: Edward Elgar.

De Geus, A. (1997) *The Living Company: Growth, Learning and Longevity in Business.* London: Nicholas Brealey Publishing.

Delany, E. (1998) 'Subsidiary Development of Multinational Subsidiaries in Ireland', in J. Birkinshaw and N. Hood (eds), *Multinational Corporate Evolution and Subsidiary Development*. London: Palgrave Macmillan, pp. 239–67.

Dranikoff, L. Koller, T. and Schneider, A. (2002) 'Divestiture: Strategy's Missing Link', *Harvard Business Review*, May: 75–83.

Duhaime, I. and Grant, J. (1984) 'Factors Influencing Divestment Decision-making: Evidence from a Field Study', *Strategic Management Journal*, 5: 301–18.

Dunning, J. (2003) 'The Eclectic (OLI) Paradigm of International Production: Past, Present and Future', in J. Cantwell and R. Narula (eds), *International Business and the Eclectic Paradigm*. London: Routledge, pp. 25–46.

Dunning, J.H. (1981) *Explaining International Production*. London: Unwin Hyman.

Dunning, J.H. (1988) 'The Eclectic Paradigm of International Production: A Restatement and Some Possible Extensions', *Journal of International Business Studies*, 30(Spring): 1–25.

Dunning, J.H. (1995) 'Reappraising the Eclectic Paradigm in an Age of Alliance Capitalism', *Journal of International Business Studies*, 26: 461–91.

Enderwick, P. (1989) 'Multinational Corporate Restructuring and International Competitiveness', *California Management Review*: 44–58.

Fenwick, M., Edwards, R. and Buckley, P.J. (2003) 'Is Cultural Similarity Misleading? The Experience of Australia Manufacturers in Britain', *International Business Review*, 12(3): 297–309.

Freitas, J.A. (1998) *Determinantes do Desinvestimento em Portugal*, Working Papers. Lisbon: GEPE/Ministério da Economia.

Frost, T., Birkinshaw, J. and Ensign, P. (2002) 'Centers of Excellence in Multinational Corporations', *Strategic Management Journal*, 23: 997–1018.

Gereffi, G. (2001) 'Shifting Governance Structures in Global Commodity Chains, with Special Reference to the Internet', *American Behavioral Scientist*, 44(10): 1616–37.

Giunta, A. and Martinelli, F. (1995) 'The Impact of Post-Fordist Corporate Restructuring in a Peripheral Region – The Mezzogiorno de Italy', in A. Amin and J. Tomaney (eds), *Behind the Myth of European Union*. London: Routledge.

Griffin, R. (2003) 'Subsidiary Divestment: The Case of CDMI Ireland 1970–2002', *Irish Journal of Management*, 24(1): 215–28.

Hamel, G. and Prahalad, C.K. (1994) 'Competing for the Future', *Harvard Business Review*, July/August: 122–8.

Hamilton, R.T. and Chow, Y.K. (1993) 'Why Managers Divest: Evidence from New Zealand's Largest Companies', *Strategic Management Journal*, 14: 479–84.

Haynes, M. Thompson, S. and Wright, M. (2000) 'The Determinants of Corporate Divestment in the UK', *International Journal of Industrial Organization*, 18: 1201–22.

Hedlund, G. (1986) 'The Hypermodern MNC: A Heterarchy?', *Human Resource Management*, 25: 9–36.

Hennart, J.-F., Kim, D.-J. and Zeng, M. (1998) 'The Impact of Joint Venture Status on the Longevity of Japanese Stakes in US Manufacturing Affiliates', *Organization Science*, 9(3): 382–95.

Holm, U. and Pedersen, T. (2000) *The Emergence and Impact of MNC Centres of Excellence – A Subsidiary Perspective*. London: Palgrave Macmillan.

Hood, N. and Young, S. (1982) *Multinational in Retreat: the Scottish Experience*. Edinburgh: Edimburgh University Press.

Hudson, R. (2001) *Development in Europe*, Paper delivered at the DIVEST Workshop, Lisbon.

Hudson, R. (2003) *Corporate Strategies, Industrial (Dis)investment and the New Geography of Uneven Development in the New Europe*, Paper delivered at the International Conference on Divestment: Corporate Strategies, the Regions and Policy Responses. Lisbon: Faculdade de Letras, University of Lisbon.

Jagersma, P.K. and van Gorp, D.M. (2003) 'International Divestments and Empirical Perspective', *Journal of General Management*, 29(1): 47–67.

Kobrin, S.J. (1988) 'Strategic Integration in Fragmented Environments: Social and Political Assessment by Subsidiaries of Multinational Firms', in N. Hood and J.-E. Vahlne (eds), *Strategies in Global Competition*, pp. 104–20.

Koening, G. (1988) 'Vulnérabilité des Entreprises: Le Cas des Filiales', *Revue Française de Gestion*: 74–84.

Kogut, B. (1991) 'Joint ventures and the Option to Expand and Acquire', *Management Science*, 37(1): 19–33.

Larimo, J. (1997) 'Determinants of Divestments in Foreign Production Operations made by Finnish Firms in OECD Countries', in K. Macharzina, M.J. Oesterle and J. Wolf (eds), *Proceedings of the 23rd Conference of EIBA*. Stuttgart: University of Höhenheim.

Li, J. (1995) 'Foreign Entry and Survival: Effects of Strategic Choices on Performance in International Markets', *Strategic Management Journal*, 16: 333–51.

MacLachlan, I. (1992) 'Plant Closure and Market Dynamics: Competitive Strategy and Rationalization', *Economic Geography*, 68(2): 128–45.

Mariotti, S. and Piscitello, L. (1997) 'Divestment as Failure or Part of a Restructuring Strategy: Evidence from the Italian TNCs', in K. Macharzina, M.J. Oesterle and J. Wolf (eds), *Proceedings of the 23rd Conference of EIBA*. Stuttgart: University of Höhenheim.

Mata, J. and Portugal, P. (1997) *The Exit Mode of Foreign Entrants: The Impact of Entry and Post-Entry Strategies*, Paper delivered at the 6th Encontro de Economia Industrial, Lisboa.

Mata, J. and Portugal, P. (2000) 'Closure and Divestiture by Foreign Entrants: The Impact of Entry and Post-Entry Strategies', *Strategic Management Journal*, 21: 549–62.

Mata, J. and Portugal, P. (2002) 'The Survival of New Domestic and Foreign-Owned Firms', *Strategic Management Journal*, 23: 323–43.

McAleese, D. and Counahan, M. (1979) ' "Stickers" or "Snatchers"? Employment in Multinational Corporations during Recession', *Oxford Bulletin of Economics and Statistics*, 41(4): 345–58.

Mudambi, R. (1999) 'TNC Internal Capital Markets and Subsidiary Strategic Independence', *International Business Review*, 8: 197–211.

O'Grady, S. and Lane, H.W. (1996) 'The Psychic Distance Paradox', *Journal of International Business Studies*, 27(2): 309–33.

Ozawa, T. (1993) 'Foreign Direct Investment and Structural Transformation: Japan as a Recycler of Market and Industry', *Business & The Contemporary World*, V(2): 129–50.

Porter, M.E. (1976) 'Please Note Location of Nearest Exit: Exit Barriers and Planning', *California Management Review*, 19: 21–33.

Prahalad, C.K. and Doz, Y.L. (1987) *The Multinational Mission: Balancing Local Demands and Global Vision*. New York: The Free Press.

Pyke, A. (2003) *Building a Geographical Political Economy of Closure: The Case of R&D in the North East Region of England*, Paper for International Conference on Divestment. Lisbon: Faculdade de Letras, University of Lisbon.

Schmid, S., Schuring, A. and Kutschker, M. (2002) 'The MNC as a Network: A Closer Look at Intra-Organizational Flows', in S. Lundan (ed.), *Network Knowledge in International Business*. Aldershot: Edward Elgar, pp. 45–72.

Shaver, J. (1995) 'The Influence of Industry Growth and Foreign Entry Rate on Foreign Direct Investment Survival', *Academy of Management Journal*, Best Papers Proceedings: 201–5.

Shaver, J.M., Mitchell, W. and Yeung, B. (1997) 'The Effect of Own-firm and Other-firm Experience on Foreign Direct Investment Survival in the United States, 1987–92', *Strategic Management Journal*, 18: 811–24.

Shin, S.-H. (2000) 'The Foreign Divestment Factors in South Korea: An Analysis of the Trading Sector', *Multinational Business Review*, Fall: 98–103.

Simões, V.C. (1987) 'Capital Extranjero y Empleo: Comparación del Comportamiento de las Mayores Empresas Industriales', *Información Comercial Española*, 643: 121–32.

Simões, V.C. (1992) 'European Integration and the Pattern of FDI Inflow in Portugal', in J. Cantwell (ed.), *Multinational Investment in Modern Europe*. Aldershot: Edward Elgar, pp. 256–97.

Simões, V.C. and Nevado, P. (2000) *TNC Centres of Excellence and Acquisitions: Long Evolutionary Paths or Capturing Opportunities?*, MESIAS project, Madrid meeting.

Simões, V.C., Biscaya, R. and Nevado, P. (2002) 'Subsidiary Decision-Making Autonomy: Competences, Integration and Local Responsiveness', in S. Lundan (ed.), *Network Knowledge in Intewrnational Business*. Aldershot: Edward Elgar.

Taggart, J. (1997) 'Evaluation of the Integration-responsiveness Framework', *Management International Review*, 4: 295–318.

Taggart, J. and McDermott, M. (1993) *The Essence of International Business*. New York, NY: Prentice Hall.

Taggart, J.H. (1998) 'Identification and Development of Strategy at Subsidiary Level', in J. Birkinshaw and N. Hood (eds), *Multinational Corporate Evolution and Subsidiary Development*. London: Palgrave Macmillan, pp. 23–49.

Taggart, J.H. and Hood, N. (1999) 'Determinants of Autonomy in Multinational Corporation Subsidiaries', *European Management Journal*, 17(2): 226–36.

Tomaney, J., Pyke, A. and Cornford, J. (1999) 'Plant Closure and the Local Economy: The Case of Swan Hunter on Tyneside', *Regional Studies*, 33(5): 401–11.

Torneden, R. (1975) *Foreign Divestment by US Multinational Corporations*. New York: Praeger.

Vale, M. (2001) *Desinvestimento e Território: Um Quadro Conceptual de Análise*, Paper delivered at the DIVEST Workshop. Lisbon: DIVEST Project.

Vale, M. (2001) *Desinvestimento: Caracterização e Literatura de Referência*, Working paper. Lisbon: DIVEST.

Van Den Bulcke, D. (1995) 'The European Works Council: A New Challenge for Multinational Enterprises', in R. Schiattarella (ed.), *New Challenges for European and*

International Business, Proceedings of the 21st Annual Conference of EIBA, Vol. 2. Urbino: Confindustria/Universitá di Urbino, pp. 426–47.

Van Den Bulcke, D. (1982) *Disinvestment Trends of Foreign and Local Owned Enterprises in the Belgian Industry*. Brussels: Institute of the Enterprise.

Van Den Bulcke, D. (1983) *Disinvestment and Loss of Employment: A Comparison between Foreign and Belgian Enterprises*, Paper presented at Workshop on European Unemployment and Productivity. Oslo: EIASM.

Van Den Bulcke, D. and Halsberghe, E. (1984) *Employment Decision-Making in MNEs: Survey Results from Belgium*, Working Paper 32. Geneva: International Labour Office.

Van Den Bulcke, D. and Volkaert, J. (1993) Disinvestment as an Instrument of Economic Sanctions: Testcase South Africa. Antwerp: Centre for International Management and Development Antwerp (CIMDA), University of Antwerp.

Van Den Bulcke, D. (1979) *Investment and Divestment Policies of Multinational Companies in Europe*. London: Saxon House.

Van Den Bulcke, D. (1985) 'Belgium', in J.H. Dunning (ed.), *Multinational Enterprises, Economic Structure and International Competitiveness*. Chichester: John Wiley.

Van Den Bulcke, D. and Halsberghe, E. (1979) *Employment Effects of Multinational Enterprises: A Belgian Case Study*, Working Paper. Geneva: International Labour Office.

Watts, H.D. (1991) 'Plant Closures in Urban Areas: Towards a Local Policy Response', *Urban Studies*, 28(5): 803–17.

Watts, H.D. and Stafford, H.A. (1986) 'Plant Closure and the Multiplan Firm: Some Conceptual Issues', *Progress in Human Geography*, 10(2): 206–27.

White, R.E. and Poynter, T.A. (1990) 'Organizing for World-Wide Advantage', in C.A. Bartlett, Y. Doz and G. Hedlund (eds), *Managing the Global Firm*. London: Routledge, pp. 95–113.

4

The Rationales for Comprehensive Approaches to European Corporate Profits Taxation

Sylvain Plasschaert

Introductory remarks

According to the generally accepted terminology, whenever an enterprise starts operating abroad through an establishment of its own, it can be labelled as a transnational corporation (TNC). While this expression connotes giant TNCs, with a worldwide reach, many, and an increasing number of TNCs are of much smaller dimensions. Anyhow, TNCs of whatever stripe become exposed to a wide variety of regulations in each of their foreign 'host' countries. Corporate taxes are amongst the most burdensome and complex of such rules.

The EU-25 member states are engaged in an evolving sequence of further economic integration. The establishment of the single market, as from 1993, has essentially removed the internal frontiers for doing business and for the free movement of goods and services amongst member states, which creates to a very high degree a 'level playing field' with similar rules of the game for competing firms. The 12 members of the EMU have gone further, as they are now encompassed by a monetary union, with a single currency, thus eliminating exchange risks.

But, in the field of corporate taxation, several tax obstacles hooked on national specific tax regulations still impede the smooth operation of level playing ground rules. No harmonization of parameters in the field of direct taxation is mandated by the European Treaties. Member states understandably want to preserve their decision-making powers in the tax field; they want to use their national tax instruments – taxable bases and tax rates – to achieve objectives in the 'Musgravian' realms of resource allocation, macroeconomic stabilization and income (re)distribution; they jealously guard fiscal autonomy as a prominent attribute of sovereignty; they also feel uncertain about how a change-over to drastically new arrangements would impact on their revenues. Moreover, agreements about tax matters at the EU level can only be reached unanimously; even the proposals submitted to the

Convention in 2003 did not question this rule, and few member states anyhow resort to their veto right.

The thorough Report which the European Commission devoted to 'Company Taxation in the Internal Market', can be viewed as a landmark as to how the fiscal regime of enterprises with cross-border activities through affiliates abroad, that is of TNCs, could evolve (European Commission, 2002). It proposed a two-track strategy to deal with the corporate tax problems in the EU. On the one hand, it identified a number of sore points in the present constellation of international corporate taxation that stand in the way of a well-functioning internal market; several actions to remedy such inadequacies have in the meantime been initiated by the Commission, although progress is very slow, owing largely to the technicalities involved. But, on the other hand, in its last section the Report opened a window to far-reaching and almost revolutionary overhauls of the present arrangements. These new schemes are called 'comprehensive' approaches; their distinguishing feature is that they cut through the per-country compartmentalization of tax bases and associated tax liabilities, and instead target the consolidated profits (and losses) of the TNC, as a whole, but only as far as the EU region is concerned. In other words, such procedures would no longer treat each of the constituent units of TNCs as 'separate entities', thus requiring the determination of that part of the overall EU-originating profits of the TNC that should be assigned to each of the countries involved. Instead, the TNC would be approached tax-wise as a 'group', say, as a single 'family' instead of as a juxtaposition of its individual members.[1]

This chapter pursues a limited objective of critically evaluating the rationales that conceivably underpin the proposals for such comprehensive or 'holistic' formats of company taxation in the EU. To acquaint the reader with such schemes, they are sketched in the following section. We also first look at how the present system of international corporate taxation operates in its basic principles, which has striking differences with the comprehensive models. The final section briefly comments on an important issue that cannot be sidestepped in the debate about the comprehensive regimes, namely whether they should be limited to specific subgroups of TNCs and which subgroups should be eligible to these holistic formats.

The three main arguments in favour of a comprehensive corporate profits tax format in the EU are reviewed here, viz. (a) the insistence of the international business world to be confronted with a (hopefully) much simpler set of fiscal rules and to substantially reduce the heavy compliance costs; (b) the need to remove tax regulations that distort competition within the single internal market; and (c) the alleged fundamental incongruity of the basic principle in the present set of corporate tax rules, namely the 'separate entity' standard, on the one hand, and the increasingly complex and coalescing relationships between the different entities that compose a TNC, on the other hand.

A sketch of the alternative comprehensive schemes

Apart from what was called a single, compulsory harmonized tax base – which would imply the substitution of all 25 corporate tax systems by a single, unified one, but which, being utterly unrealistic, was not further considered by the Commission – the Report analysed three alternative holistic schemes, which I consider in turn in their main constituent elements.

The common (consolidated) tax base (CCTB)

Under this scheme, proposed by representatives of European (big) business, the taxable bases of the affiliates within the EU would be consolidated. This implies cross-border loss compensation, but each member country would retain the right to fix its own rate on that portion of the overall consolidated profit that would be assigned to it. Such apportionment would no longer be effected by way of the present 'separate entity' approach, with all its attendant difficulties, but by a 'formulary apportionment'. Thereto, the method applied for purposes of corporate taxation at the state level in the USA is viewed as a useful reference: there, each state applies its own rate on its part of the overall profit of a company, as determined by easily ascertainable criteria, such as the value of assets, labour costs and sales. The overall taxable base would be administered by the 'residence' country of the TNC. It also follows that a new tax code, incorporating those novel tax features, would have to be drafted; it would exist alongside the 15 actual national corporate tax legislations.

The European Union company income tax (EUCIT)

This scheme, originally suggested by the present author (Plasschaert, 1997), goes one step further. EU consolidated profits would be subjected to a single tax rate schedule, which would be determined at EU level. Hence, there would be no need for a formulary apportionment of the tax revenues. It also follows that the CIT would be a EU-tax proper, whose proceeds would accrue to the EU budget itself. Here also, the new tax would exist alongside the present tax codes of the member states. It could, but should not necessarily be administered at EU level; anyhow, the taxpaying company would only have to deal with a single tax authority.

Home-state taxation (HST)

This proposal, which has already benefited from a lot of technical work by its advocates (Lodin and Gammie, 2001), is of a different pedigree as it implements the concept of 'mutual recognition'. The specific feature of the HST is that TNCs would apply their national code, as regards the definition of the taxable base, also with respect to their affiliates in the member countries that would participate in the HST scheme. Hence, that company would only have to deal with one, that is its own, administration as regards the taxable base, but each of the countries involved would apply its own tax rate as, under the CCTB, the share of the consolidated profits would be determined by a 'formulary apportionment'. The existing tax codes would be further applied, and there would be no need for an additional tax code.

It is immediately obvious that any choice in favour of one or another of the alternative models not only involves a lot of technical issues, but also cannot avoid fundamental political choices. In a Communication that accompanied the Report in October 2001, the Commission narrowed the possible choice to that between the CCTB and the HST. The EUCIT was not retained for consideration; the preservation by the member states of the competence to fix their own rates was considered to be sacrosanct. The adamant rejection of a single EU-determined tax rate (as in the EUCIT scheme) by the representatives of international business has been a major consideration: they stated that the continuation of differentiated rates builds-in a downward pressure on corporate tax rates, thanks to competition amongst member states.

The presently prevailing system(s) of international corporate taxation

Speaking about 'the' system of international corporate taxation to which TNCs are subjected amounts to a misnomer. There is not a single set of tax rules that applies to TNCs, as no supranational authority edicts universally applicable regulations on the world scene, or even only within the EU. In fact, each country applies its own rules to its own ('resident') TNCs, and to foreign ('non-resident') TNCs. But a number of common principles have been agreed upon internationally that put some order in this field, if only to avoid duplication of tax claims against the same profits. Hence, I feel inclined to refer to the present arrangements as the 'prevailing system(s)' of TNC taxation.

The basic mechanisms

In broad outline, the typically prevailing corporate tax regimes facing TNCs can be sketched as follows:

- In the host country, the affiliate *abroad* is subjected to profits tax; this is consonant with the 'source' principle which attributes the right to tax to the country where the productive activities occur. Besides, the home country is also entitled to levy its corporate tax on the (same) profits of the foreign affiliates of its own TNCs, as being part of the firm's worldwide overall taxable profits; this claim accords with the 'residence' principle.
- The legal character of the affiliate in the host country has distinct implications for the corporate tax statute of the *parent company* in the home country. One must distinguish between (a) foreign subsidiaries, which are incorporated according to the company legislation in the host country and are endowed with legal personality, on the one hand, and (b) foreign branches, which are not incorporated in the host country, but which are

nonetheless subject to corporate taxation in the host country whenever their activities are being qualified by the host country as constituting a 'permanent establishment'.

- As regards *subsidiaries*, the prevailing practice in the home country consists in including the profits of the foreign subsidiary in the taxable base of the parent company, but only to the extent that these profits are actually remitted to the parent company as 'passive income' in the form of dividends, interest payments or know-how royalties; this arrangement stems from the so-called 'deferral principle'. Besides, no compensation of the losses of subsidiaries against the overall profits of the parent company is allowed.

- Conversely, the profits of a *'permanent establishment'* – a much less frequent legal format than the subsidiary – are added to those of the parent company in accordance with the so-called 'accrual principle'. It also follows that international loss offset is allowed. The permanent establishment and the parent company are thus subsumed in an (international) fiscal group concept.

- The unabated concurrence of the tax claims by both the host and home jurisdictions on the same taxable profits would fatally undermine the propensity of firms to engage in foreign direct investments. To assuage the resulting international tax duplication, two alternative major procedures have been devised for application by the home country. Either (a) the home country *exempts* the profits made by the foreign subsidiaries from its own grasp, or (b) allows the *crediting*, that is the offsetting of the corporate taxes paid abroad against the tax liabilities, which the parent company incurs on its worldwide profits.[2] Moreover, bilateral tax conventions – in essence following a pattern devised by the OECD – typically provide for the reduction, or even the abolition, of the withholding taxes in the host country on passive incomes.

Transfer pricing intricacies

Two additional dimensions further complicate international corporate taxation for TNCs – but also for the tax authorities. The issue of how to treat so-called *transfer prices*, that is those applied on transactions of goods and services that occur between related units of the same TNC has become the most thorny problem facing TNCs according to recent surveys (Ernst and Young, 2002). Intra-TNC payment flows for goods and services between related units have grown substantially, if not as a proportion of the size of international trade,[3] at least in absolute terms in line with the further expansion of such trade.

Indeed, TNCs may be tempted to modulate the prices of internal transactions with a view to artificially siphoning off more taxable profits to the tax-wise more lenient jurisdiction, thus resulting in a net tax saving for the overall TNC. In order to thwart such manoeuvres, a growing number of countries have put in place a battery of transfer pricing regulations and trained officials for this specific purpose. Common 'guidelines' are thereby suggested by the OECD.

The basic norm is that of the 'arm's-length price' standard, which posits that prices which are being practised on an intra-TNC, 'in house' deal, should be equated with the price that would prevail on similar transactions by 'outside' unrelated parties – and amongst which collusion is not to be feared, as they pursue opposite interests.[4]

The relevant point about transfer pricing, for our purposes, is that the arm's-length price basic principle looks separately at each unit of the TNC – and even, in principle, for purposes of applying the arm's-length rules, at each individual internal transaction. Thus, the arm's-length price standard in the transfer pricing area is predicated on the same 'separate entity' concept that underpins the traditional set of rules in the area of international corporate taxation, as explained above. In both areas, a holistic approach is explicitly banned – at least, for the time being.

Tax-haven facilities

Another complicating factor – which is only briefly mentioned here – relates to the services on offer from a large number of *tax havens* (often tiny territories in which a large number of 'post-box companies', with very little economic substance, are registered) to elude tax. Elaborate schemes of 'international tax planning' allow the reduction of tax burdens, but evoke countervailing reactions by the tax authorities intent on defending their revenue sources.[5] Such schemes test the porous borderline between lawful tax avoidance and outlawed tax evasion, and give rise to an unending battle between the tax-paying enterprises and the fiscal authorities. The former want to take advantage of 'loopholes', which can be engineered from interstices between the tax rules of various jurisdictions and which the latter strive to plug by appropriate legislative prescriptions. This unending cat-and-mouse contest adds another layer of complexity.

The underlying rationales for comprehensive schemes

This section contains a critical assessment of the arguments in favour of comprehensive schemes.

Achieving less-convoluted tax legislations

There is, first, the excessive complexity of the set of national legislations to which a TNC is subjected. The complaints by business circles about the complexities of the international corporate tax system(s) have been a major consideration in suggesting moves to a comprehensive scheme. Above, the generally accepted principles in the field of multinational taxation were spelled out, but in actual practice the detailed rules and regulations, and the related administrative practices, vary greatly amongst the member states.

This forces TNCs to devote much time and expense to secure counsel on the intricacies of much of the 'small print' in the legislations in each of the countries in which it operates an affiliate.

The compliance costs imposed in the transfer pricing area to satisfy the 'arm's-length price' norm are particularly burdensome, as governments increasingly request detailed contemporaneous documentation about comparable pricing behaviour between non-related parties. The need to justify the transfer prices applied by reference to 'comparables' is understandably perceived by the taxpayers as an excessive burden, as commodities and services are often unique and, like in a dynamic marketplace, prices to outside customers are often subject to rapid adjustment.

Yet, to achieve real progress on those matters, to be vindicated and to become an attractive alternative to present arrangements, a holistic approach should result in a substantially simpler set of prescriptions and in significantly less compliance costs. It is rather unfortunate that at the time of drafting the 2002 Report, no solid data were available to estimate the costs involved in complying with the present corporate tax parameters in TNCs of differing sizes, but late in 2003 the Commission launched a 'very comprehensive compliance cost survey ... to gain a better understanding of how the need to cope with 15 separate tax systems impacts of companies, in particular on their compliance costs and their decision making' (European Commission, 2003).

There can be little doubt that operating in the EU under the present set of 'separate entity' principles, and observing the many idiosyncrasies of many national tax legislations, involves heavy compliance costs. The comprehensive schemes suggested above would reduce the complexity of tax matters is several important aspects, although to differing degrees.

The consolidation of the taxable bases would be especially highly helpful. The vexed issue of transfer pricing determination in deals between EU affiliates would thus be laid to rest as regards intra-TNC deals in the EU – although, under the CCTB and HST schemes, the factors (assets, payroll and sales) which would then act as proxies for the taxable profits, as accounted for under the present arrangements, would still allow some scope for transfer pricing manoeuvres.[6]

But the substitution of the present system(s) by a comprehensive scheme would not erase all complications. Given the complex business world, even novel tax legislation would have to retain a great number of specific provisions and distinctions. And holistic schemes would introduce their own problems; this is the case for the CCBT and the HST, as one would have to keep accounts of the factors retained for the apportionment of the taxable profits by way of a formulary approach.[7] In this sense, the EUCIT is significantly simpler.

The logic of the single internal market

The moves towards a single EU-wide market have involved the removal of about 300 national regulations that impeded the smooth movement of goods across borders in the EU. These successful measures, however, did not touch on corporate tax parameters. The question to be addressed, then, is whether and to what extent corporate tax burden differences between member countries (deriving from the joint impact of the taxable base parameters, the nominal tax rate(s) and tax incentives for investments) are acceptable or, instead, should be eliminated as being inimical to competition within the EU. This is again largely an empirical issue.

A voluminous body of research has convincingly demonstrated that lower corporate tax levels and even generous tax incentives are far from being the main determinant of foreign direct investments. The market potential of the host country provides a much more potent motivation, whereas labour-intensive productions are attracted by low wage costs, but taking thereby into account the often equally lower productivity levels.

But in the EU, in which many non-tax variables that affect competition have become substantially harmonized, differences in tax burdens are likely to have some impact on the location choices of enterprises that want to invest in a given region: today's competition between Poland, the Czech and Slovak Republics as regards the attraction of automotive projects is a case in point.

The issue about the impact of tax parameters on investment decisions and their location, however, is considerably more complex: a higher tax burden on enterprises in country A may be compensated by the supply of more 'public goods', such as infrastructure, than is the case in country B which applies a more lenient tax. Besides and foremost, the removal of all corporate tax differences would infringe excessively on the tax sovereignty of the member states. Full harmonization of corporate taxation in the EU is politically unpalatable and not supported by strong economic arguments.

The approach adopted by the Commission consisted in targeting 66 preferential tax statutes in member countries that were identified by a special *ad hoc* commission as being harmful to competition within the EU; they are now being rolled back, following agreement on a code of conduct for business taxation which is part of the 'tax package' approved in 1997.[8] In other words, the Commission distinguishes between favourable tax regimes for specific activities that are deemed discriminatory and should no longer be maintained as they amount to (indirect) forms of state aid, on the one hand, and the general tax regimes for companies, including their rate patterns that may further remain at variance, on the other hand. This move allows the elimination of a number of gross distortions of competitive conditions in the EU, and improvement of the allocation of resources in the EU. However, the elimination of such harmful tax provisions does not postulate the introduction of a comprehensive scheme.

Related to the issue of state aids via special tax statutes is that of a number of imperfections in the present EU system(s) of TNC taxation which impede the smooth operation of TNCs in the EU area and which may entail some degree of double international taxation. Such problems, often highly technical, have been identified in the panel discussions mentioned earlier, and their detailed analysis constitutes a large part of the EU Commission's 2002 Report.

Amongst the topical problems thus treated, the following should be mentioned:

- The cross-border restructuring of firms, now in full swing in the EU and elsewhere, still incurs heavy tax costs and is consequently hindered, although the 1990 'merger directive' had already addressed this problem.
- Losses in one subsidiary in a member country A cannot be compensated against profits in the parent company B or in a subsidiary in country C; a few member countries, such as Belgium, do not even allow loss-offset in a purely domestic setting. A previous proposal by the Commission has been withdrawn, as it incurred persistent rejection by several member countries. The disallowance of the compensation of losses incurred in other member countries hinders the venturing abroad of firms, as the initial years typically result in negative outcomes.
- The network of bilateral double taxation agreements between most member countries do not always achieve their objective, namely that of eliminating tax duplication.
- The Commission is also running a 'joint forum on transfer pricing' which, innovatively, groups representatives from tax administrations and from the business community. The work is proceeding slowly but is likely to yield some convergence in the attitudes and procedures amongst the member states, within the framework traced by the OECD.

On these, and a few other topical issues, the 2001 Communication has suggested remedial 'targeted measures'. In the meantime, as reported by the Commission in its Communication of 24 November 2003, further technical work and consultations are being carried out. In other words, these issues are further retaining the attention of the Commission, although the search for adequate solutions remains laborious. Further analysis of these issues would overstretch this chapter.

Here again one must admit that the eventual solutions to such topical problems can be accommodated within the present EU tax system(s) on TNCs. It follows that they do not postulate a move towards a comprehensive scheme of TNC taxation in which the 'group concept' of the TNC would be the centrepiece. On the contrary, such measures are intended to strengthen the existing scheme, still basically predicated on the 'separate entity' paradigm, although as will be recalled in a moment, some of the 'targeted measures' in specific areas of company taxation already recognize the cross-border group dimension of TNCs.

Viewing the affiliates of the TNC as a single, integrated group

A third, and potentially powerful, argument in support of a comprehensive format of corporate taxation would follow from the contention that the 'separate entity' paradigm is intrinsically inappropriate for purposes of company taxation, on account of the close interrelatedness of the various affiliates of the same TNC. In this view, a holistic approach would not be advocated primarily because of the practical difficulties of disentangling a coalesced reality, but as a matter of principle. The TNC should then be viewed tax-wise not as a sort of confederation of basically autonomous national units, but as a single entity which, accordingly, should be treated on its consolidated profits. One may surmise that the correctness of this thesis would depend on the degree to which the constituent members of a TNC family act autonomously, or, inversely, are directed by the top management at headquarters. Let us try to provide an answer to what, again, looks largely to be an empirical question.

One may first notice that large, stock exchange-listed companies usually report to their shareholders in terms of their worldwide consolidated profits. But the implementation of such a holistic concept is utterly utopian on a *world scale*, where no supranational tax authority reigns. Besides, such an approach could not satisfy the national tax authorities, who want to ascertain which portion of the overall profits should be attributed to the affiliate under their jurisdiction, and who intend to defend their revenue claims against those of other jurisdictions. But, offhand, the proposition to substitute the separate entity paradigm by the fiscal group concept is more appealing in geographical areas in which economic integration has already been achieved to a large degree, and of which the European Union is the prototype.

In the *European Union*, a high level of uniformity in the regulatory parameters that affect cross-border business has already been achieved and further progress is gradually being made. As noticed in the Commission's 2002 Report, EU companies 'now increasingly change their focus from the national State towards the Union as a coherent economic zone' and 'generally wish to realign their business structures accordingly by creating pan-European business units instead of country-based organizations' (European Community 2002: 65). The Report then mentions that this can be achieved by way of acquisitions, joint ventures, fully-fledged mergers, or the establishment of foreign branches. Often, large TNCs establish (regional) European headquarters, although the perimeter of the latter may extend beyond the EU proper; the recent entry of 10 new member states is also likely to induce a geographical repositioning of the areas to be covered by the different affiliates. One problem, however, is that it is still not easy to establish a specific EU-wide formal business structure, except by way of a holding company incorporated, say, in the Netherlands, but which basically performs a financial function with little involvement in the operations of the affiliates. In principle, as mentioned below, the commercial-law statute of the Societas Europaea (SE), which entered into force on 8 October 2004, could provide a more convenient vehicle to structure a EU-wide organization.

The issue about the degree to which business decisions and operations are centralized within TNCs or instead delegated to the managers of the foreign affiliates has been keenly investigated for more than three decades (see e.g. Hedlund, 1993). The findings on this issue cannot conceivably be homogeneous, given the wide divergences in sectoral specialization, geographic reach and size of TNCs. For example, a Belgian advertising firm, which ventures abroad for the first time by setting up a subsidiary in the Netherlands, has little in common with, say, Unilever or General Electric.

Yet, that literature provides some pointers to an exceedingly complex, and moving phenomenon. Thus, there has been an evolution from autonomous foreign subsidiaries to global product divisions. Global organizations have been the outcome of global strategies. Although, obviously, large TNCs cannot be operated fully from headquarters – as otherwise the whole organization would become unwieldy and inefficient[9] – adequate overall guidance and even control are essential to achieve congruence in the objectives. In modern TNCs such monitoring and governance require subtle mechanisms of coordination that differ significantly from vertical lines of command. Finally, some functions in the TNC are most often highly centralized: this is the case for foreign exchange management where only an overall view of the positions of each affiliate is adequate to gauge the overall foreign exchange exposure of the firm as a whole; such functions are now often entrusted to specialized subsidiaries that may be located in a country that provides them with a favourable legal and fiscal format. In the EU, the disjunction of such functions from the overall organizational pattern of the TNC is facilitated by the freedom of capital movements, and, in 'Euroland', by a common currency. Other functions, such as personnel management and advertising remain largely circumscribed by differences in national environments, languages and social legislations. Thus, TNCs typically blend centralizing and decentralized ('divisionalized') features.

Already in the 1920s, large enterprises in the USA had adopted the 'divisionalized' mould of organization whereby the various divisions are vested with the task of maximizing their own profits, as if they were legally autonomous enterprises. Besides structuring the layers of authority and responsibility, this business model is meant to stimulate the creative abilities and to allow the measurement and evaluation of their performance. This profit-centre model of the TNC, at first glance, appears similar to the basic tenet of the 'separate entity' approach in tax matters, namely that of treating each member of the TNC family separately and of quantifying the profit performance of each. Does it follow that comprehensive approaches to corporate taxation are ill-fated, as they would not reflect real-world situations?

Such inference is nonetheless unfounded, on two grounds. First, a TNC, by definition, is composed of a 'parent company' and one or more foreign affiliates. Even in TNCs which leave ample managerial powers to their affiliates, the basic fact remains that the TNC as a whole strives for market share and profits. The 'profit-centre' set-up provides a structure to achieve these overall objectives, but is not a goal in itself. One may add that the implementation of the 'profit-centre' concept is often not easy. For example, it logically implies that the divisions should feel free to procure their inputs from third parties at more favourable conditions than from a sister subsidiary; but, what if the latter happens to have unused capacity? Secondly, while TNCs are ultimately geared to achieve maximum profits, whatever their geographical source may be, national tax administrations are concerned about their own claim on a portion of the overall profits of the TNCs. This implies that, in the light of their own tax legislation and taking into account internationally agreed constraints, they are compelled to quantify the corporate tax liability of the TNC in their own country.

A high degree of integration between the various members of the TNC family is achieved when there are sizeable intra-TNC flows of raw materials, intermediate or final goods, and of specific services. Such TNCs then run into the minefield of fiscal transfer pricing problems. Moreover, the approach adopted by the tax authorities is somewhat contradictory; as a matter of fact, in raising a battery of anti-fraud regulations in the transfer pricing area, the tax legislator assumes that the various members of the same TNC family are subordinated to unified top management, which is in a position to manipulate the prices of the internal deals for tax-minimizing purposes. And yet, in order to ascertain the claims of each of the two countries involved in a transfer pricing case, the tax authorities must pierce through the links between the two related units of the TNC, and, if need be, reconstruct the internal transaction as if it had been entered into by non-related parties, at 'arm's length'.

Final comments

What conclusions can be drawn from the preceding discussion about the appropriateness of the group concept, for corporate tax purposes, within the EU framework? The adoption of a fiscal group concept, even if limited to the definition of the taxable base and not extending to the tax rate, would achieve a significant reduction in compliance costs not only for TNCs but also for the national tax administrations; a major beneficial outcome would consist in the drastic curtailment of the scope for disputes, and the related costs, in the transfer pricing area. It would also reflect the growing tendency of firms in EU member countries to pursue a pan-EU ambition and to adopt a corresponding organizational format.

Two final comments are worth adding. First, on account of the tremendous technical problems involved, the adoption of a comprehensive scheme, however useful, can only be viewed as a longer-term objective. But, secondly, as I have argued elsewhere (Plasschaert, 2002), the problem would become more manageable if a comprehensive scheme would be accessible only to well-defined categories of TNCs, instead of being open to any company as soon as it starts to operate abroad. The variety, in terms of economic substance, between the enterprises that adopt the legal form of a limited-liability company, is too wide, indeed.[10] It would follow that only specific sets of corporate vehicles with cross-border activities, and which reach a high degree of integration of their activities within the EU, should qualify. One could envisage TNCs of a large size and with a number of affiliates in EU-member countries, or stock exchange-listed companies in the EU, numbering about 7,000, which in 2005 will have adopted the same accounting rules. But, the Societas Europaea's legal corporate vehicle appears as the more suitable candidate to be equipped with a comprehensive scheme of corporate taxation with (as a minimum) a consolidated tax base. Moreover, without an appropriate tax complement, few companies are likely to convert themselves into SEs. The Commission moves cautiously along those lines, but 'continues to believe that the idea of a suitably designed pilot scheme which would provide companies created under the European Company Statutes with a common consolidated tax base at EU-level deserves to be analysed further' (European Commission, 2003: 25).

One obstacle lies in the possibly discriminatory nature of comprehensive tax statutes for only subgroups of companies, and the Commission is looking into this issue. But, I would argue that, as stressed above, the same corporate legal suit covers bodies of widely divergent composition and economic relevance. Besides, the actual national corporate tax systems also sometimes carve out special niches for specific sets of companies, such as small and medium-sized enterprises. Finally, the Commission itself is looking further into the merits and the technical aspects of the home-state taxation model, sketched above, which could be launched as a pilot project for SMEs. This, again, would engineer a special tax treatment for a limited set of companies.

Notes

1   As a member of panel II which, during a period of 18 months assisted the Commission in the preparation of its Report (but which was not involved in the actual drafting), I can testify that, in the early work of the panel, many members – who were mainly selected from the business world – were in favour of such comprehensive solutions. Although all of us realized that there would be a long way to transform a novel concept into a workable reality, an initial impetus has no doubt been imparted along that road.

2   Under the 'foreign tax credit' mechanism, and provided the profits are fully remitted to the parent company and the tax rates in the home country exceed those in the host country, capital export neutrality would ensue. The exemption method would result in capital import neutrality in the host country.

3   According to UNCTAD's 2003 *World Investment Report*, the ratio of internal to overall trade has remained fairly stable, at around one-third. The rapid growth of 'fragmented production', whereby the various stages in the production process or its components occur in different countries, would tend to raise that ratio, but such tasks are quite often outsourced to non-related subcontractors.

4   Danny Van Den Bulcke also ventured into issues of transfer pricing as early as the 1970s (Van Den Bulcke, 1976). His major contribution in this area was in fact related to the importance of intra-group trade as a venue for transfer pricing policies (Van Den Bulcke, 1976, 1985).

5   Thus, a large number of countries react against the use of controlled foreign companies, whereby passive income is channelled to tax haven subsidiaries instead of being remitted to the parent company.

6   Consolidation would yield more benefits, in terms of simplification and of inter-country comparability, if the accounting standards, presently still at variance amongst member states, were to become uniform; a move now underway in the EU for exchange-listed companies.

7   A specialist on the US apportionment system at state level has warned against its premature adoption in the EU (Martens Weiner, 2001).

8   Work on 'harmful tax competition' at the OECD has acted as a spur to the EU.

9   It is tempting to remind ourselves of the demise of the centrally-managed economies in communist states, largely due to the assignment of decision-making away from the managers in the field to bureaucrats in the planning offices.

10 Establishing a company is quite easy. Anthonissen (2003) has identified not less than about 90 addresses on the web, which invite the setting-up of offshore companies, sometimes adding that they allow use as tax shelters.

References

Anthonissen, K. (2003) 'Doorbraak en doorkijk van een rechtspersoon. Over fiscale aansprakelijkheid en fiscale transparantie', *Documentatieblad* 2003/6. Brussel: Federale Overheidsdienst Financiën.

Ernst & Young (2002), *Transfer Pricing: Global Survey*. Ernst and Young: International Tax Services.

European Commission (2001) 'Communication to the Council, the European Parliament and the European Economic and Social Committee: An Internal Market without Company Tax Obstacles; Achievements, Ongoing Initiatives and Remaining Challenges', COM (2003)726 final. Brussels: European Commission.

European Commission (2002) *Company Taxation in the Internal Market*. Luxembourg: Office for Official Publications of the European Communities.

Hedlund, G. (1993) 'Introduction: Organization and Management of Transnational Corporations in Practice and Research', in G. Hedlund (ed.), *Organization of Transnational Corporations*. The United Nations Library on Transnational Corporations, Vol. 6. London: Routledge.

Lodin, S.-O. and Gammie, M. (2001) *Home State Taxation*. Amsterdam: International Bureau for Fiscal Documentation Publications.

Martens, J.M. (2001) 'The European Union and Formula Apportionment: Caveat Emperor', *European Taxation*, 41(10): 380–9.

Plasschaert, S. (1997) 'An EU Tax on Consolidated Profits of Multinational Enterprises', *European Taxation*, 42(1): 7–17.

Plasschaert, S. (2002) 'Comprehensive Approaches to EU Company Taxation: To Which Companies Should They Apply?', *European Taxation*, 1.

Van Den Bulcke, D. (1976) 'Transfert Prijzen: Motieven, Opportuniteiten en Problemen' *Maandschrift voor Accountancy en Bedrijfskunde*, 4: 1–17.

Van Den Bulcke, D. (1985) 'Intrafirm Trade of Multinational Enterprises. Characteristics and Implications for Developing Countries', *EADI Bulletin*, 1: 95–122.

5
Managerial Responses to Borderless Risk

Alain Verbeke and James R. Dewald

The changing world

Much of the post-11 September news commentary on the 'new world of terrorism' has focused on issues of public policy, while encouraging the Western world to continue business as usual. But, is it possible to simply continue business as usual? Consider how major corporations have recently moved from actively seeking high-profile head-office locations as a reflection of their economic success to suddenly realizing that such locations may well constitute prime targets for terrorist actions. Consider also the new responsibilities placed on businesses to screen visitors to their facilities. Recently, Atco Industries revealed that individuals toured one of their gas-plant facilities carrying credentials identifying them as engineers from Iran. The credentials were since found to be false.

This chapter analyses the impact of the 11 September attacks and the subsequent changes in public policy from a different perspective: the perspective of the international business manager. For such a manager, these events mark the shift from a world of geographically well-defined risk towards a world of borderless risk. The chapter presents a new framework that can help the international manager consider strategies for resource protection in the future, given this new world of borderless risk. Four well-known top managers of large transnational corporations (TNCs), active in the oil and gas and transportation sectors and headquartered in Canada, helped to develop the conceptual framework through a series of in-depth interactions with the authors. Their perspective is likely archetypal for non-US TNCs from highly developed, small open economies. Canadian-headquartered businesses have a distinct advantage globally, being perceived as coming from a country that values diplomacy, relationships and respect for other points of view, while simultaneously fortunate enough to ride on the coattails of the United States as a major economic and military force.

The top managers participating in this strategic reflection were David O'Brien (Chairman of EnCana Corporation and former CEO of PanCanadian

Energy Corporation and Canadian Pacific Railway Limited), Gwyn Morgan (CEO of EnCana Corporation and former President and CEO of Alberta Energy Company Ltd), James W. Buckee (President and CEO of Talisman Energy Inc.) and Charles Fischer (President and CEO of Nexen Inc.). Each of these companies has its head office in Calgary and international operations throughout the world. In 2001, PanCanadian Energy Corporation and Alberta Energy Company Ltd merged to form EnCana Corporation. However, as the respective CEOs of the pre-merged firms engaged in a somewhat different response to the post-9/11 environment of borderless risk, reflecting the specific situation of PanCanadian and Alberta Energy Company, this article considers their positions of authority at that time. The combined market capitalization of the firms controlled by these top executives is more than $36 billion (November 2002).

New risks in the TNC environment

New risks for TNCs arise from three distinct sources: (1) terrorist actions; (2) public policy initiatives undertaken as a response to such actions or to prevent further terrorist activities; and (3) changes in behaviour by a wide range of TNC stakeholders, including shareholders, customers, suppliers, employees and others. This chapter focuses on the first and second sources of risks, the latter reflecting the terrorism prevention policies presently being implemented by many governments and public agencies in nations across the world.

The potential targets of terrorist actions can be classified into three types:

- Symbolic targets – the purpose being to draw attention to the cause of the terrorists, or to symbolically damage the chosen target. The 11 September attacks clearly fit into this category.
- Revenue-generating targets – this form of terrorism includes kidnapping for ransom as well as illegal activities such as money laundering to raise funds for the terrorist organizations.
- Strategic nodes – this includes attacks on strategic infrastructure such as bridges, airports, power plants, pipelines and so on, to disrupt the normal functioning of the targeted groups or organizations.

Until recently, most TNC managers had a keen awareness of the likelihood that particular forms of terrorist activity could occur in the various geographic locations where the TNC was operating, with several sources of information allowing the assessment of risks. In particular, revenue-generating terrorism is geographically very concentrated – for example, in a few regions in South America, the Middle East and the Far East – and there is no reason to believe that this situation will change. The Alberta Energy Company component of EnCana., Talisman and Nexen with substantial exploration properties in South America is well-aware of this type of terrorist activities.

Symbolic targets and strategic nodes located anywhere in the world, however, may now become the subject of attacks. Indeed, the highest probability of future attacks may well be in previously deemed 'safe' nations such as the United States and Canada. To heighten the concern, since the 23 October 1983 terrorist attack on United States and French peacekeeping contingents in Lebanon, the popularity and severity of suicide attacks has grown substantially, building up to the 11 September events (Sprinzak, 2000). These attacks, along with other terrorist activities with less-dramatic impacts (including a previous bombing at the World Trade Centre), have shifted the risk previously perceived as geographically concentrated, to one that does not respect borders.

As a response to this shift toward 'borderless' terrorism, major public policy initiatives are being undertaken, generally resulting in increased uncertainties for TNCs. These initiatives revolve around greater national security, and while much attention has been devoted to the impact greater controls may have on individual liberties, the direct impact on TNCs may be much larger. The impact of both terrorist threats and these public policy initiatives can be assessed in terms of political risk, with micro-level and macro-level components.

An example of micro-level risk through public policy initiatives has been the increased security along the Canada–United States border, which governs the largest bilateral trade flows in the world (indeed much larger than the United States–Japan bilateral trade flows). Although this does not affect the oil and gas business significantly, it does have an impact on manufacturing, transportation, retail and a variety of other industries that rely heavily on Canada–US flows of goods. This concern was echoed by all four top managers, each independently stating that the strongest impact of 11 September is being felt in North America.

The impact is particularly important in the automotive industry, where large flows of components move across the Canada–US border, within a context of just-in-time processes that leave small windows (as small as three hours) for the components to arrive at their next assembly site. With border delays increasing in excess of three hours, the total costs for business operations may become much higher than the costs of the truck driver waiting in line. Such micro-risks that affect firms in very different ways are now perceived to be gaining importance as compared to conventional macro-risks, associated with the socio-economic situation and political regimes prevailing in individual countries.

Macro-risks are assumed to affect all foreign international traders or investors in the same way. The pre-11 September global environment was one of gradual movement towards less discrimination and more liberal public policy in many countries around the world. Organizations such as the North American Free Trade Area (NAFTA), the World Trade Organization (WTO) and the Organization for Economic Cooporation and Development (OECD) were leading a global awareness shift towards valuing the creation of 'level playing fields', benefiting industries and foreign direct investors throughout both developed and developing countries, at unprecedented levels. This meant the creation of an environment with reduced institutional uncertainty for the TNC manager, and with the highest macro-risks clearly concentrated in countries that did not take part in major international liberalization efforts.

Today, the balance between micro- and macro-risks is in flux. Nations are concerned about security of resources, safe delivery of services to their residents, transfer of capital, immigration, electronic communications, and so on. In short, security has become a top priority on the agenda of many nations, resulting in a variety of impacts on specific industries and firms.

The four business leaders confirmed the pre-11 September gradual shift away from focusing proactively on government relations, guided by the belief that global trade liberalization and principles of non-discrimination would allow market forces to drive industry evolution. They also acknowledged that in the post-11 September era, government relations had again become a top priority in strategy formation. Fortunately, all four top managers saw their companies as having a solid administrative heritage in managing business–government relations. The Alberta Energy Company component of EnCana has always viewed carefully managed community/government relations as an 'art', and it has a heritage of substantial resource allocations in this area to strengthen these linkages. Likewise, one of Nexen's key sources of competitive advantage is its focus on corporate social responsibility, which includes the crafting of strong relationships with host governments as well as strong dedication to working with local communities in areas related to education and health. Nexen's most important international operation is in Yemen, and represents approximately 20 per cent of the country's GDP. While other foreign companies have suffered attacks on their facilities (such as, pipeline disruptions), Nexen has not been faced with a single terrorist problem in 15 years of operations. Nexen largely attributes this situation to the firm's corporate social responsibility initiatives, which have often resulted in a sense of 'ownership' as perceived by the local community.

Similarly, Talisman Energy maintains close relations with lead governments in international operations (for example, in Sudan), but with a much stronger emphasis on this area since the events of 11 September. One of the first priorities of Talisman's CEO, following 11 September, was to arrange for his own travel to the firm's major international operations to assess risk issues with staff and host government officials.

The Chairman of EnCana and the former CEO of PanCanadian equally devoted a significant amount of time and energy to domestic issues of security and tightened borders since 11 September. This has involved heightened discussions directly with government leaders, as well as industry cooperation through the Canadian Business Council on National Issues. Alberta Energy's former CEO also noted a heavy involvement with provincial governments to ensure proper security around key oil and gas facilities.

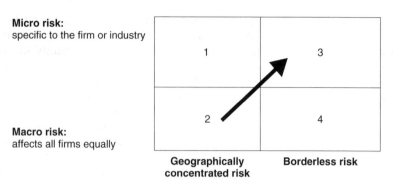

Figure 5.1   Shifts in the TNC risk paradigm

   The discussions with the four top managers indicates that they understand the creation of borderless risk as follows: it represents a shift from risk related to a particular national government's (or public agency's) intentions to effect a redistribution of wealth away from the TNC, to a phenomenon of risk beyond the direct control of legitimate institutions in sovereign nations. To a large extent, borderless risk reflects the need for public policy initiatives to focus more on heightened homeland security and security at border crossings as a response to the largely unpredictable nature of terrorist activities throughout the world. It also implies a requirement for firms to work together with public policy-makers to reduce the negative micro-level impacts of these public policy initiatives on the firm. The four top managers' perspectives as described above can be synthesized as in Figure 5.1.
   The figure describes the dual shift in risk perceived by the four TNC top executives. Here, the vertical axis makes a distinction between the occurrence of risk at the macro-level with all firms being equally affected by it, and micro-risk, that is specific to particular industries and firms. The horizontal axis distinguishes between geographically concentrated risk occurring in specific nations and regions, and borderless risk. As discussed above, at present a major shift is being perceived by the top executives from quadrant 2 to quadrant 3. The important implication for the TNC manager is that the increase of micro-level risk makes it critical to undertake strategic actions to mitigate the impacts on the firm of public policy initiatives related to possible future terrorist actions. The next section describes the key parameters that will determine corporate strategies in this area.

The management of borderless risk

In principle, each of the TNC's key resources could be substantially affected by borderless risk, namely: raw materials and intermediate products, finished products, fixed assets, information, human resources and external relations (which could include government agencies, distributors, critical suppliers, etc.). Each of these seven resource areas could be affected both by actual terrorist actions and by the public policy programmes implemented as a response to possible future terrorist activities.

Each of the four firms had already experienced negative impacts of such public policy programmes in terms of profitability and growth. The main question now faced by each business leader is where to develop firm-specific advantages (FSAs) in resource protection to compensate for new risks that threaten profitability and growth. There is no standard answer to this question, as each TNC will be faced with a different set of impacts. However, Figure 5.2 presents a conceptual framework that takes into account two critical managerial parameters. First, the likelihood of a serious negative impact on profitability and growth resulting from either the terrorist actions or the public policy initiatives aimed to prevent them, with a decomposition of this impact for each of the seven resource bundles mentioned above. Second, the extent to which the firms perceive the necessity to develop new firm-specific advantages (FSAs), that is, company-level strengths, to mitigate potentially negative impacts, again for each resource domain.

The figure represents the probability of a negative impact on profitability and growth (low, medium or high likelihood) and the most likely FSA development responses of the business leaders. These managers view the building of new FSAs in external relations, human-resource strategies and protection of finished products as top priorities. The first issue, external relations, may involve the need for stronger government relations in terms of intelligence,

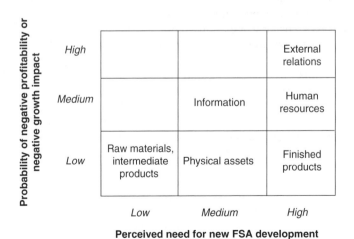

Figure 5.2   The manager's response to borderless risk

access to policy-makers and development of more effective influencing skills to deal with new public policy initiatives. The second issue reflects changes in human-resource strategies that address personnel anxiety, stress and travel risk. This includes, for example, the introduction of stress counselling, behavioural guidelines to prevent expatriate employees and their families becoming targets of revenue-generating terrorism, new employee-tracking systems and contingency plans to quickly move staff out of crisis locations if necessary. The third issue, protection of finished products, is driven primarily by the fear that terrorists could affect the distribution of products or use the products to cause severe damage (for example, oil product spills and environmental damage). This could have negative spillover effects on the targeted firm's activities at a global level, since a 'reputation' for being a terrorist target could severely affect customer loyalty and linkages with other actors in the logistics chain. Measures in this area may include very strict guidelines for transporting products by truck, ship, rail and so on. Each of the three resource areas is positioned in the right-hand sectors of Figure 5.2. Here it is interesting to observe that only the renewed focus on FSA development in external relations is actually driven by objective analysis of the likely negative impact on profitability and growth if no action were undertaken in that area. For the two other resource areas, especially for finished products, it is more subjective fear than a high likelihood of actual occurrence of problems that actually drives the FSA development process, as recognized by the top managers themselves. But in these resource areas, the business leaders view a zero tolerance for 'failure' (in the case of a terrorist attack) as the only rational response for their respective companies.

The areas of physical assets and information, positioned in the middle sectors of Figure 5.2 are viewed as somewhat less of a priority as compared to the three resource areas above. In fact, the oil and gas companies have many of their core assets (drilling operations, refineries, pipelines and so on) in areas of the world where macro-risk has always been perceived as very high (Yemen, Sudan, a number of South American countries and others). It was precisely because of this high macro-risk that some of these firms, more specifically Talisman and Nexen, were able to gain an important position in those countries as compared to the oil and gas 'mega TNCs' such as Exxon Mobil, Shell and TotalFina. Here, the key challenge is more a reassessment and fine-tuning of existing protection measures than the development of fundamentally new security strategies. The resource area of information, especially the ICT infrastructure, as well as the electronic information databases, is perceived to be at a higher risk than fixed assets, but fortunately, partly because of earlier Y2K efforts and partly because of several recent (smaller) problems generated by internet hackers, the FSA development process is again largely one of reviewing and upgrading security systems already in place.

Finally, as regards the protection of the raw materials and intermediate products themselves, both the likelihood of problems and the need to rethink existing security strategies are viewed as relatively low. It is difficult to conceive why terrorists would want to focus their attention on these resource areas as compared to the areas mentioned above. These two resource areas were positioned in the left sectors of Figure 5.2.

The decomposition of the firm's resource base into key domains and the positioning of each domain in Figure 5.2 is to a large extent company and industry-specific. The insight from the figure, however, is that senior management in TNCs should attempt to make a comprehensive evaluation of the firm's various resource bundles, in terms of risk profile and level of priority for FSA development.

Conclusion

The framework developed in this chapter should be viewed as the starting point for the identification and evaluation of actions required from the TNC manager faced with a new and decidedly very different world of borderless risk. Here, managerial attention needs to be devoted to new FSA development in a variety of resource areas, as a response to both the random threat of terrorist actions and the terrorism prevention initiatives of governments and public agencies that could seriously affect profitability and growth.

The following three elements are particularly important:

1 It is critical to understand that the world of geographically concentrated, macro-level risk is no longer dominant. Instead, TNCs now operate in a world of borderless risk, where firm-level initiatives should be developed proactively, in any location where they operate, including the most developed nations in the world, to mitigate the impact of both terrorist threats and the public policy programmes aimed to eliminate such threats.
2 Senior managers in TNCs should engage in formal assessments of the risks faced by each of their key resource areas (raw materials and intermediate products, finished products, fixed assets, information, human resources and external relations), in terms of potential negative impacts on profitability and growth.
3 The most critical resource areas requiring new FSA development in TNCs, as perceived by the business leaders who contributed to this article, appear to be government and community-based relations, human-resource management and protection of finished products. Here, it should be recognized that a mechanical cost/benefit analysis does not suffice to determine the extent to which TNCs should devote attention to these areas: the reduction of risk to zero-levels may be a reasonable option to pursue.

Reference
Sprinzak, E. (2000) 'Rational Fanatics', *Foreign Policy*, Sep/Oct: 66–73.

6
TNCs, Locational Clustering and the Process of Economic Development

John Cantwell and Katherina Glac

Introduction

Danny Van Den Bulcke has for many years been the leading authority on the impact of inward and outward foreign direct investment (FDI) on economic development in the Belgian economy. Belgium being a small country, this analysis has inevitably led him to be concerned with the constraints that might be imposed by industrial concentration in a confined geographical area, in place of the inter-firm diversity that the clustering of transnational corporations (TNCs) might produce in a bigger country, and with the development implications of relationships between generally larger TNCs and typically smaller indigenous firms in some industry in a common local vicinity (Van Den Bulcke, 1985). He has also been centrally interested in how the processes of European economic integration and the resulting relocation of TNC operations across Europe might lead to a clustering of activity in Belgium when there was a favourable interaction between inward and outward FDI (Van Den Bulcke and De Lombaerde, 1992). In this chapter, we explore how concern with such issues of clustering and local economic development has become increasingly widespread in the international business and allied literature, and now appears in discussions of TNC activity in large as well as small countries, and indeed in the context of globalization processes in general.

Since the time in the 1960s when it was central to discussions such as those around the product-cycle model (Vernon, 1966) and the role of US direct investment in Europe (Dunning, 1970), over the last 30 years the interest in location as a critical factor in international business first experienced a decline and only more recently a revival. The lessening of interest in the 1970s was largely due to the shift in emphasis in the international business literature from macro-level questions about countries and their trade and balance of payments positions, towards micro-level questions to do with the organization of cross-border operations within firms. So the focus of investigation shifted from the location to the firm. However, the international company itself has gradually come to be perceived in a wider context.

The revival of concern with location has been in part based on major changes in the economic environment, such as the increasing importance of intellectual capital as the key wealth-creating asset, increasing globalization in the form of a closer integration of activity between countries, but at the same time an increasing concentration of some specialized knowledge-based functions within selected sub-national regions, and the rise of alliance capitalism (Dunning, 1998). Alliance capitalism involves both strategic alliances and acquisition exchange deals between leading firms, but it also incorporates extended local networks in many vicinities that entail new and often closer relationships not merely between firms themselves, but between firms and other local actors (such as universities) in what have sometimes been referred to as regional and national systems of innovation. These factors taken together have contributed to a revival of the interest in location as a major topic in the international business literature, because both TNCs and host regions have recognized the importance of location as a potential source of competitive advantage that helps to ensure development and growth.

Elsewhere trade economists have rediscovered economic geography, economies of agglomeration and path-dependency, while industrial economists have become interested once more in clusters. Historically the location of economic activity was mainly a concern of economic geographers and locational economists. Due to the changes in the economic environment, however, some of the restrictive assumptions that had formed the independent foundation of the theory of international trade (notably that of perfect factor mobility across space within countries, but high factor immobility between countries) and had precluded the cross-fertilization between locational studies and the work of the international trade economists were relaxed. The more recent work in the industrial geography area considers external economies, the importance of technology and innovative activity, and the way they may be transferred across space. Trade economists have likewise begun to recognize the role of technology spillovers as a location-specific externality, rather than treating technology as readily transferable and internationally available unlike factors of production. Thus, a dialogue between these once historically separate streams of research has emerged in the recent past. As a result a better picture of the allocation of economic activity exists and forms the basis for a clearer understanding of how locational factors influence TNC activity and through feedback mechanisms in turn the host location itself (Dunning, 1998).

Because TNC activity is now increasingly being recognized as inseparable from locational factors and as influential on the characteristics of the host location, an understanding of the mechanisms of clustering and the TNC–host location interactions can prove useful for both managers as well as policy-makers concerned with firm growth and local development. This emerging interest is reflected in cross-country comparative research on the varying contexts for clusters as nuclei for local development, and how this connects to the changing structures of global intra-firm and contractual networks (Guerrieri, Iammarino and Pietrobelli, 2001). In general, clusters are a new way of thinking about the local economy (Porter, 2000) and are being recognized as crucial elements in economic development (Porter, 1998). Particularly for smaller open economies, which are usually dominated by TNC activity, the importance of cluster dynamics is of critical relevance to local industries in maintaining or enhancing their competitive position over time. The benefits that can arise out of TNC activity in a given cluster or location vary by the type of foreign-owned economic activity and do not by default lead to a virtuous cycle of local economic development (De Beule and Van Den Bulcke, 2001; Van Den Bulcke, 1985).

This chapter is therefore intended to provide an overview of some of the key readings in the field and also of the most significant recent work in these different areas, both from a theoretical and empirical point of view. It first discusses the origins of clusters as seen through theory and statistics, before turning to some empirical evidence on cluster origins and dynamics. The next section introduces the principal types of spillovers and associated cluster types that have been observed. The chapter concludes with a section on the interaction between locational hierarchies and the investments of TNCs, and the effects of such hierarchies on the strategy of TNCs and the host economies.

Origins of clusters: theory, statistics and empirical evidence

Economic activities of a common kind show a strong tendency to agglomerate in certain locations, giving rise to patterns of national and regional specialization (Caniëls, 2000). The performance and the growth of firms depend to a large extent on the conditions of the environment in which they operate, and particularly on those in the immediate proximity (Malmberg *et al.*, 1996). The phenomenon of the concentration of economic activities in space, and its persistence over time, was first observed by Marshall (1891), who listed three fundamental advantages (or externalities) which cause firms to agglomerate:

- a pooled market for skilled workers with industry-specific competencies;
- the availability of non-tradable and intermediate inputs provided by local suppliers; and
- the easy transmission of new ideas, which increases productivity through technical, organizational and production improvements.

A common location offers cultural similarities which improve the ease and the speed of knowledge diffusion, providing the right environment for the development of a common language, shared codes of communication and interaction, collective values and institutions. Therefore, more recent approaches to the analysis of the benefits of agglomeration have shifted attention away from traditional purely economic factors – such as distance and non-linearity of transport costs identified by the orthodox location theory (Hotelling, 1929; Lösch, 1954; Weber, 1929) – to the characteristics of the social and institutional localized systems, supposing that they can provide a better understanding of the geographical concentration of economic and innovative activity, as well as of the dynamics of technological specialization patterns.

The literature on the advantages of the geographical agglomeration of technological and productive activities has developed along a twofold perspective. The first, and antecedent approach has followed the Marshallian tradition in trying to identify such advantages and their implications for overall economic growth. Within this approach the spatial dimension represents a factor characterizing economic development, in relation to which the local innovation potential is assumed to be only one variable among others. The second and more recent line of research has instead addressed the localized structural factors, which shape the innovation capacity of specific geographical contexts. This has given rise to heterogeneous subnational typologies of innovative activity – all coming back to a broadly defined form of spatial organization, that is the innovative cluster.

Interorganizational network relationships – between firms and science infrastructure, between producers and users at the inter-firm level, between firms and the institutional environment – are strongly influenced by spatial proximity mechanisms that favour processes of polarization and cumulativeness (De Bresson, 1987; Lundvall, 1992; Von Hippel, 1989). Furthermore, the use of informal channels for knowledge diffusion (so-called tacit or uncodified knowledge) provides another argument for the tendency of knowledge-based activities to be geographically confined. Ellison and Glaeser (1997) offer some evidence on the geographic concentration of US manufacturing industry, which is widespread. They suggest that the explanation for geographic concentration varies by industry and that natural advantage may often play a role as industries co-agglomerate both with upstream suppliers and with downstream customers. Developing the industry-specificity of clustering further, Steinle and Schiele (2002) set out the conditions under which an industry is more likely to cluster. They distinguish between necessary conditions, which are divisibility of the process and transportability of the product, and sufficient conditions, which consist of a long value chain, multiple competencies, network innovation and volatility of the market.

A useful distinction is usually made between two different types of agglomeration forces which shape spatial organization, pushing related firms and industries to cluster spatially in one of two ways that may lead to patterns of uneven regional development, that is the emergence of centres and peripheries at the global and national level. There has been a debate as to which type of clustering predominates in a given setting and how the reasons for clustering have changed over time (Porter, 2000). On the one hand, there are general external economies and spillover effects – so-called 'urbanization economies' – which attract all kinds of economic activities into certain areas. This provokes the emergence of regional cores with broad sectoral specializations varying across different locations. These might be termed all-round centres of excellence, or higher-order centres. For an economic model of the differentiation into an industrial core and agricultural periphery under consideration of simple pecuniary externalities see Krugman (1991).

On the other hand, 'localization economies' are fostered in spatial clusters of firms undertaking similar or related activities. These kinds of forces are likely to be industry-specific and to produce cumulative mechanisms, which enable host locations to increase their production, technological and organizational competence over time (Dicken and Lloyd, 1990; Richardson, 1969). These might be termed specialized centres, or intermediate centres (by comparison with lower-order sites that lack locational attractiveness to most TNCs). As shown by Baptista and Swann (1998), agglomeration spillovers may operate for intra-industry clustering, whilst instead congestion effects may tend to dominate, offsetting positive spillovers, in the inter-industry case. For this reason general centres of excellence tend to be more geographically dispersed (to spread out over larger areas) than are specialized centres. Local interaction follows patterns of both collaboration and competition, which can produce stable mechanisms of collective knowledge accumulation, growth and development. On the one hand, as suggested by Porter's 'diamond approach', competitive pressures and the associated push to innovation provide the dynamics of the advantage, which firms derive in this virtuous circle. The competitive advantage of a regional system is thus created and sustained through highly localized processes of rivalry, which in turn are reinforced by their own capacity to attract resources from outside. On the other hand, spatial concentration boosts the intensity of interchanges and demonstration effects within the regional system, thus increasing the extent of collaboration and fostering a common attitude towards innovation (a localized system helps reduce the elements of dynamic uncertainty).

A variety of empirical and descriptive studies have examined evidence on the cluster phenomenon *per se*, focusing on different issues such as initial cluster formation and growth (De Vet and Scott, 1992; Dorfman, 1983; Feldman, 2001; Kenney and Von Burg, 1999). In their work on initial cluster formation, Feldman and Schreuder (1996), for example, focus on the pharmaceutical industry in the Mid-Atlantic region and on the very early historical origin of this cluster. They identified the basic factors that shaped the development of the industry and anchored the industry in the region as a series of historical circumstances, the influence of government actions and legislation, and the development of unique capabilities.

A slightly different and more general perspective on cluster formation is adopted by Audretsch and Feldman (1996a). Their study of US innovation data examines the clustering of innovative activity and focuses on the propensity to cluster controlling for the effects of agglomeration of production. The results indicate that the agglomeration of production remains constant over the life-cycle and is more concentrated where new technology is important. Innovative activity, however, tends to cluster more when tacit knowledge plays an important role, which is greatest in the early stages of the life-cycle. In addition, this concentration of production has a bigger influence on the agglomeration of innovation in the mature and declining life-cycle stages.

Other studies have placed emphasis on dynamic aspects such as the entry of firms into the cluster and firm growth or performance in clusters (Appold, 1995; Baptista and Swann, 1999; Maggioni, 2002; Pandit *et al.*, 2001; Prevezer, 1997; Stuart and Sorenson, 2002). In this area Swann and Pervezer (1996) began a series of research investigations into cluster dynamics, specifically the impact of cluster strength and the strength of the science base on entry into the cluster and firm growth. They show that the factors attracting entry into a cluster are different for the biotech and computing industry, and that there is also a difference between entrants and incumbents in absorbing different kinds of spillovers.

Taking a narrower focus on cluster dynamics, Malmberg *et al.* (1996) examine the impact of geographical location on the innovation process, firm competitiveness and the impact of TNC presence in the clusters on the knowledge-accumulation process. In drawing on a variety of empirical studies as well as the relevant theoretical work on the process of local knowledge accumulation and the different agglomeration forces that lead to spatial clustering it provides a very comprehensive overview of the topic.

Types of spillovers and clusters

The literature usually distinguishes between three different categories of location-specific knowledge spillovers:

- intra-industry spillovers and specialization externalities (classical clustering), which can be offset by gravitational pull and congestion effects;
- inter-industry spillovers and diversity externalities (urbanization economies in all-round centres); and
- external sources of knowledge, and science-technology spillovers.

Intra-industry spillovers are associated with the presence of a wide range of technologically active firms within a given sector, all in the same geographical area. The geographical concentration of firms engaged in similar activities leads to further local clustering of related firms and the local accumulation of relevant knowledge (Braunerhjelm *et al.*, 2000). The link between knowledge spillovers and clustering has been clearly established empirically. Not only do industries in which new knowledge plays an important part in production tend to cluster more (Audretsch and Feldman, 1996b), but firms in clusters with strong ties between similar firms also tend to innovate more than firms outside these regions (Baptista and Swann, 1998). Intra-industry spillovers relate to specialization externalities, as in Marshall's early contribution. They materialize as an appropriate agglomeration pattern that facilitates asset-sharing. The firms of each country tend to embark on a path of technological accumulation that has certain unique characteristics and sustains a distinct profile of national technological specialization (Rosenberg, 1976; Cantwell, 2000b). The kinds of linkages that grow up between competitors, suppliers and customers in any region or country are also, to some extent, peculiar to that location, and imbue the technology creation of its firms with distinctive features (Mariotti and Piscitello, 2001). For these reasons, other TNCs often need to be on-site with their own production and their innovatory capacity if they are to properly benefit from the latest advances in geographically localized technological development, to feed their innovation (Cantwell, 1989; Kogut and Chang, 1991). In addition to the more intangible effects of knowledge spillovers, Bernstein and Nadiri (1989) also find evidence for more quantifiable effects. In their empirical study of four industries they find that costs decline for the externality receiving firm as well as the rate of research and development (R&D) investment and capital accumulation. Overall the social rates of return to R&D exceed the private returns.

However, such beneficial local clustering effects require a sufficient initial cross-firm diversity of activity in a location to start the process. If a local innovative system is dominated by a single major player or strong leader company then this leader may exercise a forceful gravitational pull of the best resources, implying a particular kind of congestion effect for any other entrant (Cantwell and Kosmopoulou, 2002; Cantwell and Piscitello, 2005). There may also be a more active competitive deterrence that favours a long-established local champion in such cases.

Diversity externalities, or urbanization economies, can be related to general-purpose technologies (GPTs), entailing inter-industry spillovers (Lipsey *et al.*, 1998) associated with the existence of firms working in several different fields of productive and technological endeavour. Indeed, the more diverse the learning activities conducted in the region are, the wider the range of potential cross-overs from which the firm could potentially benefit. Such spillovers relate to diversity externalities, which favour the creation of new ideas across sectors, as originally suggested by Jacobs (1961). They are more likely to occur in an all-round 'higher-order' centre of excellence, which attracts the research-based investments of a wide variety of foreign-owned TNCs and facilitates a more favourable interaction with indigenous firms. In absence of strong competitive forces among the firms in the cluster, the milieu is particularly conducive to interaction between TNCs and local firms and thus offers greater opportunities for inter-company alliances for the purposes of technological collaboration and exchange (Cantwell *et al.*, 2001; Cantwell and Mudambi, 2000). An analysis of data from 170 US cities focusing on industry growth through knowledge spillovers in cities by Glaeser *et al.* (1992) confirms Jacob's ideas empirically. It shows that growth is mostly supported by diversity of industry and competition (which partly also supports Porter's view) and thus suggests diversity may promote innovation and knowledge spillovers to a greater extent. Further empirical evidence of urbanization economies are offered by Ciccone and Hall (1996) who develop a model to analyse the impact of employment density on labour productivity and subsequently estimate the parameters using gross state product and employment data across US states for 1988. Their results indicate that a doubling of employment density increases average labour productivity by around 6 per cent.

Locational hierarchies and TNCs

The changes in economic activity, that is the greater importance of knowledge as a key asset, the role of alliance capitalism and increased globalization, have forced TNCs to consider the implications of locating in a specific area as an integral part of their overall strategies, that is where to locate key activities such as R&D, how to distribute the charters across subsidiary networks based on the constraints and opportunities of the local markets (Birkinshaw and Hood, 1998), and how to manage the independence and simultaneous integration of the parts of the network.

The notion that the geographical dispersion of technological development enhances innovation in the network of the TNC as a whole is founded on the belief that innovation is location-specific as well as firm-specific (Cantwell, 1989). The scientific and technological traditions of each country, the shared experience of its researchers and production engineers and the communication between them across companies, the nature of its educational system, and its common business practices all contribute to the distinctiveness of the path of technology development undertaken in each location (Cantwell, 2000b; Pavitt, 1987; Rosenberg, 1976). By drawing on innovations of various kinds depending upon the conditions prevailing in the relevant local research centre, TNCs develop a more complex technological system and by accessing differentiated streams of knowledge have an important source of competitive advantage (Almeida, 1996; Dunning, 1996; Dunning and Wymbs, 1999; Fors and Zejan, 1996; Kümmerle, 1999a; Pearce, 1999). The attractiveness of locations for other research-related investments may well be strengthened in the process. The involvement of foreign TNCs in research in centres of innovation has a direct effect on broadening the scope of local technological capability, and an indirect effect through its competitive stimulus encouraging other firms to extend their local research programmes. The process helps to establish locational poles of attraction for research-related activity. According to Storper (1992) the characteristics of the increasing technological dynamism, which requires both the minimization of cost in production and avoidance of lock-in at the same time, further supports the creation of the so-called technology districts, because this geographical form is the most effective way of managing the trade-off between cost-minimization and technological flexibility.

In addition to affecting the attractiveness of a location for further research-related TNC activity, there are also more direct beneficial effects to the local economy and national system of innovation arising out of TNC activity. While the knowledge spillovers and development-enhancing effects of foreign direct investment (FDI) on a host economy have been widely discussed in the economics literature, there is now concrete empirical evidence that the connection of local firms with TNCs can give them access to international knowledge sources and thus strengthen the innovation capability of smaller enterprises, which are crucial in the earlier development stages of an economy, enhance international competitiveness, and facilitate the transformation process of transition economies (Molero and Álvarez, 2003; Palaskas and Tsampra, 2003; Inzelt, 2003). However, the long-term effects are often not clear-cut and depend in large part on the prior level of technological advancement and R&D investment of local firms, since these factors determine the level of local absorptive capacity, and thus the ability of indigenous firms to benefit from spillovers and access to external knowledge (Sanna-Randaccio and Veugelers, 2003).

The increased role of locationally dispersed sourcing of technology from major centres of excellence through the international networks of more globally integrated TNCs (Cantwell, 1995) has led to a growing interest in the asset-acquiring motive for FDI (Cantwell, 1989; Cantwell and Janne, 1999; Cantwell and Piscitello, 2000), and in the greater decentralization in the management of international R&D to capture 'home-base augmenting' benefits (Kümmerle, 1999a,b).

Internationalization has supported corporate technological diversification since the form of technological development varies between locations as well as between firms (Cantwell and Janne, 1999; Cantwell and Piscitello, 2000; Zander, 1997). By locating production in an alternative centre of innovation in its industry, the TNC gains access to a new but complementary avenue of technological development, which it integrates with its existing lines. By increasing the overlap between the technological profiles of firms competition between TNCs is raised in each international industry, but so also are cooperative agreements as the numbers of knowledge spillovers between firms increases as well. Apart from the rise in technological interrelatedness, the potential opportunities for cross-border learning within TNCs have been enhanced by an increased take-up of information and communication technologies (ICT). ICT specialization seems to amplify the firm's technological flexibility by enabling it to fuse together a wider range of formerly separate technologies.

However, the creation of technology may be locationally concentrated or dispersed according to the degree of complexity embedded in it. Some kinds of technologies are geographically easily dispersed, whilst the uncodified character of others makes cross-border learning within and across organizations much more difficult. Thus, although transnationals have shown a greater internationalization of their R&D facilities recently, it depends upon the type of technological activity involved. The development of science-based fields of activity (for example ICT, biotechnology and new materials) and an industry's core technologies appear to require a greater intensity of face-to-face interaction (Cantwell and Santangelo, 2000). Nonetheless, it may sometimes still be the case that science-based and firm- and industry-specific core technologies are dispersed internationally. The main factors driving the occasional geographical dispersion of the creation of these kinds of otherwise highly localized technologies are either locally embedded specialization which cannot be accessed elsewhere, or company-specific global strategies that utilize the development of an organizationally complex international network for technological learning (Cantwell and Santangelo, 1999).

The more typical pattern of international specialization in innovative activity within the TNC is for the development of technologies that are core to the firm's industry to be concentrated at home, while other fields of technological activity may be located abroad, and in this sense the internationalization of research tends to be complementary to the home base (Cantwell and Kosmopoulou, 2002). Thus, when science-based technology creation is internationally dispersed it is most often attributable to foreign technology acquisition by the firms of 'other' industries – for example, chemical industry TNCs developing electrical technologies abroad, or electrical equipment TNCs developing specialized chemical processes outside their home countries (Cantwell and Santangelo, 1999, 2000). From the other side of host countries as opposed to investing TNCs, a local centre of excellence for some specialized field of innovation (say in chemicals) will tend to attract investments in local chemical research not so much by foreign-owned TNCs in the chemical industry, but to a greater extent by TNCs from other industries, whose objective is to tap into the resources of the centre in order to diversify their own technological base (Cantwell and Kosmopoulou, 2002).

Evidence has now emerged that the choice of foreign location for technological development in support of what is done in the home base of the TNC depends upon whether host regions within countries are either major centres for innovation or not. The sectoral composition of technological strengths differs across regional centres, while the technological specialization of foreign-owned affiliates depends upon the rank of the regional location in the geographical hierarchy and upon its gradual change over time (Cantwell and Janne, 1999).

It is possible to distinguish between higher-order and intermediate regional centres of technological excellence (Cantwell *et al.*, 2001). Such centres arise as a consequence of the interaction and the intensity of general external economies and localization economies, which in turn depend upon the characteristics of the regional innovation system considered. Clearly, the other extreme is that of lower-order regions, that is technologically weak and backward regions that have an inadequate innovative base in order to compete with other locations and to be attractive for external flows of knowledge and technology. This differentiation has enabled us to distinguish between the form of potential knowledge spillovers and technological networks in operation between foreign-owned firms and their indigenous counterparts in different locations. These interactions are more likely to further upgrade higher-order regional locations, in which the local-for-local strategy of subsidiaries aim at exploring local knowledge and expertise, which will be integrated to widen technological competence at the corporate level through the intra-firm network (local-for-global) (Cantwell and Iammarino, 1998). Indeed, when foreign research has a more pronounced exploratory nature, it is likely to be attracted by higher-order cores, treating them as a source of general expertise and skills (Cantwell *et al.*, 2001).

Intermediate locations, with a narrower scope of technological advantages, are seen as sources of specific capabilities in some particular field and thus they might be negatively affected due to the local-for-local strategy of foreign affiliates, which follows a logic of exploitation of indigenous expertise. In other words, if the position of the region in the hierarchy falls as it becomes more narrowly focused, so the profile of technological specialization of foreign-owned firms in that region becomes more closely related to the equivalent pattern of specialization of indigenous firms in the same region.

Even in the case of higher-order regions, the broadening of specialization is just one of the possible forms of incremental change in the composition of local innovation, since regional profiles may, in other cases, be reinforced and concentrated in their established areas of technological expertise. Only some higher-order cores are able to adjust their profiles of specialization to the highest technological opportunities over time, whilst others – which experience a slower process of convergence between old and new technologies – may end up by gradually losing their competitiveness (Cantwell and Iammarino, 2001).

Core systems appear to be rooted in general purpose technologies (GPTs) – for example background engineering, mechanical methods, electronics and information and communication technologies (ICTs) – in which foreign-owned and indigenous firms' technological advantages appear to overlap in these higher-order centres. TNC subsidiaries account for an increasing share of all new technologies that are introduced in the transnational networks and that are associated with a significantly higher probability of entry into new and more distantly related fields of technology (especially GPTs), creating a long-term drift into new technological competence.

There is evidence that, for example, in chemicals the affiliates of German TNCs are technologically specialized in other European centres in accordance with the local strengths of the centre in question, and the same is true of British chemical TNCs apart from in Germany. However, British TNCs in chemicals when operating in Germany follow a pattern of technological specialization that accords with their own comparative advantages in the industry and those of their home centre, the UK. They do not appear to be especially prone to try and tap into the areas in which German expertise is relatively greatest, but rather treat Germany as a general reservoir of skills that can be used principally to extend those lines of operation on which they are already focused (and can themselves contribute most to the German system) (Cantwell and Sanna-Randaccio, 1992).

In other words, firms based in higher-order centres are more likely to establish a locationally specialized network of technological activity in support of corporate innovation than are firms that originate from lower-order centres (Cantwell and Janne, 1999). Thus, at least until recently, patterns of technological specialization within an industry seem to have been strengthened mainly by the networks of TNCs from the leading centres. This may also be partly attributable to gravitational pull and competitive deterrence effects when (local areas within) the leading centres are dominated by specific TNCs, thereby excluding these locations from the networks of other TNCs at least for diversification purposes.

Whereas most regions are not major centres and tend to be highly specialized in their profile of technological development, and hence attract foreign-owned activity in the same narrow range of fields; in the major centres much of the locally-sited innovation of foreign-owned TNCs does not match very well the specific fields of local specialization, but is rather geared towards the development of technologies that are core to the current techno-economic paradigm (notably ICT) or earlier paradigms (notably mechanical technologies) (Cantwell *et al.*, 2001). The need to develop these latter technologies is shared by the firms of all industries, and the knowledge spillovers between TNCs and local firms in this case may be inter-industry in character.

While there is now ample evidence that TNCs do tap into local knowledge networks (Kümmerle, 1999a; Zander, 1999), recent research explores in more detail under which conditions TNCs source knowledge from the centres they are located in. In his study of US patent data, Frost (2001) finds that a subsidiary is most likely to source knowledge locally if it follows an exploration strategy, that is if the sourcing is related to a technical field in which the home country is relatively disadvantaged and the host country is relatively advantaged; secondly if the technological capabilities of the subsidiary are strong; thirdly if the subsidiary is large; and lastly if the firm has an overall wide presence in the host country and its membership in technical networks. Cantwell and Mudambi (2003) report some related findings on the connection between local inter-firm and global intra-firm knowledge networks. An analysis of US patents granted to UK subsidiaries of non-UK TNCs and survey data indicates that local industry-cluster diversity (the inverse of concentration) and resource munificence positively affects the likelihood of a subsidiary receiving a competence-creating mandate, and thus sourcing knowledge locally. The degree to which a competence-creating subsidiary sources knowledge locally is also positively affected by whether the subsidiary was acquired, since acquisition increases the chances that a highly potentially creative subsidiary can contribute novel lines of technology to their new group. In contrast, for purely competence-exploiting subsidiaries acquisition affects local knowledge-sourcing negatively, since they are likelier to lose out in the process of post-acquisition elimination of R&D duplication, and this tends to leave them relatively more dependent on knowledge sources from elsewhere in their new group.

Conclusion

The economic landscape has undergone many significant changes in the last few decades, the most extensive of which is globalization. In its wake certain kinds of economic activity have become more and more easily dispersed across space, and distance matters less in the transfer of goods and people. However, at the same time 'sticky places within such slippery space' (Markusen, 1996) are emerging, especially with respect to knowledge-intensive activities. Thus, the location decision is an increasingly important issue for the transnational firm and more and more closely interacts with and is inseparable from the analysis and strategic planning of internalization and ownership-specific advantages (Cantwell, 2000a; Dunning, 1998, 2000), through the efficient management of cross-border transactions and the creative development of in-house corporate competence. With the rising awareness by TNCs of locational advantages as a competitiveness-enhancing and sustaining factor, the understanding of the very specific processes and phenomena involved in a variety of locational types has become fundamental, and they are no longer just something that is 'in the air' as Marshall had once noted over 100 years ago.

At the same time that TNCs are becoming more aware of locational issues, policy makers are also rediscovering location as an issue of importance. As indicated throughout this chapter, the interplay between TNC activity and the development of a host economy is complex and does not always result in a virtuous cycle, thus preventing the use of one-size-fits-all recommendations and approaches. A careful analysis of the individual characteristics of a place, its history, its resource availabilities and capabilities seems critical if locational dynamics are to be leveraged for developmental purposes. However, further research is needed to clarify if even the most thought-out interventions and policies will ultimately have the desired impact or if, intrinsically, clusters are not susceptible to policy-led manipulation.

References

Almeida, P. (1996) 'Knowledge Sourcing by Foreign Multinationals: Patent Citation Analysis in the US Semiconductor Industry', *Strategic Management Journal*, 17: 155–65.

Appold, S.J. (1995) 'Agglomeration, Interorganizational Networks, and Competitive Performance in the US Metalworking Sector', *Economic Geography*, 71(1): 27–54.

Audretsch, D.B. and Feldman, M.P. (1996a) 'Innovative Clusters and the Industry Life Cycle', *Review of Industrial Organization*, 11: 253–73.

Audretsch, D.B. and Feldman, M.P. (1996b) 'R&D Spillovers and the Geography of Innovation and Production', *American Economic Review*, 86(3): 630–40.

Baptista, R. and Swann, G.M.P. (1998) 'Do Firms in Clusters Innovate More?', *Research Policy*, 27: 525–40.

Baptista, R. and Swann, G.M.P. (1999) 'A Comparison of Clustering Dynamics in the U. S. and UK Computer Industries', *Evolutionary Economics*, 9: 373–99.

Bernstein, J.I. and Nadiri, M.I. (1989) 'Research and Development and Intra-Industry Spillovers: An Empirical Application of Dynamic Duality', *Review of Economic Studies*, 56(2): 249–67.

Birkinshaw, J. and Hood, N. (1998) 'Multinational Subsidiary Development: Capability Evolution and Charter Change in Foreign-Owned Subsidiary Companies', *Academy of Management Review*, 23(4): 773–95.

Braunerhjelm, P., Faini, R., Norman, V., Ruane, F. and Seabright, P. (eds) (2000) *Integration and the Regions of Europe: How the Right Policies can Prevent Polarization.* London: Centre for Economic Policy Research.

Caniëls, M.C.J. (2000) *Knowledge Spillovers and Economic Growth: Regional Growth Differentials across Europe.* Cheltenham: Edward Elgar.

Cantwell, J.A. (1989) *Technological Innovation and Multinational Corporations.* Oxford: Basil Blackwell.

Cantwell, J.A. (1995) 'The Globalisation of Technology: What Remains of the Product Cycle Model?' *Cambridge Journal of Economics*, 19(1): 155–74.

Cantwell, J.A. (2000a) 'A Survey of Theories of International Production', in C.N. Pitelis and R. Sugden (eds), *The Nature of the Transnational Firm.* London and New York: Routledge.

Cantwell, J.A. (2000b) 'Technological Lock-in of Large Firms since the Interwar Period', *European Review of Economic History*, 4(2): 147–74.

Cantwell, J.A. and Iammarino, S. (1998) 'TNCs, Technological Innovation and Regional Systems in the EU: Some Evidence in the Italian Case', *International Journal of the Economics of Business*, 5(3): 383–408.

Cantwell, J.A. and Iammarino, S. (2001) 'EU Regions and Multinational Corporations: Change, Stability and Strengthening of Technological Comparative Advantages', *Industrial and Corporate Change*, 10(4): 1007–037.

Cantwell, J.A., Iammarino, S. and Noonan, C.A. (2001) 'Sticky Places in Slippery Space – the Location of Innovation by TNCs in the European Regions', in N. Pain (ed.),

Inward Investment, Technological Change and Growth: The Impact of TNCs on the UK Economy. London and New York: Palgrave Macmillan.

Cantwell, J.A. and Janne, O.E.M. (1999) 'Technological Globalisation and Innovative Centres: The Role of Corporate Technological Leadership and Locational Hierarchy', *Research Policy*, 28(2–3): 119–44.

Cantwell, J.A. and Kosmopoulou, E. (2002) 'What Determines the Internationalisation of Corporate Technology?', in M. Forsgren, H. Håkanson and V. Havila (eds), *Critical Perspectives on Internationalisation.* Oxford: Pergamon.

Cantwell, J.A. and Mudambi, R. (2000) 'The Location of TNC R&D activity: The Role of Investment Incentives', *Management International Review*, 39(Special Issue 1): 123–47.

Cantwell, J.A. and Mudambi, R. (2003) 'On the Nature of Knowledge Creation in TNC Subsidiaries: An Empirical Analysis Using Patent Data', paper presented at the DRUID Summer Conference, Copenhagen, June.

Cantwell, J.A. and Piscitello, L. (2000) 'Accumulating Technological Competence – Its Changing Impact on Corporate Diversification and Internationalisation', *Industrial and Corporate Change*, 9(1): 21–51.

Cantwell, J. A. and Piscitello, L. (2005) 'The Recent Location of Foreign-Owned R&D Activities by Large TNCs in the European Regions: The Role of Spillovers and Externalities', *Regional Studies*, 38(1): 1–16.

Cantwell, J.A. and Sanna-Randaccio, F. (1992) 'Intra-Industry Direct Investment in the European Community: Oligopolistic Rivalry and Technological Competition', in J.A. Cantwell (ed.), *Multinational Investment in Modern Europe: Strategic Interaction in The Integrated Community.* Cheltenham: Edward Elgar.

Cantwell, J.A. and Santangelo, G.D. (1999) 'The Frontier of International Technology Networks: Sourcing Abroad the Most Highly Tacit Capabilities', *Information Economics and Policy*, 11(1): 101–23.

Cantwell, J.A. and Santangelo, G.D. (2000) 'Capitalism, Profits and Innovation in the New Techno-Economic Paradigm', *Journal of Evolutionary Economics*, 10(1–2): 131–57.

Ciccone, A. and Hall, R.E. (1996) 'Productivity and the Density of Economic Activity', *American Economic Review*, 86(1): 54–70.

De Beule, F. and Van Den Bulcke, D. (2001) 'Industrial Clusters and Japanese Manufacturing Affiliates in the Belgian Small Open Economy', in D. Van Den Bulcke and A. Verbeke (eds), *Globalization and the Small Open Economy.* Cheltenham: Edward Elgar.

De Bresson, C. (1987) 'I poli tecnologici dello sviluppo', *L'industria*, 3: 301–408.

De Vet, J.M. and Scott, A.J. (1992) 'The Southern California Medical Device Industry: Innovation, New Firm Formation and Location', *Research Policy*, 21: 145–61.

Dicken, P. and Lloyd, P.E. (eds) (1990) *Location in Space. Theoretical Perspectives in Economic Geography.* New York: HarperCollins.

Dorfman, N.S. (1983) 'Route 128: The Development of a Regional High Technology Economy', *Research Policy*, 12: 299–316.

Dunning, J.H. (1970) *Studies in International Investment.* London: Allen & Unwin.

Dunning, J.H. (1996) 'The Geographical Sources of Competitiveness of Firms. Some Results of a New Survey', *Transnational Corporations*, 5(3): 1–21.

Dunning, J.H. (1998) 'Location and the Multinational Enterprise: A Neglected Factor?', *Journal of International Business Studies*, 29(1): 45–66.

Dunning, J.H. (2000) 'Regions, Globalization, and the Knowledge Economy: The Issues Stated', in J.H. Dunning (ed.), *Regions, Globalization, and the Knowledge-Based Economy.* Oxford and New York: Oxford University Press.

Dunning, J.H. and Wymbs, C. (1999) 'The Geographical Sourcing of Technology-Based Assets by Multinational Enterprises', in D. Archibugi, J. Howells and J. Michie (eds),

Innovation Policy in a Global Economy. Cambridge and New York: Cambridge University Press.

Ellison, G. and Glaeser, E.L. (1997) 'Geographic Concentration in US Manufacturing Industries: A Dartboard Approach', *Journal of Political Economy*, 105(5): 889–927.

Feldman, M.P. (2001) 'The Entrepreneurial Event Revisited: Firm Formation in a Regional Context', *Industrial and Corporate Change*, 10(4): 861–91.

Feldman, M.P. and Schreuder, Y. (1996) 'Initial Advantage: The Origins of the Geographic Concentration of the Pharmaceutical Industry in the Mid-Atlantic Region', *Industrial and Corporate Change*, 5(3): 839–62.

Fors, G. and Zejan, M. (1996) 'Overseas R&D by Multinationals in Foreign Centers of Excellence', Working paper 111. Stockholm: Economic Research Institute, Stockholm School of Economics.

Frost, T.S. (2001) 'The Geographic Sources of Foreign Subsidiaries' Innovations', *Strategic Management Journal*, 22(2): 101–23.

Glaeser, E.L., Kallal, H.D., Scheinkman, J.A. and Shleifer, A. (1992) 'Growth in Cities', *Journal of Political Economy*, 100(6): 1126–52.

Guerrieri, P., Iammarino, S. and Pietrobelli, C. (eds) (2001) *The Global Challenge to Industrial Districts: Small and Medium-Sized Enterprises in Italy and Taiwan.* Cheltenham: Edward Elgar.

Hotelling, H. (1929) 'Stability in Competition', *The Economic Journal*, 39(153): 41–57.

Inzelt, A. (2003) 'Foreign Involvement in Acquiring and Producing New Knowledge: the Case of Hungary', in J.A. Cantwell and J. Molero (eds), *Multinational Enterprises, Innovative Strategies and Systems of Innovation*. Cheltenham: Edward Elgar.

Jacobs, J. (1969) *The Economy of Cities.* New York: Vintage.

Kenney, M. and Von Burg, U. (1999) 'Technology, Entrepreneurship and Path Dependence: Industrial Clustering in Silicon Valley and Route 128', *Industrial and Corporate Change*, 8(1): 67–193.

Kogut, B. and Chang, S.J. (1991) 'Technological Capabilities and Japanese Foreign Direct Investment in the United States', *Review of Economics and Statistics*, 73: 401–13.

Krugman, P.R. (1991) 'Increasing Returns and Economic Geography', *Journal of Political Economy*, 99(3): 483–99.

Kümmerle, W. (1999a) 'The Drivers of Foreign Direct Investment into Research and Development: an Empirical Investigation', *Journal of International Business Studies*, 30(1): 1–24.

Kümmerle, W. (1999b) 'Foreign Direct Investment in Industrial Research in the Pharmaceutical and Electronic Industries – Results from a Survey of Multinational Firms', *Research Policy*, 28: 179–93.

Lipsey, R.G., Bekar, C. and Carlaw, K. (1998) 'What Requires Explanation?' in E. Helpman (ed.), *General Purpose Technologies and Economic Growth*. Cambridge: MIT Press.

Lösch, A. (1954) *The Economics of Location.* New Haven, CT: Yale University Press.

Lundvall, B.Å. (1992) *National Systems of Innovation.* London: Pinter.

Maggioni, M.A. (2002) 'Empirical Analyses of the Location of High-Tech Firms and of Cluster Development', in M. Maggioni (ed.) *Clustering Dynamics and the Location of High Tech Firms*. Heidelberg, New York: Physica-Verlag.

Malmberg, A., Sölvell, Ö. and Zander, I. (1996) 'Spatial Clustering, Local Accumulation of Knowledge and Firm Competitiveness', *Geografiska Annaler Series B: Human Geography*, 78(2): 85–97.

Mariotti, S. and Piscitello, L. (2001) 'The Role of Territorial Externalities in Affecting Internationalisation of Production by SMEs', *Entrepreneurship and Regional Development*, 13: 65–80.

Markusen, A. (1996) 'Sticky Places in Slippery Space: a Typology of Industrial Districts', *Economic Geography*, 72(3): 293–313.

Marshall, A. (1891) *Principles of Economics*. London: Macmillan.

Molero, J. and Álvarez, I. (2003) 'The Technological Strategies of Multinational Enterprises: Their Implications for National Systems of Innovation', in J.A. Cantwell and J. Molero (eds), *Multinational Enterprises, Innovative Strategies and Systems of Innovation*. Cheltenham: Edward Elgar.

Palaskas, T. and Tsampra, M. (2003) 'National Innovation Systems: Absorptive Capacity and Firm Competitiveness', in J.A. Cantwell and J. Molero (eds), *Multinational Enterprises, Innovative Strategies and Systems of Innovation*. Cheltenham: Edward Elgar.

Pandit, N.R., Cook, G.A.S. and Swann, G.M.P. (2001) 'The Dynamics of Industrial Clustering in British Financial Services', *The Service Industries Journal*, 21(4): 33–61.

Pavitt, K.L.R. (1987) 'International Patterns of Technological Accumulation', in N. Hood and J.E. Vahlne (eds), *Strategies in Global Competition*. London: Croom Helm.

Pearce, R.D. (1999) 'Decentralized R&D and Strategic Competitiveness: Globalised Approaches to Generation and Use of Technology in TNCs', *Research Policy*, 28: 157–78.

Porter, M.E. (1998) 'Clusters and Competition: New Agendas for Companies, Governments, and Institutions', in M.E. Porter, *On Competition*. Boston, Mass.: Harvard Business School Press.

Porter, M.E. (2000) 'Location, Competition and Economic Development: Local Clusters in a Global Economy', *Economic Development Quarterly*, 14(1): 15–34.

Prevezer, M. (1997) 'The Dynamics of Industrial Clustering in Biotechnology', *Small Business Economics*, 9(3): 255–71.

Richardson, H.W. (ed.) (1969) *Elements of Regional Economics*. Harmondsworth: Penguin.

Rosenberg, N. (1976) *Perspectives on Technology*. Cambridge and New York: Cambridge University Press.

Sanna-Randaccio, F. and Veugelers, R. (2003) 'Global Innovation Strategies of TNCs: Implications for Host Economies', in J.A. Cantwell and J. Molero (eds), *Multinational Enterprises, Innovative Strategies and Systems of Innovation*. Cheltenham: Edward Elgar.

Steinle, C. and Schiele, H. (2002) 'When do Industries Cluster? A Proposal on how to Assess an Industry's Propensity to Concentrate at a Single Region or Nation', *Research Policy*, 31: 849–58.

Storper, M. (1992) 'The Limits to Globalization: Technology Districts and International Trade', *Economic Geography*, 68: 60–93.

Stuart, T. and Sorenson, O. (2002) 'The Geography of Opportunity: Spatial Heterogeneity in Founding Rates and the Performance of Biotechnology Firms', *Research Policy*, 36: 1–25.

Swann, G.M.P. and Pervezer, M. (1996) 'A Comparison of the Dynamics of Industrial Clustering in Computing and Biotechnology', *Research Policy*, 25: 1139–157.

Van Den Bulcke, D. (1985) 'Belgium', in J.H. Dunning (ed.), *Multinational Enterprises, Economic Structure and International Competitiveness*. Chichester and New York: Wiley & Sons.

Van Den Bulcke, D. and De Lombaerde, P. (1992) 'The Belgian Metalworking Industries and the Large European Internal Market: The Role of Multinational Investment', in J.A. Cantwell (ed.), *Multinational Investment in Modern Europe: Strategic Interaction in the Integrated Community*. Cheltenham: Edward Elgar.

Vernon, R. (1966) 'International Investment and International Trade in the Product Cycle', *Quarterly Journal of Economics*, 80(2): 190–207.

Von Hippel, E. (1989) *The Sources of Innovation*. Oxford: Oxford University Press.

Weber, A. (1929) *Theory of the Location of Industries*. Chicago: University of Chicago Press.

Zander, I. (1997) 'Technological Diversification in the Multinational Corporation: Historical Evolution and Future Prospects', *Research Policy*, 26(2): 209–28.

Zander, I. (1999) 'How do you Mean "Global"? An Empirical Investigation of Innovation Networks in the Multinational Corporation', *Research Policy*, 28(2–3): 195–213.

7
The Role of Developing Countries and Emerging Economies in International Inter-Firm R&D Partnering

Daniëlle Cloodt and John Hagedoorn

Introduction

This chapter presents an analysis of major historical trends and sectoral patterns in international inter-firm R&D partnering from 1971 to 2000. The focus is on collaboration between independent companies through formal agreements, such as contractual agreements and joint ventures. We will mainly look at partnerships where R&D is at least part of the collaborative effort. It is well-established that the ongoing process of globalization has greatly influenced the growth of these international inter-firm R&D partnerships, and this is especially the case in technology-intensive industries that undergo a process of rapid technological development. Increased global competition together with enlarged complexity of technology and the associated risks and costs of innovative activities have stimulated many firms to enter into international R&D partnerships.

In the following we will pay specific attention to differences between the developed economies of the Organization for Economic Cooperation and Development (OECD), newly industrialized countries (NICs), less-developed countries (LDCs), and, in particular, the East European previously state-run economies and former communist countries (FCC). The opening of FCC markets resulted largely in the disappearance of regulations such as internal trade barriers and national protectionism, for instance the liberalization of foreign direct investment (FDI), discriminatory regional agreements, privatization and deregulation of industries (Van Den Bulcke, 1988; Kang and Johansson, 2000; Van Den Bulcke and Zhang, 1998; Zhang and Van Den Bulcke, 2000). Because of this, the pool of markets and potential partners for international partnerships has expanded to China, Eastern Europe and the former Soviet Union (Hagedoorn and Sedaitis, 1998).

The MERIT-CATI database (see the Appendix) will be used to discover a number of general trends and patterns in international R&D partnering. This database is one of the few still existing databases that generate both cross-sectional and longitudinal insight. It allows us to study patterns in R&D partnerships in several industries, in different regions of the world over an extended period of several decades (Hagedoorn *et al.*, 2000; Hagedoorn, 2002).

The chapter is organized as follows: first, we will explain the rationale behind inter-firm partnering and provide some definitions. Second, we will give a general overview of trends in international R&D partnerships since 1971, using the MERIT-CATI database. We will present growth data, as well as the distribution of major organizational features of R&D partnerships. Third, specific sectoral patterns of international R&D partnerships will be analysed because partnerships are known to be somewhat sector-specific as the propensity to enter into partnerships differs by industry. Fourth, we will present an in-depth discussion of the patterns in R&D partnerships of companies from different regions in general, and with companies from FCC countries in particular. Finally, we will discuss some of the main conclusions that can be drawn from this contribution.

R&D partnerships: definition, their rationale and organizational settings

Traditionally, firms have been understood to be independent and self-contained units. During the 1970s and early 1980s, however, a number of companies started to replace their traditional practices, such as mergers and foreign direct investment, with new forms of organization, such as joint ventures, joint development agreements and other types of partnerships (Duysters and Hagedoorn, 2000). This process was triggered by fundamental changes in the structure of the global economy and by the ongoing process of technological change (Haklisch, 1989).

Strategic partnerships are often seen as an essential part of international corporate strategies (Ohmae, 1990; De Woot, 1990). It has been indicated in the literature that strategic partnerships can make up for the lack of economic power, competence or foreign experience of at least one of the partners. Furthermore, they are also increasingly used as scanning devices that allow firms to monitor new markets without the need to invest the full amount of resources (Duysters and Hagedoorn, 2000).

This chapter focuses on international R&D partnerships. We define R&D partnerships as the set of different modes of innovation-based inter-firm collaboration where two or more independent firms share part of their R&D activities (see for instance Hagedoorn, 2002; Hagedoorn *et al.*, 2000). These partnerships are expected to have an impact on the long-term product-market combinations of the companies involved. R&D partnerships can be divided into two categories: contractual partnerships such as joint R&D pacts and joint development agreements, and equity-based partnerships such as joint ventures. Joint ventures are organizational units created and controlled by two or more parent companies, thereby increasing the organizational interdependence of the parent companies. Joint ventures, including those with a specific R&D programme, are one of the older modes of inter-firm partnering and have become well-known during the past decades (Berg *et al.*, 1982; Hagedoorn, 1996; Hladik, 1985). According to Hagedoorn (1996) and Narula and Hagedoorn (1999), joint ventures seem to have become gradually less popular if compared to other forms of partnering due to their organizational costs in combination with high failure rates (Kogut, 1988; Porter, 1987).

Contractual agreements cover technology and R&D sharing between two or more companies in combination with joint research or joint development projects. The costs are shared between the partners. Although these contractual R&D partnerships have a limited time-horizon, due to their project-based organization, each partnership appears to need a relatively strong commitment of companies and a solid interorganizational interdependence during the joint project. Compared to joint ventures, however, the organizational dependence between companies in a contractual R&D partnership is smaller and the time-horizon of the actual project-based partnership is almost by definition shorter (Hagedoorn, 1993). These contractual forms of R&D partnerships have become very important modes of inter-firm collaboration as their share has far exceeded that of joint ventures (Hagedoorn, 2002; Narula and Hagedoorn, 1999; Osborn and Baughn, 1990).

The literature mentions two important categories of motives for engaging in inter-firm partnerships: the cost-economizing motive, and the strategic motive (see for instance Narula, 1996). The cost-economizing motivation applies when at least one company enters the partnership mainly to lower the cost of some of its R&D activities by sharing the costs with one or more other companies. This cost-economizing rationale appears to particularly play a role in capital and R&D-intensive industries where the cost of single, large R&D projects are beyond the reach of many companies (Hagedoorn, 1993).

The strategic motive concerns organizational interdependence, such that there is a "strategic benefit" that accrues to either partner as the result of shared capital, technology or other resources. There must be some expected long-term positive effects of the agreement of the product-market positioning of at least one of the partners (Hagedoorn, 1993). Collaboration is seen as a means of shaping competition by improving a firm's comparative competitive position (Hagedoorn *et al.*, 2000; Narula, 1996).

The strategic rationale becomes important if, for instance, companies decide to selectively enter into R&D partnerships that are not related to their core activities, while keeping their main R&D activities within their own domain (Teece, 1986). The strategic intent of R&D partnerships is also apparent in those cases where companies jointly perform R&D in new, high-risk areas of R&D of which the future importance for their technological capabilities remains unclear for a considerable period of time. As mentioned before, the reduction and sharing of costs of R&D play an important role in the cost-economizing rationale. The strategic rationale, however, lies rather in the reduction, minimizing and sharing of uncertainty in R&D. Other strategic motives that can be seen as driving factors behind the choice for engaging in a R&D partnership are, among others, the increased complexity and intersectoral nature of new technologies, cross-fertilization of scientific disciplines and fields of technology, monitoring technological opportunities, monitoring of the evolution of technologies, technological synergies, and the access to scientific knowledge or to complementary technology (Hagedoorn, 1993). Other motives for participating in these research partnerships are found in gaining technical ability to diversify horizontally into new product lines, to vertically integrate production activities, and to leapfrog competition within their primary line of business (Hagedoorn *et al.*, 2000).

For many R&D partnerships, however, cost-economizing and strategic motives are intertwined; that is, they are often both strategically motivated as well as cost-economizing, although some agreements are clearly biased towards one motivation (Das *et al.*, 1998; Eisenhardt and Schoonhoven, 1996; Hagedoorn, 1993; Hagedoorn *et al.*, 2000, Lorenzoni and Lipparini, 1999; Mowery *et al.*, 1998; Narula, 1996). However, it is important to realize there is a dynamic aspect to all of this as the motives of a company can change over time due to both developments in the company itself, its environment and changes within the partnership (Harrigan, 1988).

General patterns in international R&D partnerships

Previous research (Chesnais, 1988; Hagedoorn, 2002; Hergert and Morris, 1988; Hladik, 1985; Mariti and Smiley, 1983; OECD, 1986, 1992) has established that there was a small growth of inter-firm partnerships during the 1960s and 1970s. During the 1980s there seems to have been a boom in the growth of inter-firm partnerships through all sorts of agreements, and this general pattern is also found for the particular group of partnerships studied in this chapter, that is international R&D partnerships (see Figure 7.1).

At the beginning of the 1970s the number of yearly established international R&D partnerships, found in the MERIT-CATI database, remained at a low level of around 15 made each year. Although these numbers are relatively small, they already attracted some attention in the literature, because this phenomenon puzzled academic observers (Hladik, 1985). Most of these partnerships were organized as joint ventures and the existing literature assumed

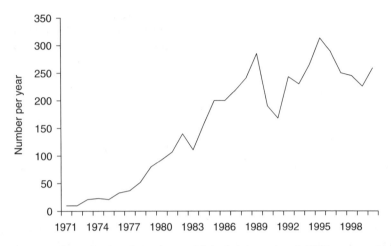

Figure 7.1 The growth of newly established international R&D partnerships, 1971–2000

Source: MERIT-CATI database.

that companies would simply exclude R&D from joint ventures because of the risk involved in such sensitive activities. During the 1970s there was a gradual increase in newly made international R&D partnerships from around 15 per year in the early 1970s to nearly 20 by the middle of the decade. At the end of the 1970s there was a sudden increase to 80 new international R&D partnerships formed per year.

This phenomenon appears to have developed even further during the next decade, the 1980s, which marked a steep increase in new R&D partnerships from about 90 per year in the early 1980s to almost 300 made each year at the end of the 1980s and the turn of the decade. The movement to all kinds of partnerships since the 1970s and early 1980s was triggered by fundamental changes in the structure of the global economy and by the ongoing process of technological change. Some examples are homogenization of markets, fierce competition and ongoing globalization tendencies. Ever-increasing costs of R&D and the increasing complexity of products combined with a strong increase in the speed of technological developments are the main drivers from a technological perspective (Haklisch, 1989).

The early 1990s showed a decrease in the newly made international partnerships to about 170 per year. From then onwards there was an increase to another peak in 1995 with a record of nearly 315 new established international R&D partnerships. From 1995 to 1999, we can witness a decrease again to nearly 230 partnerships in 1999, still considerably higher than the figures found for most years since the early 1980s. In 2000, the number of partnerships again increased to almost 260 newly established international R&D partnerships.

In other words, there is a clear pattern of growth in the newly made R&D partnerships if one looks at the historical data since 1971. In the early years there was a steady growth pattern with an acceleration since the 1980s. Explanations for this overall growth pattern of newly made international R&D partnerships are generally related to motives that lead to collaborations on R&D by companies. The main drivers for this growth are related to important industrial and technological changes in the 1980s and 1990s that have led to increased complexity of scientific and technological development, higher uncertainty surrounding R&D, increasing costs of R&D projects, and shortened innovation cycles that favour collaboration (see Contractor and Lorange, 1988; Dussauge and Garette, 1999; Hagedoorn, 1993, 1996; Mowery, 1988; Mytelka, 1991; Nooteboom, 1999; OECD, 1992).

In the above we indicated that previous contributions had already established that joint ventures seem to have become gradually less popular if compared to other forms of partnering. If we consider the specific trend for international R&D partnerships during the past three decades, we arrive at a similar conclusion. Looking at the overall trend in Figure 7.2, we notice a sharp decline in the share of joint ventures in international R&D partnering from on average an 85 per cent share in the early 1970s to 15 per cent in 2000. During the mid-1970s the share of R&D joint ventures was still at a level of about 70 per cent, whereas in the early 1980s this share reached around 55 per cent. In the late 1980s, the share of joint ventures increased to

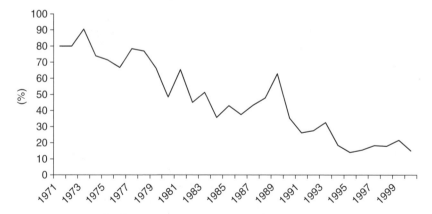

Figure 7.2 The share (%) of joint ventures in all newly established international R&D partnerships, 1971–2000

Source: MERIT-CATI database.

nearly 65 per cent, after which the downward trend reached a level of 20 per cent during the first half of the 1990s, until it arrived at a small share of 15 per cent at the end of the decade. These overall trends in newly established international R&D partnerships indicate two major developments. First, companies seem to increasingly prefer contractual partnerships to joint ventures. Second, the growth in partnerships since the early 1980s is largely caused by an overwhelming increase in the absolute numbers of contractual partnerships.

Sectoral patterns in international R&D partnerships

According to the literature, inter-firm partnerships are associated with so-called high-tech sectors and other sectors, where learning and flexibility are important features of the competitive landscape (Ciborra, 1991; Dussauge and Garette, 1999; Eisenhardt and Schoonhoven, 1996; Gomes-Casseres, 1996; Harrigan and Newman, 1990; Oster, 1992). The literature also reveals that many R&D partnerships are concentrated in a limited number of, mainly R&D intensive, industries (see for instance, Dussauge and Garette, 1999; Hagedoorn and Schakenraad, 1993; Link and Bauer, 1989; Mytelka, 1991). As this chapter concentrates on international R&D partnership, one can expect that, given the asymmetrical distribution of R&D efforts across industries, this particular group of partnerships will also be concentrated in R&D-intensive industries. In order to discuss the importance of sectoral differences in R&D partnering, R&D intensity indicators will be used to differentiate between industries. High-tech sectors (with an R&D intensity ranging from 10 per cent to 15 per cent) include: pharmaceuticals including biotech, information technology, aerospace and defense, and heavy electrical equipment. Medium-tech sectors (with an average R&D intensity ranging from 3 per cent to 5 per cent): chemicals, automotive, consumer electronics, and instrumentation and medical technology. Finally, low-tech sectors (with an R&D intensity below 1 per cent) include: food and beverages, metals, and oil and gas (see OECD, 1997).

During the whole period, that is from 1971 to 2000, the share of high-tech sectors was 68 per cent. The share of medium-tech sectors accounted for 30 per cent. Finally, low-tech sectors had a share of 2 per cent during this period. From Figure 7.3 it can be seen that the above-mentioned expected dominance of R&D partnering by high-tech, that is R&D-intensive, industries has only gradually developed as it did not become apparent until the mid-1980s. During the 1970s, R&D partnerships in high-tech industries still counted for only between 20 per cent and 50 per cent. During that same period, medium-tech industries had a share of between at least 50 per cent and 80 per cent. Although the share of medium-tech sectors is high, we witness a decrease over time.

The 1980s and 1990s marked a period where the growth of R&D-intensive industries is reflected in the increasing importance of these high-tech industries

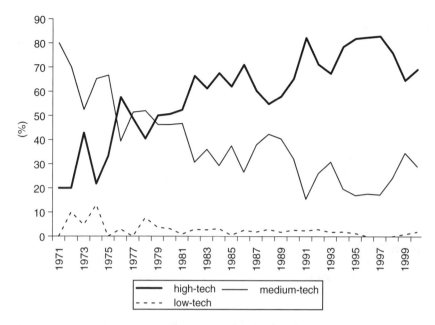

Figure 7.3 The share (%) of high-tech, medium-tech and low-tech industries in all newly established international R&D partnerships, 1971–2000

Source: MERIT-CATI database.

in R&D partnering. From 1980 to 1997, the share of high-tech industries in newly established international R&D partnerships increased from about 50 per cent to over 80 per cent, after which there was some decline. During the same period, the share of medium-tech industries in these partnerships decreased sharply from about 50 per cent to less than 20 per cent from 1980 to 1997, after which we can witness an increase again. In 2000, the share of newly established international R&D partnerships in the medium-tech sector was nearly 30 per cent. The share in the high-tech sector was more than twice as much, that is nearly 70 per cent.

As high-tech industries have become so dominant in international R&D partnering, we also looked at the trends in the share of individual high-tech sectors (see Figure 7.4). The information technology sector (including computers and office equipment, telecom, semiconductors, industrial automation and software) has become important in terms of its total R&D effort, which is reflected in its share in international R&D partnering. With a few exceptional years during the 1970s and the mid-1990s, the information technology sector takes by far the largest share in the sectoral distribution of R&D partnerships. During the first half of the 1970s, it had an average share of about 6 per cent of all these partnerships, rising quickly to around 20 per cent at the end of the 1970s. The early 1980s mark a period in

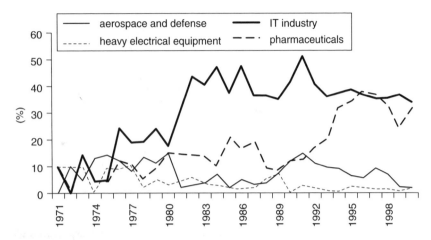

Figure 7.4 The share (%) of high-tech industries in all newly established international R&D partnerships, 1971–2000

Source: MERIT-CATI database.

which there was a very sharp increase in the share of the information technology sector from around 20 per cent in the early 1980s to on average 45 per cent during the rest of the decade. In the early 1990s there was again a decrease after which the average share of the information technology industry remains on average around 35 per cent.

Since the early 1970s there was a gradual increase in the share of pharmaceutical R&D partnerships, rising from about 10 per cent during most of the 1970s to 15 per cent during most of the 1980s. After a decline to about 10 per cent at the turn of the decade, the share of pharmaceutical R&D partnerships rose to nearly 40 per cent in 1996, after which we can again witness a decline. In 2000, the share of the pharmaceutical industry in international R&D partnerships was above 30 per cent, that is very close to the share of the information technology industry.

While the information technology sector and the pharmaceutical industry have become so dominant in international R&D partnering in high-tech industries, the share for the third and fourth high-tech industries, that is the aerospace and defense sector and the heavy electrical equipment sector, has remained relatively small. During the 1970s their shares were around 10 and 5 per cent, respectively. During most of the 1980s, the share of the aerospace and defense sector was around 5 per cent and peaked at 15 per cent in 1991, after which it decreased again. During the rest of the 1990s its share decreased to only 2 per cent in 2000. The share of the heavy electrical equipment sector was also around 5 per cent during the 1980s, while it decreased to 2 per cent during the 1990s.

With respect to the most important trends in medium-tech sectors, it can be said that the chemical sector dominates international R&D partnering in those industries. There is a decreasing trend in its share, starting at 50 per cent in 1971 to 10 per cent in 2000. The consumer electronics sector started quite dominant with about 30 per cent during the early 1970s, which decreased to 2 per cent at the end of the decade. During the 1980s and 1990s it remained at a level of around 2 per cent. The share of the automotive industry in medium-tech sectors remains around 5 per cent during the period from the 1970s to the early 1990s. Since 1995 there has been an increase, resulting in a share of 12 per cent in 2000. The share of the instrumentation and medical technology sector remained around 5 per cent from 1971 to 2000.

Finally, it will come as no surprise that low-tech industries (for instance food and beverages, metals, and oil and gas) do not seem to play an important role in all of this. The share of low-tech industries fluctuated around 6 per cent during the first half of the 1970s, after which their share remained at about 2 per cent.

Patterns in international R&D partnerships of companies from different economic regions

To take a closer look at international differences in R&D partnering, we now differentiate between partnerships and companies from different economic regions and trading blocks. The first group of countries that we distinguish consists of the OECD countries, that is the Triad (North America, Western-Europe and Japan), and Australia, New Zealand, Turkey and South Korea. Partnerships and companies from the so-called newly industrialized countries (NIC) include Taiwan, Singapore, Malaysia, Hong Kong, some Latin American countries (Brazil, Argentina, and Mexico) and Israel. Partnerships and companies from the so-called less-developed countries (LDC) include Latin American countries (with the exception of those mentioned above), Asian countries (with the exception of those mentioned above) and Africa. Finally, partnerships and companies from East European previously state-run economies and former communist countries (FCC) refer to Bulgaria, Croatia, the Czech Republic (including former Czechoslovakia), Hungary, Kazakhstan, Poland, the People's Republic of China, the Russian Federation (including the former Soviet Union), Slovakia, Ukraine, Vietnam and (former) Yugoslavia.

When analysing trends and patterns in international R&D partnerships, we will use the following division: intra-OECD partnerships include all partnerships between companies from the OECD. Next, OECD-NIC partnerships, OECD-LDC partnerships, and OECD-FCC partnerships refer to partnerships in which at least one of the partners is from the OECD, whereas also at least one of the other partners is from a NIC, LDC or FCC country respectively. Finally, non-OECD partnerships include all partnerships in which none of the partnering companies is from the OECD. Looking at the overall pattern in R&D partnering during the period under study, that is 1971–2000 (see Figure 7.5), it becomes clear that companies from the OECD have participated in over 99 per cent of these newly established international R&D partnerships. More than 90 per cent of the R&D partnerships are made between companies from the OECD. When taking a closer look at the distribution of these R&D partnerships for individual countries, it becomes clear that the USA plays a very dominant role. More than 70 per cent of all international R&D partnerships have at least one US company as a partner (see also Plasschaert and Van Den Bulcke, 1992). Japan comes second with almost 28 per cent of all international R&D partnerships having at least one Japanese company. The leading countries in Europe are the United Kingdom and Germany (both around 18 per cent), France (13 per cent) and the Netherlands (11 per cent).

Additional statistics, not presented in this chapter, reveal that the dominance of the USA has gradually increased from a share in international R&D partnerships of around 60 per cent in the 1970s to around 65 per cent and 75 per cent in the next two decades. Interestingly, the development in the share of Japanese companies has followed an opposite direction; it decreased from more than 40 per cent in the first decade of this study to respectively less than 35 per cent and around 20 per cent in the following two decades. Finally, Germany's share witnessed an increase from 13 per cent in the first decade to over 20 per cent in 1990–2000. Most other countries underwent relatively small changes.

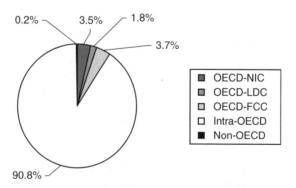

Figure 7.5 Distribution of newly established international R&D partnerships by economic region, 1971–2000

Source: MERIT-CATI database.

Additional material also indicates that there has been a more or less gradual decline in the share of joint ventures in intra-OECD R&D partnerships, from 80 per cent in 1971 to nearly 15 per cent in 2000. The share of joint ventures in the total of OECD-NIC, OECD-LDC and OECD-FCC partnerships started at 100 per cent in the 1970s and this also decreased to nearly 15 per cent in 2000. The share of joint ventures in non-OECD R&D partnerships has remained rather high throughout the period 1971–2000. The share of joint ventures was around 65 per cent during the 1970s, while it decreased to around 50 per cent during the 1990s.

These findings are consistent with previous literature. Freeman and Hagedoorn (1994) analysed the extent to which diverging international patterns in the distribution of technological capabilities are also found in inter-firm technology cooperation. They reported that over 95 per cent of research relationships have been established within the Triad, suggesting a straightforward relationship between the degree of technological sophistication of an industry and the degree of participation of firms from less-developed countries. Not surprisingly, the higher the R&D intensity of the industry, the lower the participation of companies from developing and emerging economies, as such firms are seldom in possession of knowledge-intensive resources that would be attractive to a Triad partner.

Freeman and Hagedoorn (1994) also concluded that in high-tech industries the share of the intra-Triad research relationships established during the 1980s remained high, whereas the growth of inter-firm research partnerships with partners from outside the Triad was primarily found in partnerships with companies from Asian countries, such as South Korea, Taiwan, Singapore and Hong Kong. Furthermore, one of their major conclusions was that inter-firm partnering had not led to a catching up of the LDC countries and most of the NIC countries, as it is much more part of a process of concentration of technological competencies within the developed economies (Freeman and Hagedoorn, 1994; Hagedoorn, 1996).

Additionally, Duysters and Hagedoorn (2000) found that technological complementarity between partners turns out to be the major driving force behind the growth of international strategic technology partnerships. The most advanced NIC countries have increasingly become aware of the importance of building up technological competencies in knowledge-intensive sectors; technological know-how from companies in the developed economies is crucial to establishing a prominent (technological) position in high-tech markets. NIC companies were gradually becoming interesting partners for companies from the developed economies due to their technology-intensive assets, particularly in electronics and related industries.

Therefore it is not surprising that compared with other international partnerships, Triad-NIC partnerships are increasingly found in high-tech sectors. The use of contractual agreements, dominating intra-Triad alliance formation since the 1980s, has also become widespread practice for Triad-NIC partnerships in the 1990s. This could indicate that these partnerships have reached a general level of sophistication that is coming close to that of many domestic and international R&D partnerships between major trading partners. If one considers these major changes, then it is clear that several NIC countries have developed from 'junior' partners in the early 1970s to important players in the 1990s (Duysters and Hagedoorn, 2000).

Patterns in international R&D partnerships of companies from FCC countries

As mentioned in the introduction, it is interesting to take a closer look at the FCC countries. According to Sadowski and Hagedoorn (1997), inter-firm partnering with firms from capitalist countries were the exception for companies from FCC countries prior to the opening of their economies to the West. According to our data, the number of R&D partnerships with FCC countries was very low during most of the 1970s and 1980s (see Figure 7.6). Their total number increased rapidly during the late 1980s and early 1990s, although it remained a 'bumpy ride'. The establishment of R&D partnerships reached a peak in 1989, but the subsequent two years showed a sharp decrease. One year later, the establishment of inter-firm partnerships began to increase again, and in 1993 there was a second peak, albeit much lower than in 1989. From then onwards the amount of international R&D partnerships decreased again, with a third but relatively small peak in 1999.

Throughout this period, joint ventures played a dominant role in the formation of R&D partnerships with companies from FCC countries,

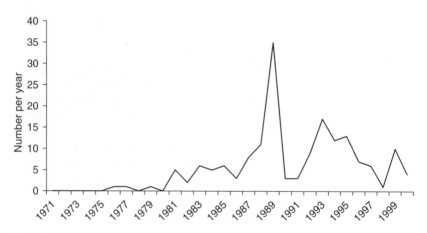

Figure 7.6 Number of newly established international R&D partnerships with companies from FCC countries, 1971–2000

Source: MERIT-CATI database.

although contractual partnerships gradually gained importance. From the 87 R&D partnerships formed between 1971 and 1990, 86.2 per cent were joint ventures. From the 82 partnerships that were established between 1991 and 2000, 53.7 per cent were joint ventures. Since the late 1980s, the importance of contractual R&D partnerships increased, and although the number is still very small, it is interesting to note that in the year 2000 all newly established R&D partnerships were contractual arrangements.

During the period 1971–2000 there was a strong dominance of high-tech sectors, taking 59.9 per cent of the international R&D partnerships with companies from FCC countries, followed by medium-tech sectors taking 38.4 per cent. Low-tech industries do not play a significant role. It is interesting to note that partnerships made in the information technology sector have dominated international R&D partnering with companies from FCC countries throughout this period. Sadowski and Hagedoorn (1997) indicated that most of these partnerships were state-regulated partnerships created to improve the telecommunications infrastructure in FCC countries. Other important sectors were chemicals, and aerospace and defence industries, followed by automotive, heavy electrical equipment and pharmaceuticals (see Figure 7.7).

Since the late 1980s, companies from Russia and China have played a dominant role in international R&D partnering with FCC countries (see Figure 7.8). More than 40 per cent of the R&D partnerships were established with companies from China and around 35 per cent with companies from the Russian Federation (including the former Soviet Union). These countries are followed by Hungary with almost 10 per cent, and Bulgaria, (former)

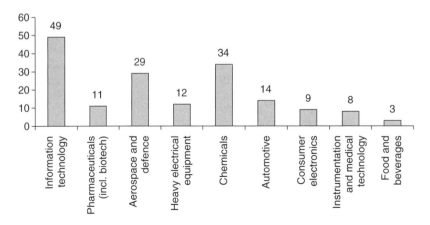

Figure 7.7 Number of newly established international R&D partnerships with companies from FCC countries per sector, 1971–2000

Source: MERIT-CATI database.

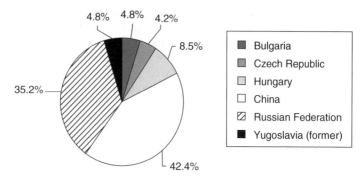

Figure 7.8 Distribution of newly established international R&D partnerships with companies from FCC countries, 1971–2000

Source: MERIT-CATI database.

Yugoslavia, and the Czech Republic (including former Czechoslovakia) with less than 5 per cent. The share of the other countries such as Poland, Croatia, Slovakia, Vietnam, Ukraine and Kazakhstan is very small.

Most of the R&D partnerships with Russian companies have been established in high-tech sectors, especially in information technology and chemicals. During the 1990s, the role of the high-tech sector in Russia became even stronger with the opening of the defense and aircraft sectors (Sadowski and Hagedoorn, 1997). Between 1992 and 1995, most of the R&D partnerships with Russian companies were formed in the aerospace and defense industries.

In terms of the form of R&D partnering with Russian companies, we notice a radical change. During the 1980s, 89 per cent of these international partnerships would be a joint venture, whilst during the 1990s more than 60 per cent of the newly established partnerships were of a contractual nature. Hagedoorn and Sedaitis (1998) indicated that partnerships with older Russian companies dating from the days of the centrally planned economy usually took the joint-venture form, whereas new firms were inclined to engage in contractual partnerships.

The creation of international R&D partnerships with Chinese companies has gained importance since the early 1980s (see also Zhang and Van Den Bulcke, 2000), and changes in Chinese regulations to encourage foreign investments (Van Den Bulcke and Zhang, 1998) probably played a role. During the 1980s, 86 per cent of all R&D partnerships in China were equity-based and most of them were established in the medium-tech sector. During the 1990s, around 67 per cent of the partnerships established with Chinese companies were still joint ventures. During this second wave of partnership formation, medium-tech and high-tech sectors gained importance. Chemicals and information technology have become the most dominant sectors in R&D partnering with Chinese companies. These findings with respect to the dominance of joint ventures and particular industries are supported by previous literature on the internationalization of the Chinese economy (see for instance, Van Den Bulcke and Zhang, 1998).

Conclusions

Despite an overall increase in international R&D partnerships, their importance has become relatively more concentrated within major economic regions instead of becoming overwhelmingly global (see also Duysters and Hagedoorn, 1996). Such partnerships are dominated by companies from the world's most developed economies, and companies from OECD countries participate in nearly 99 per cent of all the international R&D partnerships and more than 90 per cent of these are within the OECD. US companies in particular play a dominant role in international R&D partnering. More than 70 per cent of all partnerships have been established with at least one US company, whereas more than 65 per cent of these partnerships are made between at least one US company and the OECD. This picture parallels the current worldwide distribution of R&D resources and capabilities (Freeman and Hagedoorn, 1994). The dominance of the USA also reflects its leading role in R&D and production in major high-tech industries such as the information technology industry and pharmaceutical biotechnology (OECD, 1992).

The overall growth in international R&D partnerships during the past decades is largely due to the growth in the number of contractual agreements. The dominant position of joint ventures in inter-firm R&D agreements is now almost completely taken over by contractual agreements as about 85 per cent of the recently established international partnerships are of a contractual nature. In general, the demand for flexibility has increased in many industries, where inter-firm competition is affected by increased technological development, innovation races and the constant need to generate new products. Contractual international R&D partnerships enable companies to increase their strategic flexibility through short-term joint R&D projects with a variety of partners.

The role of technological development is also apparent in the sectoral background of international R&D partnering. Over the last three decades, there has been a gradual increase in the share of high-tech industries in international R&D partnering. During the late 1990s, nearly 70 per cent of the newly established international R&D partnerships could be found in the information technology and pharmaceutical industries. There is an over-representation of contractual partnerships in these sectors, which again stresses the role of flexibility in inter-firm R&D partnering.

Two FCC countries, the Russian Federation and China, have witnessed a significant increase in newly established international R&D partnerships since the late 1980s. There is a strong dominance of R&D partnerships in high-tech industries, such as aerospace and defense, information technology, and in a large medium-tech industry, the chemicals sector. Although equity joint ventures are still important modes of partnering with companies from the Russian Federation and China, contractual modes of research partnerships have become very relevant in these industries.

As already mentioned, international R&D partnering appears to be heavily concentrated within the developed countries (OECD). Sadowski and Hagedoorn (1997) indicate that many companies from the developing countries and the FCC countries are locked-out from R&D partnerships concentrated in information technology and biotechnology. The maintenance of an advanced civilian technological infrastructure in order to approach worldwide technology standards is a prerequisite for FCC firms that wish to participate in international R&D partnering. We expect that structural changes in FCC countries, such as the opening of the defense and aircraft sectors and all kinds of deregulations to encourage foreign investments (Van Den Bulcke and Zhang, 1998), will foster the internationalization of the FCC economies and their further participation in international partnering.

Appendix: the MERIT-CATI database

The Cooperative Agreements and Technology Indicators (CATI) database is a relational database which contains separate data files that can be linked to each other and provide both disaggregated and combined information from several files. So far information on thousands of technology-related inter-firm partnerships has been collected for the period 1960–2000. Systematic collection of such information started in 1987, although many sources from earlier years are consulted to establish a retrospective view. Various sources are consulted: newspaper and journal articles, books dealing with the subject, and in particular specialized journals which report on business events. Company annual reports, the Financial Times industrial companies yearbooks, and Dun & Bradstreet's 'Who Owns Whom' provide information about dissolved equity ventures and investments, as well as ventures that were not registered when surveying partnerships.

This method of information gathering, which one can refer to as 'literature-based alliance counting', has its drawbacks and limitations due to the lack of publicity for certain arrangements, and the low profile of certain groups of companies and fields of technology. Despite these shortcomings, which are largely unsolvable even in a situation of extensive and large-scale data collection, this database is able to produce a clear picture of the joint efforts of many companies and enables researchers to perform empirical research which goes beyond case studies.

The database contains information on each agreement and some information on companies participating in these agreements. The first entity is the inter-firm cooperative agreement. Cooperative agreements are defined as common interests between independent (industrial) partners which are not connected through (majority) ownership. In the CATI database only those inter-firm agreements are being collected that contain some arrangements for transferring technology or doing joint research. Joint research pacts and second-source data are clear-cut examples. Information is also collected on joint ventures in which new technology is received from at least one of the partners, or joint ventures having some R&D programme. Mere production or marketing joint ventures are excluded. In other words, this material is primarily related to R&D collaboration and technology cooperation, that is those agreements for which a combined innovative activity or an exchange of technology is at least part of the agreement.

References

Berg, S.V., Duncan, J. and Friedman, P. (1982) *Joint Venture Strategies and Corporate Innovation*. Cambridge, MA: Oelgeschlager.

Chesnais, F. (1988) 'Technical Cooperation Agreements between Firms', *STI Review*, 4: 51–120.

Ciborra, C. (1991) 'Alliances as Learning Experiments: Cooperation, Competition and Change in High-Tech Industries', in L.K. Mytelka (ed.), *Strategic Partnerships and the World Economy*. London: Pinter, pp. 51–77.

Contractor, F.J. and Lorange, P. (1988) 'Why Should Firms Cooperate? The Strategy and Economics Basis for Cooperative Ventures', in F.J. Contractor and P. Lorange (eds), *Cooperative Strategies in International Business*. Lexington, MA: Lexington Books, pp. 3–30.

Das, S., Sen, P.K. and Sengupta, S. (1998) 'Impact of Strategic Alliances on Firm Valuation', *Academy of Management Journal*, 41: 27–41.

De Woot, P. (1990) *High Technology Europe: Strategic Issues for Global Competitiveness*, Oxford: Blackwell.

Dussauge, P. and Garette, B. (1999) *Cooperative Strategy: Competing Successfully through Strategic Alliances*. Chichester: Wiley.

Duysters, G. and Hagedoorn, J. (1996) 'Internationalization of Corporate Technology through Strategic Partnering: An Empirical Investigation', *Research Policy*, 25: 1–12.

Duysters, G. and Hagedoorn, J. (2000) 'International Technology Collaboration: Implications for NIEs', in L. Kim, and R.R. Nelson (eds), *Technology, Learning & Innovation: Experiences of Newly Industrializing Economies*. Cambridge: Cambridge University Press, pp. 193–215.

Eisenhardt, K.M. and Schoonhoven, C.B. (1996) 'Resource-based View of Strategic Alliance Formation: Strategic and Social Effects in Entrepreneurial Firms', *Organizational Science*, 7: 136–50.

Freeman, C. and Hagedoorn, J. (1994) 'Catching Up or Falling Behind: Patterns in International Interfirm Technology Partnering', *World Development*, 22: 771–80.

Gomes-Casseres, B. (1996) *The Alliance Revolution: The New Shape of Business Rivalry*. Cambridge, MA: Harvard University Press.

Hagedoorn, J. (1993) 'Understanding the Rationale of Strategic Technology Partnering: Inter-Organizational Modes of Cooperation and Sectoral Differences', *Strategic Management Journal*, 14: 371–85.

Hagedoorn, J. (1996) 'Trends and Patterns in Strategic Technology Partnering since the early Seventies', *Review of Industrial Organization*, 11: 601–16.

Hagedoorn, J. (2002) 'Inter-firm R&D Partnerships: An Overview of Major Trends and Patterns Since 1960', *Research Policy*, 31(4): 477–92.

Hagedoorn, J., Link, A.L. and Vonortas, N. (2000) 'Research Partnerships', *Research Policy*, 29: 567–86.

Hagedoorn, J., and Schakenraad, J. (1993) 'A Comparison of Private and Subsidized Inter-Firm Linkages in the European IT industry', *Journal of Common Market Studies*, 31: 373–90.

Hagedoorn, J. and Sedaitis, J.B. (1998) 'Partnerships in Transition Economies: International Strategic Technology Alliances in Russia', *Research Policy*, 27: 177–85.

Haklisch, C.S. (1989) *Technical Alliances in the Semiconductor Industry: Effects on Corporate Strategy and R&D*, in Background Papers for Conference on Changing Global Patterns of Industrial Research and Development, Stockholm, 20–22 June .

Harrigan, K.R. (1988) 'Joint Ventures and Competitive Strategy', *Strategic Management Journal*, 9: 141–58.

Harrigan, K.R. and Newman, W.H. (1990) 'Bases of Interorganization Co-operation: Propensity, Power, Persistence', *Journal of Management Studies*, 27: 417–34.

Hergert, M., and Morris, D. (1988) 'Trends in International Collaborative Agreements', in F.J. Contractor and P. Lorange (eds), *Cooperative Strategies in International Business*. Lexington, MA: Lexington Books.

Hladik, K.J. (1985) *International Joint Ventures*. Lexington, MA: Lexington Books.

Kang, N. and Johansson, S. (2000) 'Cross-border Mergers and Acquisitions: Their Role in Industrial Globalisation', *STI Working Paper*. Paris: OECD.

Kogut, B. (1988) 'Joint Ventures: Theoretical and Empirical Perspectives', *Strategic Management Journal*, 9: 319–32.

Link, A.N. and Bauer, L.L. (1989) *Cooperative Research in US Manufacturing: Assessing Policy Initiatives and Corporate Strategies*. Lexington, MA: Lexington Books.

Lorenzoni, G., and Lipparini, A. (1999) 'The leveraging of Interfirm Relationships as a Distinctive Organizational Capability: a Longitudinal Study', *Strategic Management Journal*, 20: 317–38.

Mariti, P. and Smiley, R.H. (1983) 'Co-operative Agreements and the Organization of Industry', *Journal of Industrial Economics*, 31: 3437–51.

Mowery, D.C. (ed.) (1988) *International Collaborative Ventures in US Manufacturing*. Cambridge, MA: Ballinger.

Mowery, D.C., Oxley, J.E. and Silverman, B.S. (1998) 'Technological Overlap and Interfirm Cooperation: Implications for the Resource-based View of the Firm', *Research Policy*, 27: 507–23.

Mytelka, L.K. (1991) *Strategic Partnerships and the World Economy*. London: Pinter.

Narula, R. (1996) 'Forms of International Cooperation between Corporations' in C. Jepma and A. Rhoen (eds), *International Trade: A Business Perspective*. Harlow: Longman, pp. 98–122.

Narula, R. and Hagedoorn, J. (1999) 'Innovating through Strategic Alliances: Moving Towards International Partnerships and Contractual Agreements', *Technovation*, 19: 283–94.

Nooteboom, B. (1999) *Inter-firm Alliances: Analysis and Design*. London: Ballinger.

Organisation for Economic Co-operation and Development (OECD) (1986) *Technical Cooperation Agreements Between Firms: Some Initial Data and Analysis*. Paris: OECD.

OECD (1992) *Technology and the Economy*. Paris: OECD.

OECD (1997) *Revision of the High Technology Sector and Product Classification*. Paris: OECD.

Ohmae, K. (1990) *TRIAD Power*. New York: Free Press.

Osborn, R.N. and Baughn, C.C. (1990) 'Forms of Interorganizational Governance for Multinational Alliances', *Academy of Management Journal*, 33: 503–19.

Oster, S.M. (1992) *Modern Competitive Analysis*. New York: Oxford University Press.

Plasschaert, S. and Van Den Bulcke, D. (1992) 'Changing Dynamics of International Production: Globalisation and collaborative Schemes in Multinational Enterprises', in J. Van Den Broeck and D. Van Den Bulcke (eds), *Changing Economic Order*. Groningen: Wolters-Noordhoff Publishers, pp. 93–116.

Porter, M.E. (1987) 'From Competitive Advantage to Corporate Strategy', *Harvard Business Review*, May–June: 43–59.

Sadowski, B. and Hagedoorn, J. (1997) 'General Trends in International Technology Partnering: The Prospects for European Economies in Transition', in J.B. Sedaitis (ed.), *Commercializing High Technology: East and West*. Lanham (MD): Rowman & Littlefield, pp. 253–267.

Teece, D.J. (1986) 'Profiting from Technological Innovation: Implications for Integration, Collaboration, Licensing and Public Policy', *Research Policy*, 15: 285–305.

Van Den Bulcke, D. (1988) Deregulation of Foreign Direct Investment in Developing Countries, in D. Van Den Bulcke (ed.), *Recent Trends in International Development: Direct Investments, Services, Aid and Human Rights*, Institute for Administrative Studies (College for Developing Countries), State University of Antwerp, Antwerp.

Van Den Bulcke, D. and Zhang, H. (1998) 'Foreign Equity Joint Ventures in China: Interactions between Government Policies and Multinational Investment Strategies', in P.K.M. Tharakan and D. Van Den Bulcke (eds), *International Trade, Foreign Direct Investment and the Economic Environment*. London: Palgrave Macmillan.

Zhang, H. and Van Den Bulcke, D. (2000) 'Internationalisation of Ethnic Chinese-Owned Enterprises: A Network Approach', in H.W. Yeung (ed.), *The Globalisation of Chinese Business Firms*. London: Palgrave Macmillan.

8
Tigers, Pussycats and Flying Geese: The Faunal Characteristics of Economic Growth in South-East Asia

Ludo Cuyvers and Michel Dumont

Introduction

In this contribution we discuss the impressive economic growth record of the so-called high-performing Asian Economies (HPAE). If debates on the determinants of East Asian economic growth performance (for example free trade versus state intervention) are far from concluded (Cuyvers and Van Den Bulcke, 1989), there seems to be a bit more unanimity as to the role international technology transfer and spillovers played in the development process. The question then, of course, remains why the HPAE, in contrast with so many other developing countries, succeeded in benefiting from these spillovers. Institutional factors and policy instruments that enhance the absorptive capacity of firms (such as investment in education and human capital) may explain why international trade and intraregional growth dynamics contributed to economic growth to the extent that it did in the HPAE.

In an empirical section we use global vector error-correction estimation to establish the causal links between different macro-economic variables whilst, contrary to most previous studies, controlling for intraregional interdependence.

The 'flying geese' theory offers an explanation for the sequential economic development in East Asia. Industrial development and technological catch-up started with 'lead goose' Japan, which, as it reached higher levels of economic and technological development, transferred know-how and production plants to neighbouring countries. As the four Asian tigers or 'follower geese' (Hong Kong, South Korea, Singapore and Taiwan) took off to follow the 'mother goose', they initiated the same development process in second-tier countries (the pussycats) like Indonesia, Malaysia and Thailand (Kojima, 2000). Due to a lack of data we were unfortunately not able to assess the

FDI-led growth assumption. FDI is, in the 'flying geese' theory, considered to be a principal mechanism for economic development.

For the period 1960–99, we find evidence in favour of the export-led growth assumption in Hong Kong, Indonesia, South Korea and Malaysia. Only for Hong Kong there is a significant positive feedback of growth on exports.

Imports had a positive impact on growth in tiger countries Hong Kong and South Korea, but a significant negative effect on growth in pussycat countries Indonesia and Malaysia. Regional economic growth positively affects domestic growth, which supports the importance of intra-regional growth dynamics and shows the need to control for the mutual interdependence between countries in establishing causal links.

The economic performance of high-growth Asian countries

In Table 8.1, we compare the average growth of GDP per capita in the eight HPAE[1] in the 1960–2000 period to average growth for a number of OECD countries and China. In the 1960s Japan and the four tigers already occupied the first five positions in terms of average economic growth. Thailand apparently also had a relative high growth, whereas the two other pussycats Malaysia and Indonesia were still lagging behind. In the 1970s and the 1980s the eight HPAE all witnessed higher economic growth than the considered

Table 8.1 Average real GDP per capita (in constant prices) growth, 1960–2000

1960–69		1970–79		1980–89		1990–2000	
Singapore	10.3	Singapore	8.3	Taiwan	6.6	China	7.7
Japan	9.6	Taiwan	8.2	South-Korea	6.3	Singapore *	5.8
Hong Kong	7.7	South-Korea	7.0	Hong Kong	5.8	Taiwan **	5.5
Taiwan	6.7	Hong Kong	6.9	Thailand	5.2	South-Korea	5.2
South-Korea	6.3	Indonesia	5.6	China	5.1	Malaysia	4.5
Italy	5.1	Malaysia	5.1	Singapore	5.0	Thailand	4.3
Thailand	5.0	Thailand	4.7	Indonesia	4.3	Indonesia	3.0
France	4.7	Japan	4.0	Japan	3.3	Hong Kong	2.7
Belgium	4.4	Italy	3.2	Malaysia	3.0	Netherlands	2.4
Netherlands	3.7	Belgium	3.2	Italy	2.6	USA	2.2
USA	3.4	France	3.1	UK	2.2	Belgium	1.9
Malaysia	3.1	USA	2.7	Belgium	2.2	UK	1.8
UK	2.3	China	2.7	USA	2.1	Japan	1.4
China	1.8	Netherlands	2.4	France	2.0	Italy	1.3
Indonesia	1.1	UK	2.2	Netherlands	1.6	France	1.3

Notes: * Average over 1990–96; ** average over 1990–98.

Source: Own calculations from data in Heston, Summers and Aten (2002).

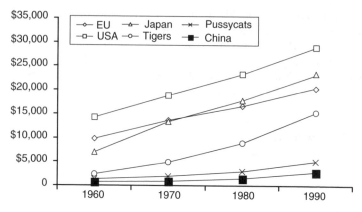

Figure 8.1   Average decade GDP per capita, 1960–2000
Source: Data in Heston, Summers and Aten (2002).

OECD countries. In the 1990s Japan slipped into a recession from which it has yet not fully recovered. China, on the other hand, witnessed substantial growth in the 1980s, and in the 1990s had the highest economic growth. Most Asian countries appear to have recovered rather smoothly from the 1997 Asian crisis, given the substantial growth rates in recent years, after negative growth in 1997 in most HPAE.

As shown in Figure 8.1, which plots the average GDP per capita for each decade in the period 1960–2000, the four 'tigers' have, in the wake of Japan, gained on most developed countries, especially on EU countries, to the extent that some of them reached the international frontier in a number of high-tech disciplines. Pussycats Indonesia, Malaysia and Thailand thus far do not seem to have caught up with the OECD countries and their arrearage with regard to Japan and the 'tigers' even appears to have increased, if anything.

Obviously, the performance of these Southeast Asian countries marks them off from most other developing countries, although it is still unclear to what extent their success can be explained by intraregional growth dynamics (for example the 'flying geese' hypothesis) and to what extent proper national characteristics can guarantee future economic growth and technological progress, should the lead goose or some follower geese make a forced landing.

Accumulation of capital and/or technological progress

From a theoretical perspective, diverging views have been put forward to explain the regionally clustered growth and swift development of the HPAE.[2]

In 1993 the World Bank published *The East Asian Miracle*, in which the performance of the fastest-growing East Asian countries was demonstrated and explained. Although the HPAE did have some fundamental characteristics in common at the onset of their development, the World Bank clearly states that it is questionable to talk about a single 'Asian model'. In spite of the title of the report, the World Bank does not consider the East Asian economic performance to be miraculous in the sense that it can be explained by a balanced policy focused on macro-economic stability and the promotion of investments in both physical and human capital. This view fits within the neo-classical growth theory which can explain how less-developed countries can, through the accumulation of capital, catch up with developed countries which face diminishing returns on production factors.

The problem with this explanation, however, is why apart from East Asian countries so few developing countries actually succeeded in converging to the level of industrialized countries. More recent endogenous growth models can explain how developed countries may, due to dynamic economies of scale, extend their lead over developing countries. This offers a possible explanation for the growing arrearage of most developing countries but cannot explain the catch-up of Japan and the four tigers unless one considers important technology spillovers from industrialized countries. But why then, did only East Asian countries benefit from such spillovers?

The World Bank concedes that the performance of HPAE cannot entirely be ascribed to a well-considered 'free market–free trade' policy, and that most of these countries established a relatively high degree of state intervention, which, certainly where Northeast Asia is concerned, resulted in higher and more balanced growth than would have been possible without intervention (World Bank, 1993: 5–6). Certain sectors were goal-directedly subsidized, exports were promoted and domestic markets of import substitutes were protected although the necessary foreign capital goods were imported without high tariffs. Governments highly invested in applied research and the transfer of knowledge between the public and the private sector was activated.

Wade (1994) reflects on the possibility that the intraregional relocation of firms from Japan and the four tigers induced high growth afterwards in Southeast Asia.[3] The acclaimed liberal policy towards FDI has led to considerable investments from East Asian firms in Southeast Asia, which resulted in a high dependence on foreign export-oriented TNCs. Two-thirds and more of Southeast Asian production is exported and is therefore not destined to the domestic market, which is more the case in East Asia.[4] Wade claims that Southeast Asian governments did too little to reinforce the link between foreign and domestic firms, and as a consequence technology spillovers of FDI are limited and foreign firms operate within 'enclaves' (Wade, 1994: 65–9).

The assumption that exports and investments boosted economic growth (for example due to economies of scale, stimulation of technological change and efficiency spillovers from export sectors to non-exporting sectors: Yamada, 1998) cannot be proven in an unambiguous way because of the well-known problem of 'reverse causation'. High economic growth may equally well have stimulated exports as the other way round. Rodrik (1994) and Young (1994) pointed to the high investment rates with respect to physical and human capital in the HPAE. These investments may have boosted economic growth and productivity, increasing the ability of a country to compete on the world market and thus to increase its exports. Khalafalla and Webb (2001) argued that economic growth involves structural changes, which will change the trade pattern, shifting comparative advantage and terms of trade, resulting in a different mix of exports and imports. Krishna, Ozyildirim and Swanson (2003) mention a number of studies that suggest that it is not so much export-oriented firms that become more productive, but rather productive firms that export.

Openness to trade is apparently not a characteristic that discriminated well between HPAE and other developing countries at the onset of the East Asian high-growth era (Sarel, 1996: 16–20). Rodrik (1994) examined for which parameters East Asian countries were significantly different from other developing countries at the onset of their growth, and found evidence of the importance of school enrolment and relative equal income and land distribution. The World Bank (1993) reveals that the HPAE in 1965 scored higher on primary and secondary education levels and participation than other developing countries. Kim and Lau (1994) and Young (1994) concluded that the hypothesis that no technological progress occurred in East Asia cannot be rejected. Technological progress is generally measured through 'total factor productivity' (TFP), that is the part of economic growth that cannot be explained by factor accumulation.

The World Bank (1993) estimated that the accumulation of labour and capital explains two-thirds of economic growth of the HPAE. So accumulation explains, according to the World Bank, the considerable difference between HPAE performance and the economic growth record of Latin America and Sub-Saharan Africa, which due to a lack of investment missed out on growth opportunities (World Bank, 1993: 53). However, accumulation does not suffice to explain the catch-up of Japan and the four tigers, or, to quote Dowling and Summers (1993: 171): 'While capital accumulation was critical to rapid growth it was only a necessary condition which had to be augmented by technological transfer.'

In a comprehensive survey on TFP estimations in Asian countries Dowling and Summers (1998) explain the diverging estimates by the high sensitivity to the period that is considered, the assumed capital share in income, whether embodied technological progress is considered or not, and also by the level of economic growth itself. The World Bank (1993) distinguishes between technological change, which relates to movements at the technological frontier, and technological efficiency, which relates to the degree to which a country converges towards that frontier. Technological efficiency, as a proxy of catch-up, is obviously the more relevant measure for developing countries. The World Bank's estimates of technological efficiency discriminate between groups of HPAE countries. Productivity-driven HPAE are characterized by high TFP contributions and positive technological efficiency estimates in Hong Kong, Japan, Taiwan and Thailand. The investment-driven HPAE have low TFP and negative efficiency estimates and thus seem to lag behind with regard to the technological frontier. Singapore, Malaysia, Indonesia and to a lesser extent also South Korea belong to this group (World Bank, 1993: 57–8).

Striking in these results is the presence of two tigers in the second group and of 'second-tier' Thailand in the first group. Especially Singapore catches the eye with the by far most negative estimate of efficiency of all the HPAE. The estimates for Singapore suggest that economic growth can almost entirely be attributed to accumulation of production factors. The estimates from the World Bank, however, show that the situation of Singapore is not similar to that of other HPAE and that at least for a number of them there are undeniable indications of technological 'catch-up'. Moreover, even the TFP-based conclusion of the poor technological performance of Singapore is not unquestioned (see for example Felipe, 2000). Although the view that economic growth in the Asian tiger countries can predominantly be explained by factor accumulation has been reiterated recently by Bar-Shira *et al.* (2003), the discussion on TFP in HPAE has clearly not resulted in unequivocal conclusions. Dowling and Summers (1998) rightly point out that even a small TFP contributes more to growth in the fast-growing HPAE than in the considerably more slow- growing industrialized countries.

In our view it seems only fair to say that statistical 'reality' is still too blurred to resign in the tyranny of (some) numbers as Young (1995), and others with him, urges us to do.

The international transfer of technological knowledge and know-how to East Asia

There is ample evidence that the transfer of technological knowledge and know-how from the USA and Europe contributed to the growth performance of the HPAE and the technological catch-up of a number of them (see for example Mowery and Oxley, 1997, and Igel, 1997). Looking at the different channels of technology transfer that have been important to (South-) East Asian countries, the considerable differences between the HPAE stands out.

The channels through which technology is transferred seem less important than the factors that determine the absorption and diffusion capacity. This capacity which is primordial for the efficiency of technology transfer can be reinforced through investment in own R&D, education and formation and policies that facilitate the absorption and diffusion between firms, and

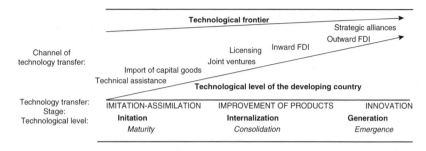

Figure 8.2   The time dimension of technology transfer and technological catch-up
Sources: Based on Ramanathan (1997) and Kim and Dahlman (1992).

between firms and research institutions (see for example Pavitt, 1985; Igel, 1997; Mowery and Oxley, 1997).

Kim and Dahlman (1992) and Ramanathan (1997) argue that according to the development stage, some transfer mechanisms may be more appropriate than others, and in Figure 8.2 we show the three development stages considered by these authors. At the first stage (initiation), countries primarily use mature technologies to initiate the process of industrialization. The most important mechanisms at this stage are the purchase of plants and equipment, technical information and expert services. Imitation and assimilation can possibly already be backed up by own R&D efforts. At the next stage (internalization), mechanisms like licensing and joint ventures become more important, as firms which transfer their technology will want to control its use. Transnationals will also be more easily tempted to invest in these countries as the technological level has increased and (labour) costs will still be relatively low. Own R&D efforts will focus on the development of new products or the improvement of existing products.

Finally, during the last stage (generation), the firm (country) will have reached the technological frontier in a specific technological domain. Now, foreign firms will be reluctant to transfer their technology to firms (countries) that have reached this stage, as these will now be (potential) competitors. Strategic alliances will become important mechanisms at this stage, and investing abroad will allow firms that have reached this stage to monitor technological progress in foreign markets.

In Table 8.2 we summarize, on the basis of the literature, the importance that the different channels of international technology transfer have played in the eight HPAE. Blanks in the table imply that we did not find any explicit information on the (non-) importance of the given transfer mechanism for that country.

As is apparent from Figure 8.3, which shows average openness measured as exports plus imports relative to GDP, the tiger countries were the most open

Table 8.2 Importance of channels of international technology transfer and spillovers to HPAE

	Japan	South Korea	Taiwan	Hong Kong	Singapore	Thailand	Indonesia	Malaysia
Inward FDI	Limited	Important	Relatively limited	Important	Very important	Relatively limited	Relatively limited	Important
Import substitution	1950–60s	1950–60s	1950–60s	No	1959–65	1960–70s		Limited
Imports of capital goods	Important (import often limited to 1 specimen)	Important		Very important	Very important	Limited		Limited
Reverse engineering/imitation	Important	Important	Important					
Export promotion		Important		From 1967		From mid-1980s		Important from 1970
Alliances, M&A	Important	Important (semi conductors)						
Licensing	Important in the beginning	Important (chemical industry, electrical and non-electrical machinery)				Important		
Education/formation abroad	Very important	Important						
Outward FDI	Important	Important						

Sources: Lynn (1985), Ozawa (1985), Westphal, Kim and Dahlman (1985), World Bank (1993), Kochhar *et al.* (1996), Bae (1997), Kim (1997), Mowery and Oxley (1997) and Ramanathan (1997).

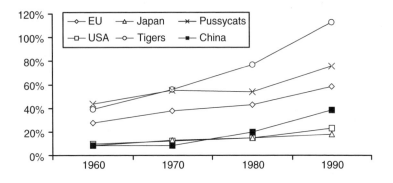

Figure 8.3   Average decade openness (exports + imports /real GDP), 1960–2000
Source: Data in Heston, Summers and Aten (2002).

countries although this is explained by the extreme values for Hong Kong and Singapore, as Taiwan and South-Korea had levels of openness closer to the low level of Japan and the USA. The pussycat countries also had a relative high degree of openness.

At the start of their industrialization, the imports of capital goods have been of primordial importance to most HPAE. In the 'flying geese' model of Kojima (2000), the basic pattern of economic development starts with industrial products being imported from more developed countries. These imports later on decrease in favour of domestic production, and in the last stage domestic producers start exporting the type of goods that used to be imported (Kojima, 2000: 377–9).

Economies like Hong Kong and Singapore pursued a strongly marked free trade policy. Other countries like Japan and South Korea were much more restrictive with regard to imports and heavily relied on import-substituting industrialization. The description, by Ozawa (1985), of the well-considered policy of Japan's MITI with regard to the imports of capital goods is very illustrative: usually only one type of a new capital good was imported while for the rest capital goods had to be purchased from Japanese producers, working under license of a foreign company. To ease the duplication and imitation of foreign capital goods, important efforts were made of own adaptive R&D.

Ozawa remarks that this policy, which in the long term can be regarded as very successful, was not appropriate according to the theory of comparative advantage as a country like Japan, that was initially highly endowed with labour but not with capital or raw materials, started to concentrate on capital-intensive sectors (Ozawa, 1985: 230–1). In South Korea as well, the imports of capital goods were accompanied by import-substitution and the protection of the domestic market, the latter policy especially in favour of capital-good users (Kim and Dahlman, 1992: 443).

Caves (1974) considered three potential benefits of FDI: improvement of allocative efficiency; increase in technical efficiency; and the technology transfer from the home country to the host country. However, FDI may exclusively relate to production for foreign or domestic demand without any transfer or technological spillovers in the host country, which, as mentioned before, Wade (1994) suggests may be the case in a number of pussycat countries.

Asian countries participate more in alliances with the USA, Europe or Japan than with other developing Asian countries. The emergence of a Japan-centred bloc of alliances, excluding US or European firms, does not seem to be confirmed by the data (Mowery and Oxley 1997: 147–8). The Triad countries account for more than 80 per cent of international technology-based alliances, although some smaller Asian countries are increasingly getting involved (European Commission, 1997: 617). As pointed out by Ramanathan (1997), joint research activities and strategic alliances are only an option to those firms in countries that have reached an advanced technological level and are less obvious for firms and countries that are still in an early stage of the development process.

Global vector autoregression model of Asian growth performance

The most popular hypothesis about exports having led economic growth in the HPAE is commonly tested in a vector autoregression (VAR) framework. Causal links can then be established with exogeneity tests, although the causal interpretation is not straightforward and conclusions seem to be highly sensitive to the type of causality model or technique that is used (see for example Jacobs *et al.*, 1979; Roberts and Nord, 1985; Gordon and Sakyi-Bekoe, 1993). More recent studies have improved over earlier studies in controlling for non-stationary time series that are involved (see Bahmani-Oskooee and Alse, 1993; Ahmad and Harnhirun, 1996; Dutt and Ghosh, 1996; Khalafalla and Webb, 2001; and Krishna, Ozyildirim and Swanson, 2003). However, even when the appropriate cointegration techniques are applied there are no conclusive results, for the same HPAE, as to the direction of the causality. Some studies find support for the export-led growth hypothesis, other studies for the growth-led exports assumption and some find evidence of mutual causality. Dutt and Ghosh (1996) blame the diverging conclusions on different time periods, different sample intervals and the use of incomplete error-correction specifications.

We try to establish the causal linkages between economic growth and potential determinants like imports and exports. Contrary to most previous studies we consider the interdependence between the HPAEs to test for intraregional growth dynamics. Moreno and Trehan (1997) find evidence that a country's long-term growth depends on the development in neighbouring countries and that being close to a large market contributes significantly to growth. As a consequence, high-growing countries tend to cluster geographically. This seems to link on to the 'flying geese' view of economic development in East Asia, with Japan as the large market (see for example Kojima, 2000).

Krishna, Ozyildirim and Swanson (2003) found that for nine out of 25 considered countries all VAR models were *confused*. Malaysia, Singapore and South Korea were among the nine countries for which the models could not accurately predict turning points of GDP growth, that is the criterion of *confusion*. The authors reason that for these countries models may be miss-specified due to missing variables and suggest to consider a trade-weighted partner GDP index as well as common shocks (for example US GDP).

We apply a global error-correction model as proposed by Pesaran *et al.* (2001), that considers interactions between countries and regions through three channels. First, exogenous counterparts of the endogenous (country) variables are computed. For instance, for each country not only own-exports are considered, but also the exports of the other countries. The latter variables can be constructed as trade-weighted sums of all other countries' exports. Common global exogenous variables (US GDP and oil prices) are also considered in each country-specific model.

For each country a general vector autoregressive (VAR) specification is given as (Pesaran *et al.*, 2001: 10):

$$x_{i,t} = \alpha_{i0} + \alpha_{i1} t + \Phi_i x_{i,t-1} + \Lambda_{i0} x_{i,t}^* + \Lambda_{i1} x_{i,t-1}^* + \Psi_{i0} d_t + \Psi_{i1} d_{t-1} + \varepsilon_{it} \quad (8.1)$$

where $t = 1, 2, \ldots T$ (time periods)   and $i = 0, 1, \ldots N$ (countries); $x_{i,t}$ is a vector of country-specific variables, t allows for a deterministic trend, $x_{i,t}^*$ is a vector of a weighted sum of foreign variables, specific to country i, and d_t is a vector of variables common to all considered countries, which is assumed to be exogenous to the global economy.

The following assumptions are implied for the residuals:

$$\varepsilon_{it} \sim iid\ (0, \Sigma_{ii})$$
$$E(\varepsilon_{it} \varepsilon_{it}') = \Sigma_{ij} \quad \text{for } t = t'$$
$$= 0 \quad \text{for } t \neq t' \quad (8.2)$$

so that contemporaneous shocks between countries can be correlated.

Each kth variable of the vector $x_{i,t}^*$ is constructed as a weighted sum using country-specific weights:

$$x_{i,t}^{*K} = \sum_{j=0}^{N} w_{ij}^K x_{j,t}^K \quad (8.3)$$

The global VAR model allows for interdependence between countries through three mechanisms (Pesaran *et al.*, 2001: 6):

- Direct dependence of $x_{i,t}$ on $x^*_{i,t}$ and $x^*_{i,t-1}$
- Dependence on the common global exogenous variables d_t and d_{t-1}
- Contemporaneous dependence of shocks in country i on shocks in country j (see equation 8.3).

To account for the non-stationarity of most variables and to test for cointegration, a vector error-correcting specification is used (Pesaran *et al.*, 2001: 28):

$$\Delta x_{i,t} = \alpha_{i0} + \alpha_{i1} t - (I_{k_i} - \Phi_i) x_{i,t-1} + (\Lambda_{i0} + \Lambda_{i1}) x^*_{i,t-1}$$
$$+ (\Psi_{i0} + \Psi_{i1}) d_{t-1} + \Lambda_{i0} + \Lambda x^*_{i,t} + \Psi_{i0} \Delta d_t + \varepsilon_{it} \tag{8.4}$$

with I_{k_i} as an identity matrix of order k_i (i.e. the number of variables in vector $x_{i,t}$).

Imposing some restrictions, the reduced form specification of equation (8.4) can be given as (Pesaran *et al.*, 2001: 28):

$$\Delta x_{i,t} = \gamma_{i0} - \Pi_i v_{i,t-1} + \Lambda_{i0} \Delta^*_{i,t} + \Psi_{i0} \Delta d_t + \varepsilon_{it} \tag{8.5}$$

where $v_{i,t-1}$ contains the lagged values of $x_{i,t}$, $x^*_{i,t}$ and d_t.

The rank of Π_i determines the number of long-run relationships that exist between the considered variables. If all variables would be integrated of order one (that is the time series are stationary after differencing once) and would not appear to be cointegrated (that is there is no long-run stable co-movement pattern of the considered time series) then Π_i would equal zero and equation (8.5) would reduce to a first-difference specification. An error-correction specification distinguishes long-run equilibrium changes from short-run deviations from the long-run equilibrium.

The advantage of the model proposed by Pesaran *et al.* (2001) is that it estimates causal relationships, accounting for regional and global interdependency between countries which especially for the growth performance of geographically clustered countries may have been substantial.

Data on economic growth, imports and exports were retrieved from the World Bank 2001 World Development Indicators CD-ROM.[5] We were able to costruct time series for the period 1960–99 for Hong Kong, Indonesia, Japan, South Korea, Malaysia and Thailand. For Singapore and Taiwan there was not sufficient information to apply the procedure.

Exogenous foreign variables were constructed using bilateral trade shares (data from the World Trade Analyzer provided by Statistics Canada). For exports we multiplied the bilateral export shares of a given country with the bilateral export shares of the other country. As such the weights proxy for export competitiveness, the weights being higher the more two countries have similar trade patterns. For the other variables we used bilateral export shares.

Bahmani-Oskooee and Alse (1993) used quarterly data with the obvious advantage, over annual data, of larger time series. Quarterly data (for example on GDP) are, however, constructed from annual data, so no real information is added to the data set. Moreover, we follow Dutt and Ghosh (1996) in that the causal links in this type of analysis will probably take a couple of years rather than a couple of quarters to show up. The relationships that we are looking for indeed relate to long-term mechanisms such as different channels of technology transfer (imports and exports) enhancing economic growth, and economic growth increasing the technological level and consequently trade competitiveness, and less on some short-term links some of which are rather trivial.

As common global variables we considered US GDP, taken from the World Development Indicators, and crude oil prices for which data were kindly provided by James Williams (WTRG Economics).

All time series need to be integrated of the same order for a cointegration relationship to exist. Phillips-Perron unit root tests[6] show that all time series are integrated of order 1, except for GDP of Thailand for which the hypothesis of a unit root in the first difference could not be rejected, not even at the 10 per cent level. We therefore will not consider Thailand. For a small number of first-differenced variables the unit-root null hypothesis could only be rejected at the 10 per cent level, but we consider these series as approximately integrated of order 1. Cointegration rank tests identify the number of linearly independent long-term (cointegration) relationships. For cointegration to exist the rank of the coefficient matrix, of the variable levels in an error-correction specification, cannot have full rank (Greene, 2000: 794). Trace tests show that for all countries, except for Japan, the hypothesis that the rank equals zero (that is, there is no cointegration vector) is rejected although for Malaysia only at the 10 per cent level. Dutt and Ghosh (1996) also failed to find a cointegration relationship between exports and economic growth for Japan. Japan is not considered in the global model though, given its importance in the region. It is considered in the trade-weighted exogenous variables, which all appear to be integrated of order 1.

In Table 8.3 we report the short-term (ST) and long-term (LT) causal relationships that can be established with a global vector error-correction specification. With regard to the link between a given country's exports (EXPD) and economic growth (GDPD) we find evidence of a long-term mutual positive causal link for Hong Kong. For Indonesia, South Korea and Malaysia results support the export-led growth assumption. For Malaysia economic growth seems to have had a negative LT impact on exports. It should be pointed out that evidence of cointegration for Malaysia was only found at the 10 per cent significance level. Imports (IMPD) have had only a ST positive

Table 8.3 Causal relationships in the global vector error-correction model

Hong Kong	Causality	Sign (5
ST/LT	IMPF → EXPD	−
ST/LT	IMPF → IMPD	−
ST	GDPF → IMPD	+
ST	IMPD → GDPD	+
ST/LT	IMPF → GDPD	−
LT	IMPD → EXPD	−
LT	GDPD ← → EXPD	+
LT	EXPD → IMPD	+
LT	GDPF → GDPD	+
Indonesia		
ST	GDPD ← → EXPD	+
ST	GDPD → IMPD	+
ST	IMPF → IMPD	+
ST/LT	IMPD → GDPD	−
ST/LT	EXPF → GDPD	−
ST/LT	GDPF → GDPD	+
LT	IMPF → EXPD	+
LT	EXPD → GDPD	+
South Korea		
ST/LT	IMPD → EXPD	−
ST	EXPD → IMPD	+
ST	GDPD → IMPD	−
ST/LT	EXPF → IMPD	−
ST	GDPF → IMPD	+
ST	EXPD → GDPD	+
ST	IMPD → GDPD	+
ST/LT	EXPF → GDPD	−
Malaysia		
ST/LT	GDPD → EXPD	−
ST/LT	GDPF → EXPD	+
ST/LT	GDPD → IMPD	−
ST	IMPF → IMPD	+
ST/LT	EXPD → GDPD	+
ST	IMPD → GDPD	−
LT	IMPD → EXPD	+
LT	GDPF → GDPD	+

Note: GDPD: domestic GDP per capita; GDPF: weighted GDP of trade partners; IMPD/ EXPD: imports (exports) of the given country; IMPF/ EXPF: weighted sum of trade partners' imports (exports). Control variables US GDP and crude oil prices have significant coefficients in a number of equations but are not reported here. The results are given for the model with a lag of three years, which proved to be optimal.

impact on growth for Hong Kong and South Korea, and they had a negative impact for Indonesia (ST and LT) and Malaysia (ST). Economic growth seems to have reduced the need for imports, as assumed by the sequential pattern in Kojima (2000), given the negative sign in South Korea and Malaysia, but to have increased imports in the short term for Indonesia.

Turning to intraregional interdependence, reflected primarily in the impact of trade-weighted variables, economic growth in the region (GDPF) appears to have a long-term positive impact on domestic economic growth (GDPD) of Hong Kong, Indonesia and Malaysia, supporting the 'flying geese' assumption. Trade-weighted exports of partner countries (EXPF), which can be seen as a proxy for intraregional export competition, has had a negative effect on domestic economic growth, both in the short term and the long term, for Indonesia and South Korea. Trade-weighted imports of nearby countries (IMPF), which can be considered as a measure of regional openness, has a positive impact on domestic growth in Indonesia but a surprisingly negative impact on both exports and economic growth in Hong Kong.

Conclusions

Though macro-economic stability and investments in physical and human capital may explain a large part of economic growth in East Asian High Performing Economies (HPAE), the World Bank concedes that some degree of state intervention contributed to the high and balanced growth record, especially in comparison with other newly industrialized countries and developing countries.

Technology transfer and spillovers from the USA and Europe substantially contributed to the HPAE growth performance. The channels that are most appropriate to transfer knowledge and know-how depend on the stage of technological development. Throughout the development process, the HPAE have shown that investments in own R&D activities and human-capital formation, that is investments in the absorptive capacity, are probably more important to economic growth than is the nature of the channels through which knowledge is transferred or spills over.

The results of a global vector error-correction model, which takes intraregional dependence into account, suggests that exports have led economic growth in Hong Kong, Indonesia, South Korea and Malaysia with only a significant positive feedback of growth on exports for Hong Kong.

Imports had a positive impact on growth in tiger countries Hong Kong and South Korea, but a significant negative effect on growth in pussycat countries Indonesia and Malaysia. The latter finding might be an indication of the 'export enclaves' in pussycat countries (Wade, 1994); that is, foreign-owned plants produce more for exports than they do for the domestic market. The imports needed for the production may, due to the few links between the foreign-owned subsidiaries and domestic firms and their sole use for export goods, contribute little to domestic technological development and economic growth.

Regional economic growth has a significant long-term effect on domestic growth. This goes to show that it is important to consider the impact of neighbouring countries. Previous research has also found that high-growing economies tend to cluster geographically and that the vicinity of a high-growing large market can foster economic growth. Omitting intraregional determinants may bias estimations of causal relationships. The results support the 'flying geese' theory of economic development, which considers that the industrialization process was transmitted from Japan to the tiger countries and in a later stage to the pussycat countries. Unfortunately, we were, due to a lack of sufficient data, not able to test the importance of FDI in this transmission process.

In spite of some significant links that we find, all variables reflecting international trade and intraregional interdependence combined explain less than one-half of variance in economic growth. Possible domestic variables like investment in human capital and education were beyond the scope of this study. As previous work has showed, these are probably highly important to economic growth, as they determine the ability to absorb, diffuse and use the knowledge and technology that is transferred or that spills over from the most developed countries. It may very well be that institutional factors and policy instruments that focused on the capacity to absorb technology, whichever channel it was transferred through, made international trade and intraregional growth dynamics contribute to economic growth to the extent that it did in the high-performing Asian economies.

Notes

1   The World Bank (1993) considers eight high-performing Asian economies (HPAE): Japan, Hong Kong, South Korea, Singapore, Taiwan, Indonesia, Malaysia and Thailand. In this category a distinction is made between forerunner Japan, the four Asian 'Tigers' (South Korea, Taiwan, Hong Kong and Singapore) and the 'second-tier' countries Indonesia, Malaysia and Thailand (henceforth the Asian pussy cats). The World Bank report does not deal with China although its high growth performance is acknowledged.

2   Landes (1999) even suggests that the success of the HPAE in micro-assembly can to some extent be ascribed to the manual dexterity that comes from eating with chopsticks.

3   Puga en Venables (1999) describe a model that stresses agglomeration of economic development and the role of trade policy. They find that both import-substitution and free trade offers low-wage countries the possibility to boost specific sectors. Free trade is in their model found to generate a larger welfare effect than import-substitution. The model focuses on the development of HPAE to show how industrialization gradually evolved from Japan to Taiwan and South Korea first and later on to 'second-tier' countries like Malaysia. This supports the 'flying geese' theory of the sequential development of Asian economies (see e.g. Kojima, 2000).

4 In Malaysia foreign firms control 90 per cent of exports in machinery, electrical appliances and consumer electronics (Wade, 1994: 66).
5 We also gathered data on FDI but there was insufficient information to construct time series that were long enough for the estimation procedure. As a consequence, we are not able to test the FDI-led growth assumption of the 'flying geese' model proposed by Kojima (2000).
6 Phillips and Perron (1988) proposed a unit-root test that generally proves to be more powerful than the more popular Augmented Dickey–Fuller test, especially if residuals are serially correlated. Estimation results are available from the authors.

References

Ahmad, J. and Harnhirun, S. (1996) 'Cointegration and Causality between Exports and Economic Growth: Evidence from the ASEAN Countries', *Canadian Journal of Economics*, 29: 413–16.

Bae, Z.-T. (1997) 'Role of R&D in Technology Transfer', in P. Gougeon and J. Gupta (eds), *Contemporary Issues in Technology Transfer*. Paris: Editions ESKA, pp. 47–59.

Bahmani-Oskooee, M. and Alse, J. (1993) 'Export Growth and Economic Growth: An Application of Cointegration and Error-Correction Modeling', *The Journal of Developing Areas*, 27: 535–42.

Bar-Shira, Z., Finkelshtain, I. and Simhon, A. (2003) 'Cross-Country Productivity Comparisons: The "Revealed Superiority" Approach', *Journal of Economic Growth*, 8(3): 301–23.

Caves, R.E. (1974) 'Multinational Firms, Competition and Productivity in Host-Country Markets', *Economica*, 41: 176–93.

Cuyvers, L. and Van Den Bulcke, D. (1989) 'Some Reflections on the Outward Oriented Development Strategy of the Far Eastern Developing Countries', in W. Adriaansen and G. Waardenburg (eds), *A Dual World Economy*. Groningen: Wolters Noordhoff.

Dowling, M. and Summers, P.M. (1998) 'Total Factor Productivity and Economic Growth Issues for Asia', *Economic Record*, 74(225): 170–85.

Dutt, S.D. and Ghosh, D. (1996) 'The Export-Growth-Economic Growth Nexus: A Causality Analysis', *Journal of Developing Areas*, 30: 167–82.

European Commission (1997) *Second European Report on S&T Indicators 1997*. Luxemburg: EU.

Felipe, J. (2000) 'On the Myth and Mystery of Singapore's "Zero TFP", *Asian Economic Journal*, 14(2): 187–209.

Fishlow, A. and Gwin, C. (1994) 'Overview: Lessons from the East Asian Experience', in A. Fishlow, (ed.), *Miracle or design? – Lessons From the East Asian Experience*, Overseas Development Council Policy essay no. 11, Washington DC, pp. 1–12.

Gordon, D.V. and Sakyi-Bekoe, K. (1993) 'Testing the Export-Growth Hypothesis: Some Parametric and Non-Parametric Results for Ghana', *Applied Economics*, 25: 553–63.

Greene, W.H. (2000) *Econometric Analysis*, Prentice-Hall: New Jersey.

Heston, A., Summers, R. and Aten, B. (2002) *Penn WorldTable Version 6.1*, Center for International Comparisons at the University of Pennsylvania (CICUP).

Igel, B. (1997) 'International Technology Transfer as a Success Factor in Economic Development', in P. Gougeon and J. Gupta (eds), *Contemporary Issues in Technology Transfer*. Paris: Editions ESKA, pp. 133–57.

IMF (1999, 2001) *World Economic Outlook*, Washington: IMF.

Jacobs, R.L., Leamer, E.E. and Ward, M.P. (1979) 'Difficulties with Testing for Causation', *Economic Inquiry*, 17: 401–13.

Khalafalla, K.Y. and Webb, A.J. (2001) 'Export-led Growth and Structural Change: Evidence from Malaysia', *Applied Economics*, 33: 1703–15.

Kim, J.-I and Lau, L.J. (1994) 'The Sources of Economic Growth in the East Asian Newly Industrialized Countries', *Journal of the Japanese and International Economies*, 8(3): 235–71.

Kim, J.-I and Lau, L.J. (1995) 'The Role of Human Capital in the Economic Growth of the East Asian Newly Industrialised Countries', *Asia-Pacific Economic Review*, 1(3): 3–22.

Kim, J.-I and Lau, L.J. (1996) 'The Sources of Asian Pacific Economic Growth', *Canadian Journal of Economics*, 29 (special issue): S 448–54.

Kim, L. (1997) *Imitation to Innovation: The Dynamics of Korea's Technological Learning.* Boston, MA: Harvard Business School Press.

Kim, L. and Dahlman, C.J. (1992) 'Technology Policy for Industrialization: An Integrative Framework and Korea's Experience', *Research Policy*, 21: 437–52.

Kochhar, K., Dicks-Mireaux, L. and Horvath, B. (1996) *Thailand: The Road to Sustained Growth*, IMF Occasional Paper no. 146, Washington.

Kojima, K. (2000) 'The "Flying Geese" Model of Asian Economic Development: Origin, Theoretical Extensions, and Regional Policy Implications', *Journal of Asian Economics*, 11: 375–401.

Krishna, K., Ozyildirim, A. and Swanson, N.R. (2003) 'Trade, Investment, and Growth: Nexus, Analysis, and Prognosis', *Journal of Development Economics* 70(2): 479–500.

Landes, D. (1999) *The Wealth and Poverty of Nations*. London: Abacus.

Lynn, L.H. (1985) 'Technology Transfer to Japan: What We Know, What We Need to Know, and What We Know That May Not be So', in N. Rosenberg and C. Frischtak (eds), *International Technology Transfer: Concepts, Measures and Comparisons.* New York: Praeger, 255–76.

Moreno, R. and Trehan, B. (1997) 'Location and the Growth of Nations', *Journal of Economic Growth*, 2: pp. 399–418.

Mowery, D.C. and Oxley, J. (1997) 'Inward Technology Transfer and Competitiveness: The Role of National Innovation Systems', in D. Archibugi and J.Michie (eds), *Technology, Globalisation and Economic Performance*. Cambridge: Cambridge University Press, pp.138–71.

Ozawa, T. (1985) 'Macroeconomic Factors Affecting Japan's Technology Inflows and Outflows: The Postwar Experience', in N. Rosenberg and C. Frischtak (eds), *International Technology Transfer: Concepts, Measures and Comparisons*. New York: Praeger, pp. 222–54.

Pavitt, K. (1985) 'Technology Transfer among the Industrially Advanced Countries: An Overview', in N. Rosenberg and C. Frischtak (eds), *International Technology Transfer: Concepts, Measures and Comparisons*. New York: Praeger, pp. 222–54.

Pesaran, M.H., Schuermann, T. and Weiner, S.M. (2001) *Modelling regional interdependencies using a global error-correcting macroeconometric model*, Working Paper, mimeo.

Phillips, P. and Perron, P. (1988) 'Testing for Unit Root in Time Series Regression', *Biometrika*, 75: 335–46.

Puga, D. and Venables, A.J. (1999) 'Agglomeration and Economic Development: Import Substitution vs. Trade Liberalisation', *Economic Journal*, 109 (April): 292–311.

Ramanathan, K. (1997) 'An Analytical Framework for Technology Transfer', in P. Gougeon and J. Gupta (eds), *Contemporary Issues in Technology Transfer*. Paris: Editions ESKA, pp. 21–46.

Roberts, D.L. and Nord, S. (1985), 'Causality Tests and Functional Form Sensitivity', *Applied Economics*, 17: 135–41.

Rodrik, D. (1994) 'King Kong Meets Godzilla: The World Bank and the East Asian Miracle', in A. Fishlow (ed.), *Miracle or Design? Lessons from the East Asian Experience*, Policy Essay no. 11. Washington DC: Overseas Development Council, pp. 13–53.

Sarel, M. (1996) *Growth in East Asia – What We Can and What We Cannot Infer*, Economic Issues no. 1, Washington: IMF.

Wade, R. (1994) 'Selective Industrial Policies in East Asia: Is The East Asian Miracle Right?', in A. Fishlow (ed.), *Miracle or Design? Lessons from the East Asian Experience*, Policy Essay no. 11. Washington DC: Overseas Development Council, pp. 55–79.

Westphal, L.E., Kim, L. and C.J. Dahlman (1985) 'Reflection on the Republic of Korea's Acquisition of Technological Capability', in N. Rosenberg and C. Frischtak (eds), *International Transfer of Technology: Concepts, Measures and Comparisons*. New York: Praeger, pp. 167–221.

World Bank (1993) *The East Asian Miracle: Economic Growth and Public Policy*, New York: Oxford University Press.

World Bank (1997) *World Development Report*, Washington: World Bank.

Yamada, H. (1998) 'A Note on the Causality between Export and Productivity: An Empirical Re-examination', *Economics Letters*, 61: 111–14.

Young, A. (1994) 'Lessons from the East Asian NICs: A Contrarian View', *European Economic Review*, 38: 964–73.

Young, A. (1995) 'The Tyranny of Numbers: Confronting the Statistical Realities of the East Asian Growth Experience', *Quarterly Journal of Economics*, 110(3): 641–80.

9
Effects of Foreign Direct Investment on the Agglomeration of China's Electronics Industry

Haiyan Zhang

Introduction

Together with Professor Daniel Van Den Bulcke, I have been studying the developments of the Chinese economy since the beginning of the 1990s, especially with regard to the issues of foreign direct investment. The fact that our first publication dealt with joint ventures (Van Den Bulcke and Zhang, 1994), is probably very appropriate because during all those years we formed some kind of academic joint venture. This chapter fits in to a larger research project about economic concentration and clusters in the Chinese manufacturing sector. It also follows two other joint publications about Chinese industrial sectors, that is, the pharmaceutical industry (Van Den Bulcke *et al.*, 1999) and the automotive sector (Van Den Bulcke and Zhang, 2000).

Although China was a late and slow starter in developing its electronics industry as compared to its neighbouring economies, such as Japan, Taiwan, Hong Kong, South Korea and Singapore, it has achieved dramatic growth over the last 20 years. In 2001, China's electronics industry employed 2 million people, realized US$107 billion of sales and created US$25 billion of added value, which represented respectively 4, 10 and 7 per cent of the total Chinese manufacturing industry. The growth of China's electronics industry has been quite spectacular as the gross industrial output value (GIOV) of the industry increased by more than 30 per cent per year during the period 1995–2001. As a result, the added value of the electronics industry reached 1.34 per cent of China's GDP in 2001, up from 0.78 per cent in 1995.

China's electronics industry has become strongly integrated into the global production network. The export and import values of the industry reached US$55.16 and US$83.93 billion in 2001, accounting for more than 10 per cent of worldwide electronics production and 25 per cent of China's exports and imports. More than half (in terms of output value) of China's electronics production was exported, of which about three-quarters was realized by foreign-invested enterprises (FIEs). The inward FDI stock in the Chinese electronics sector amounted to US$10 billion, which represented about half of the total capital of the industry. The dominance of foreign-invested enterprises in exports of electronic products has largely been due to the transfer of export-oriented factories to mainland China by Hong Kong and Taiwan firms in the past two decades, and the recent increasing investment by Western TNCs to produce in China for their home and even the global market.

The size of China's large domestic market has motivated market-seeking FDI from industrial countries, while its low labour costs have attracted efficiency-seeking FDI from Asian NIEs (Van Den Bulcke *et al.*, 2003). The annual survey of China's Ministry of Information Industry has shown that transnational corporations established 865 manufacturing subsidiaries in the Chinese electronics industry by the end of 2001, which accounted for about one-quarter of surveyed Chinese electronics manufacturing firms. These FIEs controlled one-third of the total assets of this industry, employed about a half million people and realized more that half of its total industrial output, sales and added value (Table 9.1). The importance of FIEs in the Chinese electronics industry continually increased between 1996 and 2001 not only with regard to its output, employment and exports, but also with regard to the upgrading of its industrial structure and performance. In 1996 40 per cent of the FIEs' output was related to consumer electronics, in which Hong Kong and Taiwan transferred a large part of their basic technological manufacturing activities to China.

Between 1996 and 2002 the proportion of consumer electronics in the total output of FIEs decreased, while the share of the branch of investment electronics increased from 30 to 45 per cent as a result of the entry and expansion of Western transnational companies in the Chinese telecommunication and IT industry. Also, a number of specific performance characteristics illustrate that FIEs are doing extremely well as compared to domestic enterprises: their productivity is higher as compared to the industrial average in terms of added value per employee and their plant size is larger than other firms in the industry. FIEs are also more capital-intensive as measured by the ratio of fixed capital per employee. Yet, the innovation ratio of FIEs (measured by the new products in the total added value) as well as the ratio of engineers to total employees is lower than the average of the industry, indicating that FIEs are less engaged in innovation activities in China, while the domestic firms have experienced a rapid restructuring process.

The performance of China's electronics industry as compared to other Chinese industries is not only reflected in its integration into the world production network and markets through FDI and foreign trade, but also in its growing spatial agglomeration (Table 9.2). The eight provinces and municipalities which showed clustering trends in the Chinese electronics industry – Guangdong, Jiangsu, Shanghai, Beijing, Tianjin, Sichuan, Fujian and

Table 9.1 Foreign invested enterprises in China's electronics industry, 1996 and 2001

Indicators	1996 FIEs	1996 As % of the total industry	2001 FIEs	2001 As % of the total industry
Number of companies	759	22.21	865	28.25
Number of employees	271,767	16.31	486,399	31.05
Industrial output (billion RMB, constant prices of 1990)	133	43.67	742	54.47
Added value (billion RMB)	26	47.89	92	51.65
Sales (billion RMB)	106	47.75	450	53.87
Export value (billion RMB)	47	74.46	215	78.91
Assets (billion RMB)	106	33.80	287	36.78

Industrial structure (%)	FIEs	All enterprises	FIEs	All enterprises
Investment electronics	29.53	33.42	44.41	40.54
Consumer electronics	39.89	35.54	24.86	33.43
Devices and components	30.58	31.04	30.69	26.02

Ratios	FIEs	All enterprises	FIEs	All enterprises
New products in output (%)	22.29	30.84	26.20	37.09
Exports in sales (%)	44.34	28.25	47.90	32.70
Engineers in total employment (%)	10.55	11.84	11.33	17.34
Added value per employee (thousand RMB)	96	32	189	114
Size of plant (sales in million RMB)	147	63	493	270
Fixed assets per employee (thousand RMB)	126	60	178	128

Annual change between 1996 and 2001	FIEs	All enterprises
Industrial output (%) (constant prices of 1990)	91.58	69.21
Employment (%)	15.80	−1.20
Export (%)	71.49	66.33

Source: *Yearbook of the Chinese Electronics Industry* (1997, 2002).

Table 9.2 Agglomeration in China's electronics industry, 1996 and 2001

	1996		2001	
Indicators	Regions with agglomeration*	As % of the total industry	Regions with agglomeration	As % of the total industry
Number of companies	1,731	54.13	1,658	50.66
Number of employees	937,683	56.26	915,739	58.46
Industrial output (billion RMB, constant prices of 1990)	226	74.29	1,028	75.42
Added value (billion RMB)	41	76.95	131	73.08
Sales (billion RMB)	168	75.62	623	74.50
Export value (billion RMB)	51	80.47	237	86.54
Assets (billion RMB)	215	68.41	520	66.61

Industrial structure (%)	Regions with agglomeration	Other regions	Regions with agglomeration	Other regions
Investment electronics	32.37	36.43	44.87	27.26
Consumer electronics	39.68	23.58	29.44	45.68
Devices and components	27.95	39.99	25.69	27.06

Ratios	Regions with agglomeration	Other regions	Regions with agglomeration	Other regions
New products in output (%)	32.24	28.98	35.12	27.57
Exports in sales (%)	26.64	17.70	31.10	14.25
Engineers in total employment (%)	12.13	11.77	16.06	18.32
Added value per employee (thousand RMB)	48	14	148	60
Size of plant (sales in million RMB)	110	25	427	97
Fixed assets per employee (thousand RMB)	69	52	154	113

Annual change between 1996 and 2001	Regions with agglomeration	Other regions
Industrial output (%) (constant prices of 1990)	70.00	55.15
Employment (%)	−0.47	−2.14
Export (%)	73.54	39.91

Notes: * Guangdong, Jiangsu, Shanghai, Beijing, Tianjin, Sichuan, Fujian and Shaanxi.

Source: *Yearbook of the Chinese Electronics Industry* (1997, 2002).

Shaanxi – accounted for 75 per cent of the total industrial output, 87 per cent of exports and 64 per cent of employment in 2001 (*Yearbook of China's Industrial Economy*, 2002). These regions experienced a higher growth rate in the electronics industry as compared to the rest of China in terms of industrial output value and exports between 1996 and 2001, although their employment in the industry has slightly declined. The industrial structure of these regions has also significantly changed during this period as the share of investment electronics in the total industrial output increased from 32 to 45 per cent, while the share of consumer electronics decreased from 29 to 40 per cent. These structural changes can be regarded as a shift in these regions from low-cost manufacturing (or assembling) of consumer products to the production of more sophisticated IT products. These regions are also more performant than the rest of China in terms of innovation, exports, economies of scale, labour productivity and capital intensity.

The importance of FIEs in the performance of China's electronics industry on the one hand, and the agglomeration trends of the industry in a limited number of regions on the other hand, are two focuses of this study. The major research questions are as follows: Are there spatial agglomerations in China's electronics industry? What is the interdependence between spatial agglomeration and FDI in China's electronics industry? Does the spatial agglomeration affect the specific features of the industry, such as capital intensity, labour productivity, market structure, innovation capabilities and international competitiveness? Although this study does not intend to survey the determinant factors of the spatial agglomeration of China's electronics industry as such, it tries to emphasize the role of TNCs in these clustering trends.

The chapter is divided into four sections. The next section presents a literature review on FDI and industrial clusters, after which we map the geographical agglomeration of China's electronics industry and survey the importance of FIEs in the industry and their specific characteristics. The aggregated firm level data is then analysed to emphasize the agglomeration economies in the Chinese electronics industry on the one hand, and to assess the effects of FDI on the geographical agglomeration of Chinese electronics industries on the other hand.

Literature review

Agglomeration effects

The agglomeration economies consist of the economic benefits associated with the spatial concentration of economic activities in general and industrial clusters in particular. According to Marshall (1882), the external effects of agglomeration are various types of benefits and cost savings obtained outside the market that may lead to increased productivity of a firm. These effects may consist of the availability of skilled labour, the access to specialized suppliers of intermediary goods, but also localized knowledge spillovers, or simply the so-called 'atmosphere'. These economic benefits allow an increase in the productivity of firms in a static perspective and augment the capacity for innovation and sustained productivity growth in a more dynamic perspective.

Krugman has emphasized the importance of clustering in economic growth in his writings on trade and geography (Krugman, 1991, 1995; Krugman and Venables, 1995), while Porter approached the role of clustering in the competitiveness of industries and companies from a business-management point of view (Porter, 1990, 1996). The major concern of these studies on linkages between industrial clusters and national competitiveness is to assess enhanced competition and technological spillovers as the mechanism through which the productivity of the host economy is improved. It needs to be stressed that competitiveness of the individual firm is a very important element in this concept as competitive firms make up a competitive cluster and economic self-interest is ultimately the glue that binds the cluster together (Enright, 1996).

Saxenian (1994) and Porter (1990, 1998) identified the existence of a number of competitive clusters on the basis of small-sample qualitative studies and documented the existence of agglomeration externality mechanisms. At the industry level, there is also evidence of a positive relationship between agglomeration and competitiveness in terms of, for example, increased labour productivity (see for example, Henderson, 1986; Ciccone and Hall, 1996), enhanced human capital (labour quality), rapid industrial restructuring (plant size and specialisation), increased competition (international and local) and innovation (investment and capability).

During the last few decades, TNCs have increasingly invested in foreign industrial clusters to augment their knowledge base through obtaining direct access to foreign pools of skilled human resources and knowledge (Dunning, 2000; Rugman and Verbeke, 2001). FDI by TNCs has been driven by knowledge-seeking and/or strategic asset-seeking motivation, while foreign subsidiaries have been more and more considered as 'asset-augmenting investments' (Dunning, 1998), 'scanning units' (Bartlett and Ghoshal, 1986; Westney, 1990) and 'transplanted home bases' (Porter, 1990).

The positive impact of foreign industrial clusters on the asset-creating and competitiveness of TNCs has become the focus of several studies (Birkinshaw and Hood, 1998, 2000; Birkinshaw, 2000; Enright, 2000; Peters and Hood, 2000), which provide a rich set of conceptual and practical insights into the contribution of foreign industrial clusters in general and foreign subsidiaries in particular to the competitive position of TNCs. The importance of TNCs in foreign cluster formation, functioning and upgrading constitutes another interesting segment of the literature, which focuses on the dependent, independent and interdependent relationships between foreign clusters and TNCs (Enright, 2000; Cantwell and Santangelo, 1999). Yet, the dynamic interaction and co-evolution between indigenous clusters and foreign subsidiaries is a complex phenomenon, of which the causality and sequential development are difficult to identify.

Impact of TNCs on clusters

The discussion about the impact of TNCs on foreign industrial clusters is derived from the literature on the relationship between TNCs and the host economy, which suggests that the major impacts of TNCs on the host country are related to the employment, transfer of technology, knowledge spillovers, balance of payments, exports, foreign exchange, demand expectations, competition and entrepreneurship stimulation. Extending from this literature, Dunning suggests that foreign TNCs play a major role in the formation, structure and development of industrial clusters, especially for knowledge-based clusters, exports processing zones and technology parks (Dunning, 2000).

The impact of TNCs on industrial clusters depends on the nature and form of the assets of the investing company, the location-bound resources and capabilities of the host clusters and the organizational mechanisms through which they interact (Enright, 2000). This argument is clearly based on Dunning's eclectic paradigm which is frequently used in the literature for explaining the phenomenon of FDI. Young, Hood and Peters found that TNCs – which have a wide product franchise, strong export orientation, highly skilled production process and personnel, substantial local content and deep involvement for building up local research capabilities – are most likely to contribute positively to the regional development as 'developmental TNCs' (Young, Hood and Peters, 1994).

Zander and Sölvell (2000) emphasized that the TNC can be considered as a boundary-spanning vehicle, furthering the integration of regions through international trade, foreign direct investment and international knowledge exchange. Cantwell and Iammarino (1997) found that the concentration of technological activity by foreign affiliates is correlated to the concentration of the same activity carried out by local firms. Therefore, TNCs appear especially prone to perform R&D investments in foreign locations with a strong technological activity, and this leads to a further strengthening of indigenous R&D activities, thus illustrating the co-evolution of domestic firms and foreign subsidiaries in host-country clusters.

A number of empirical studies have shown that certain clusters have resulted from the agglomeration of the facilities of foreign subsidiaries, especially in the case of 'satellite platform clusters', while other contributions have identified the substantial influence of transnationals on individual clusters located both in industrial and developing countries. The dominant role of foreign TNCs in cluster formation and development have been illustrated, for instance, by the cases of German and Swiss firms in the New York–New Jersey–Pennsylvania pharmaceutical cluster (Enright, 1991) and foreign TNCs in the development of Venezuela's oil and petrochemical cluster (Enright, Frances *et al.*, 1996). Subsidiaries of foreign TNCs may also perform the role of regional headquarters and have strong cluster ties among themselves and with local cluster participants. Yet, in some cases clusters dominated by foreign subsidiaries are likely to behave as satellites of the foreign parent companies, with few spillover effects accruing to indigenous cluster participants.

Birkinshaw studied the specific link between the process of upgrading in industrial clusters and the level of foreign ownership of those clusters in order to emphasize the importance of FDI on industrial clusters at different level of cluster maturity (or life-cycle) and cluster dynamism (Birkinshaw, 2000). His empirical survey on the Stockholm IT cluster showed that foreign investment has an important role to play in shaping the potential for upgrading in a cluster, especially in rapidly growing industries with considerable scope for expansion. Yet, in mature industries that are consolidating, the relative positions of various clusters and their strengths and weaknesses are well-known and foreign ownership has little impact on the cluster dynamics.

Enright (2000) developed an interdependent model – as compared to independent and dependent approaches – to analyse the interactions between TNCs and industrial clusters. His empirical study on Hong Kong's financial-services cluster showed that the benefits that foreign TNCs have brought to the local industrial cluster went well-beyond the direct benefits of employment, output and skill transfer, as well as the indirect benefits of spillovers into other industries identified with the presence of foreign TNCs. The impact of foreign TNCs was especially related to market-creating, cluster-creating, infrastructure-creating, linkage-creating and information-creating. Foreign firms in local industrial clusters can be regarded as 'contributing subsidiaries' (Birkinshaw and Hood, 1998) in that they strongly contribute in terms of strategy-setting and developing and deploying substantial skills and capabilities. The ability to attract FDI in an emerging cluster, especially from large TNCs with a high visibility, may signal at the international level that the cluster is credible; this may result in a foreign investment snowball effect benefiting the cluster as a whole.

To achieve and sustain their ability to compete, firms seem increasingly to have to rely on their capacity to internationally relocate and disperse their production activities (or some stages of them). The firm's location decision depends not only on the general (at the country level), but also on the specific (at the regional level) characteristics of the industrial and socio-economic structure of the location, as globalization tends to emphasize the significance of location choices. Moreover, the globalization process can be depicted as a higher degree of interdependency among the geographically dispersed units of global (transnational) firms. This leads to a stronger geographical concentration of both production and technological activities of TNCs, which have been defined as 'the key-ring in the chain from global to local' (Cantwell and Iammarino, 1998). Therefore, as globalization processes are likely to strengthen regional differences, local environments will play an increasingly important role in the TNCs' value-added activities.

Impact of clusters on TNCs

TNCs tend to locate their international operation where they may benefit from suitably specialized factors that are complementary to their own major strengths in order to enjoy localized spillovers from the dynamic host system of innovation. On the other hand, the comparative advantage in innovation of the local system is enhanced over time through the presence of foreign-owned affiliates (Birkinshaw and Hood, 2000).

The literature on location factors has shown that TNCs can gain access to a number of specific location factors by concentrating their value-added activities in a particular region/country. The location factors can be natural and created resources, strategic assets, market information and production knowledge. Recent research has applied these approaches to cluster studies and concluded that clusters can be considered as an important variation of the geographic or location-based advantages that influence international production. Dunning has used 'asset-augmenting investment' to describe the situation in which TNCs invest abroad to gain access to specific capabilities present in a foreign cluster in order to enhance the assets that the corporation already possesses (Dunning, 1998a, 1998b, 2000).

From the TNC perspective, participation in a foreign cluster may lead to several benefits: the access to knowledge, which otherwise would have remained out of reach; the potential leveraging of this knowledge throughout the firm's internal network; the transfer of global best practices; the monitoring of rivals active in the foreign clusters, and so on. The impact of foreign clusters on TNCs can be analysed at two levels: from the perspective of the subsidiary located in the foreign cluster, and from that of the TNC group. From the subsidiary perspective, Birkinshaw and Hood (1998) showed that subsidiaries located in leading-edge clusters tended to have higher value-added activities, to be more internationally oriented and to be better embedded into local environments than subsidiaries that were not located in such clusters. With regard to the spillover effects of foreign clusters on TNC groups – that is through foreign subsidiaries located in the clusters to their parent companies or groups – the role of foreign subsidiaries varies according to their function within TNC groups (Enright, 1998), the structural context imposed by the parent company, the entrepreneurial capacity of subsidiary management and the local environment (Birkinshaw and Hood, 2000).

In the case where foreign subsidiaries are set up as 'listening posts', they may be used to collect information and knowledge from the clusters and disseminate it to the parent companies and other subsidiaries. In an advanced stage, they can serve as a vehicle to transfer skills and capabilities from the cluster to the rest of the group. In the case of standalone investments, foreign subsidiaries often serve as the centre for a particular business segment of TNCs at a global or regional scale, especially within satellite platform clusters. The TNC may also benefit from advantages that a foreign cluster might have in developing and producing a particular product or service that can be transferred to the existing business units of the group through its subsidiaries in the cluster (Enright, 2000). In industrial leading-edge industrial clusters, two major types of foreign subsidiaries have been observed. The first consists of scanning units that tap selectively into sources of advantage in foreign national industrial clusters. They are often R&D units with limited development capability of their own, which allow them to contribute to, as well as draw from, the knowledge base of the cluster (Porter, 1990). The agglomeration effects have been regarded as positive to promote this type of localized innovation process (Zander and Sölvell, 2000). The second function as transplanted home bases, which consist of top management, R&D activities and main manufacturing operations of an entire production division. In addition to this type of high-profile subsidiary, there are also likely to be many more traditional subsidiaries in leading-edge clusters, for example market-seeking units that are located in the clusters because the country represents an important market for the firm's products. Others will be resource-seeking units that are located in the cluster to access specialized inputs, well-trained labour or low-cost factor inputs.

TNCs tend to perform R&D investments in foreign locations with strong technological capabilities, and this leads to a further strengthening of indigenous R&D activities. There is an increase of knowledge-seeking FDI by TNCs, because the intra-firm specialization and the related local embeddedness of know-how make it difficult to achieve international innovation processes within the TNC without participating in foreign clusters. Yet, being in a foreign cluster does not necessarily create positive effects on the innovation process of TNCs for the following reasons. Different sub-units within the TNC may have a specialized knowledge base and a specific technological trajectory, which may be inconsistent with the knowledge absorbed in a foreign cluster. In addition, the TNC unit involved in the knowledge absorption process may be faced with difficult choices between maximizing convergence of its own operations with the other parts of the TNC network, and maximizing convergence with the functioning of the localized knowledge cluster in which it is physically embedded (Cantwell and Santangelo, 1999).

Methodology, data and cluster mapping

Two major arguments developed in this study are (1) the characteristics of a given industry should vary in different regions as a result of their differences in geographical agglomeration (effects of agglomeration economies); and (2) the characteristics of a given industry should vary in different regions as a result of the difference in the degree of foreign participation in the industry (impact of foreign direct investment). These two arguments can be examined in a matrix, showing the different degrees of geographical agglomeration (horizontal dimension) and foreign participation (vertical dimension) as shown in Figure 9.1.

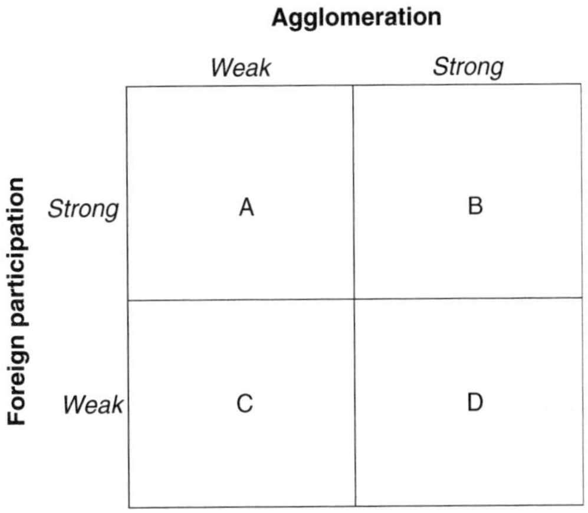

Agglomeration

Figure 9.1 Typology of clusters based on agglomeration and foreign participation

Quadrant A in the figure represents the situation in which there is a higher presence of FDI in a given industry as compared to the rest of the economy in a particular region, but the industry itself is not (or not yet) agglomerated. The attractiveness of the region to FDI seems related to the potential rather than current industrial cluster. Yet the possible positive effect of FDI on the formation of a new industrial cluster cannot be excluded. Quadrant B illustrates the situation where the FDI and clusters are all highly present; yet, although it is difficult to identify the sequence in the co-development of these two factors, the existence of interaction or interdependence between these two factors cannot be ignored.

Quadrant D presents the situation where the industrial clusters are developed without a high participation of FDI. In quadrant C, neither FDI nor clusters are influential. The failure in attracting FDI and in building up substantial industrial structure may result from the disadvantages of the region for a given industry. The absence of an appropriate industrial or regional development might also be at the origin of this disadvantaged position of the region.

A number of characteristics of the Chinese electronics industry will be analysed in the following sections according to the above-mentioned four situations in order to assess the effects of agglomeration economies and FDI as well as their interaction:

- *Human capital intensity* The proportion of engineers to the total employees is used as a ratio to measure the intensity of the human capital in a given industry located in a given region. A high ratio is interpreted as indicating that the industry in this region relies more on the inputs of qualified labour as compared to other regions that are ranked less high.

Higher intensity of human capital usually implies higher innovation capability.

- *Labour productivity* The added value per employee is used as a ratio to measure the labour productivity; that is, the output of the industry in a given region relative to its input of the labour force.
- *Local competition* The competition index is usually calculated as the ratio of the number of firms to the total value added in the industry in a given region divided by the national average value of this ratio. A higher score implies that firms in the related industry in the region are smaller in size as compared to the national average, and thus exposed to more local competition (Glaeser *et al.*, 1992).
- *Industrial structure* The electronics industry consists of three subsectors, namely consumer electronics, investment electronics and electronic parts and components. The importance of these subsectors in the industry is measured by their relative proportion in the industrial output of the industry in a given region.
- *Economies of scale* The ratio of the industrial sales revenue to the number of firms indicates the size of the manufacturing plants in a given region. A higher ratio implies that the region benefits more from economies of scale than other regions.
- *Innovation capabilities* The level of innovative capability is calculated as the ratio of new products to the total industrial output. Yet, it could also indicate the importance of a restructuring process in terms of products.
- *International competitiveness* The international competitiveness of a given region is measured by the ratio of exports to total sales. A higher ratio implies that the region has a stronger competitive position in the international market as compared to other regions.
- *Entrepreneurship development* The level of entrepreneurship development is measured by the ratio of private capital to the total capital of the industry in a given region. A higher ratio in a particular region is supposed to indicate that entrepreneurship in this region is more dynamic and developed as compared to other regions.
- *Capital intensity* A measure of the relative use of capital, compared to other factors, such as labour, in the production process. It is often measured by the ratio of the net value of fixed capital stock to the average number of employees.

Data

The location quotient (LQ) of employment (see below), which is used to measure geographical agglomeration and the concentration of FDI, is calculated on the basis of data from *China Industry Economy Statistical Yearbook* (2002), while the comparative analysis of the electronics industry in different regions is based on the industry/province level data collected by the Ministry of Information Industry (MII) (*China's Electronics Industry Yearbook*,

1997 and 2002). It has to be noted that the data of these two sources were collected by company level surveys and that these aggregated figures concern only large and middle sized enterprises in China's electronics industry. Small firms, especially township and village enterprises (TVEs) and privately owned enterprises are not included. Yet, such small and private enterprises play a very important role in a number of regions such as Zhejiang, Jiangsu and Fujian.

Statistical methods

Measuring industrial agglomeration

By using industrial cluster analysis researchers attempt to identify areas of a given economy in which the output, productivity and growth of an industry are higher than in other areas or regions. One would like to use data about the industries' exports of goods and services out of a given area or region and consequently bring wealth back into it, to identify regional clusters, but most regions lack accurate data about shipments out of the area. In order to overcome this hurdle, a proxy calculation, the so-called location quotient (LQ), is largely used as a standard approach. This method identifies the industries that employ more workers in the region than the national average for that same industry, and assumes that this indicates that the industry is producing more goods and services than the region alone can consume; thus exporting the excess product out of the region. A location quotient is defined as the following ratio:

$$LQ_i = \frac{(e_i/e)}{(E_i/E)}$$

where e_i is the area employment in industry i; e is the total employment in the area; E_i is employment in the benchmark economy in industry i; and E is the total employment in the benchmark economy. Normally, the benchmark economy taken is usually the nation as it is considered to be the closest available approximation to a self-sufficient economy. The location quotient also relates to the Employment Concentration Factor (ECF) in the literature (SDAOF, 1999). ECF is determined by calculating the percentage of employment in a four-digit SIC code industry within a specified region to total regional employment, compared to that of national employment, that is the national average. If an industry's ECF is larger than 1.0, it can be assumed that some portion of its production is exported out of the region. An ECF of 3.0 would mean that employment in this particular industry is three times more concentrated in the region than for the nation as a whole.

Measuring the concentration of FDI

The above-mentioned location quotient (LQ) method is also used to assess the concentration degree of FDI in a particular industry in a given region as compared to other regions. It is determined by calculating the percentage of FDI in a four-digit SIC code industry within a specified region to total FDI in the region, compared to the national average. If the FDI in an industry exceeds 1.0, it can be assumed that the relevant industry in this region has some attractiveness as compared to others, while a lower score means that this industry is less attractive.

One-way analysis of variance (ANOVA)

This is used to compare regional differences on the basis of the indicators discussed above, for labour productivity, innovative capability, local and global competitiveness, and so on.

Results

Geographical agglomeration and FDI concentration

The cluster analysis of China's electronics industry on the basis of LQ shows that the local employment in the electronics industry is higher than expected (that is, LQ > 1) in eight of 29 regions, namely Guangdong (3.53), Beijing (2.21), Tianjin (1.89), Shanghai (1.73), Fujian (1.72), Shaanxi (1.32), Jiangsu (1.25) and Sichuan (1.24). Consequently, it can be concluded that these regions have a higher concentration of the electronics industry as compared to other regions in China.

The LQ analysis of FDI in China's electronics industry in different regions shows that seven of 29 regions have a higher foreign participation in their electronics industries as compared to the national average, of which five regions show also strong cluster trends. These regions are Tianjin, Beijing, Guangdong, Shanghai and Jiangsu. Figure 9.2 presents a classification of the Chinese regions according to geographical agglomeration and foreign participation in the electronics industry.

Comparative analysis

Industrial structure

The regions with agglomeration trends are specialized in manufacturing of investment electronics (42% of the total output) as compared to other regions which are more representative for the production of parts and devices (36%) (Table 9.3). The specialization of the agglomerated regions in investment electronics is clearly related to the high participation of FDI, as investment electronics accounted for 45 per cent of the total output value in the regions where there is a strong concentration of FDI. By contrast, in the region without concentration of FDI the relative share is only 35 per cent (Table 9.4). The effects of FDI on the industrial structure are also evident in the agglomerated regions: investment electronics accounts for 46 per cent of the total output value in the regions where there is a concentration of

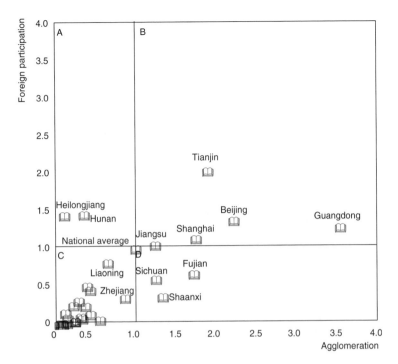

Figure 9.2 Geographical agglomeration and FDI concentration of China's electronics industry, 2001

FDI, while the relative ratio is 37 per cent in the region without FDI concentration (Table 9.5).

Market competition

The regions without concentration of FDI and agglomeration trends, i.e. quadrant C, have the highest degree of industry/ market competition as the local competition ratio reached 1.9 as compared to less than 0.5 in other regions. This means that agglomeration as well as FDI has a negative effect on local competition, or a positive effect on the monopolistic situation.

Regional industrial growth

The comparative analysis shows that the agglomeration economies as well as FDI have a positive impact on regional industrial growth. The eight regions with strong agglomeration trends (group BD) have higher growth rates in terms of industrial output (70%) as compared to other regions (55%) where the agglomeration phenomenon in the electronics industry was not observed (Table 9.3). On the other hand, the regions with strong concentrations of FDI recorded a higher industrial growth rate during the

Table 9.3 Agglomeration effects in China's electronics industry, 2001

Descriptive analysis	Regions without agglomeration (AC) (N = 21)			Regions with strong agglomeration (BD) (N = 8)			ANOVA test	
	Mean	Std. deviation	Std. error	Mean	Std. deviation	Std. error	F	Sig.
Growth rate of output	55.15	41.98	9.63	70.00	34.13	12.07	0.779	0.386
Productivity (RMB thousand)	60.28	42.67	0.93	148.35	61.14	2.16	19.440	0.000
Human capital ratio	18.32	8.66	1.81	16.06	4.65	1.64	0.485	0.492
Export ratio	14.25	19.64	4.39	31.10	17.70	6.26	4.434	0.045
Innovation ratio	27.57	18.74	4.09	35.12	17.68	6.25	0.966	0.334
Degree of market competition	1.90	3.56	0.76	0.32	0.07	0.02	1.544	0.224
Fixed assets to employees	11.35	5.09	1.11	15.40	8.56	3.03	2.494	0.126
Growth of investment electronics	73.93	68.54	15.72	178.98	238.73	84.4	3.212	0.085
Growth of consumer electronics	170.95	390.32	89.55	142.33	309.10	109.28	0.034	0.856
Growth of parts and devices	40.76	46.60	10.69	70.40	43.95	15.54	2.351	0.138

Table 9.4 Effects of foreign direct investment in China's electronics industry, 2001

Descriptive analysis	Regions with concentration of FDI (AB) (N = 7)			Regions without concentration of FDI (CD) (N = 22)			ANOVA test	
	Mean	Std. deviation	Std. error	Mean	Std. deviation	Std. error	F	Sig.
Growth rate of output	78.68	28.57	10.80	52.86	41.53	9.29	2.295	0.142
Productivity	147.85	73.78	2.79	64.44	42.40	0.90	14.167	0.001
Human capital ratio	18.23	5.69	2.15	17.59	8.43	1.72	0.035	0.853
Export ratio	29.19	16.68	6.30	15.69	20.64	4.50	2.441	0.130
Innovation ratio	37.57	20.69	7.82	27.14	17.45	3.72	1.741	0.198
Degree of market competition	0.46	0.26	0.10	1.79	3.51	0.73	0.989	0.328
Fixed assets to employees	17.25	8.13	3.07	10.95	4.97	1.06	6.225	0.019
Growth of investment electronics	79.20	70.48	15.76	178.92	258.10	97.55	2.609	0.119
Growth of consumer electronics	160.02	382.62	85.56	169.48	324.99	122.83	0.003	0.954
Growth of parts and devices	37.52	38.20	8.54	83.89	55.80	21.09	6.006	0.022

Table 9.5 Effects of foreign direct investment on the agglomeration of China's electronics industry, 2001

Descriptive analysis	Regions with concentration of FDI and strong agglomeration (B) (N = 5)			Regions with strong agglomeration without concentration of FDI (D) (N = 3)			ANOVA test	
	Mean	Std. deviation	Std. error	Mean	Std. deviation	Std. error	F	Sig.
Growth rate of output	85.92	28.12	12.58	43.48	28.38	16.39	4.245	0.085
Productivity	185.87	42.55	1.90	85.82	8.80	0.51	15.225	0.008
Human capital ratio	17.26	5.22	2.33	14.07	3.42	1.97	0.868	0.387
Export ratio	37.66	9.98	4.46	20.17	24.70	14.26	2.129	0.195
Innovation ratio	40.92	16.61	7.43	25.44	17.83	10.29	1.549	0.260
Degree of market competition	0.33	0.08	0.04	0.32	0.04	0.03	0.036	0.855
Fixed assets to employees	18.94	9.26	4.14	9.50	1.20	0.69	2.898	0.140
Growth of investment electronics	218.13	305.18	136.48	113.72	54.65	31.55	0.324	0.590
Growth of consumer electronics	217.63	385.05	172.20	16.81	8.37	4.83	0.765	0.415
Growth of parts and devices	79.67	48.42	21.66	54.96	38.72	22.35	0.555	0.484

period 1996–2001, that is 78.7 per cent per year as compared to 52.9 per cent in the rest of China (Table 9.4). The impact of FDI on regional industrial growth is even higher when the industry is agglomerated: the growth rate in the regions with a high concentration of FDI and industry agglomeration reached 86 per cent per year (group B) as compared to 45 per cent of the regions where the industry is strongly agglomerated, but without a strong presence of FDI (group D, that is in the provinces of Shaanxi, Sichuan and Fujian) (Table 9.5). Yet, although the differences in regional industrial growth in the above-mentioned cases are important, the ANOVA test of variance does not provide significant statistical evidence.

Labour productivity

The analysis of labour productivity shows that the added value per employee in the regions with strong agglomeration is more than twice as high as compared to the region without industrial agglomeration (that is, RMB148,000 as compared to RMB60,000), indicating a positive impact of agglomeration economies on labour productivity. The ANOVA test confirms the regional differences. The impact of FDI on labour productivity is also evident as the added value per employee in the regions with strong concentration of FDI reached RMB148,000 while that of the regions without high participation of FDI amounted to only RMB64,000. Within the regions with strong agglomeration, those with a high concentration of FDI recorded RMB186,000 added value per employee in 2001, about twice as high as for the regions with only a weak presence of FDI.

Human capital

The ratio of the number of engineers to total employment measures the quality of labour. A high ratio indicates a high proportion of engineers in the total labour force and is assumed to create high innovation capabilities. The geographical agglomeration in China's electronics industry seems to have very limited impact on the labour quality, as the regional difference is quite small; that is, 18 for the regions with agglomeration and 16 for those without agglomeration trends. The difference between regions with or without a high concentration of FDI is even less significant. This shows that both the FDI and industry agglomeration did not result in a pool of highly qualified labour in China's electronics industry. A possible explanation is that the agglomeration of China's electronics industry as well as FDI in this industry is related to manufacturing and assembling of low-cost electronics, which only requires skilled workers rather than qualified engineers.

Innovation capability

Both agglomeration economies and FDI have a positive effect on the innovation of a region. The ratio of new products to total output, which is used to measure the innovation capabilities of a region, is relatively higher in a region where there is concentration of FDI and/or an agglomeration trend. Yet, the ANOVA test does not provide convincing statistical evidence. About one-third (35%) of the industrial output in regions with industrial agglomerations is related to new products as compared to 28 per cent in other regions. In regions with FDI concentration, the relative ratio is 38 per cent as compared to 27 per cent in other regions. Within the regions with agglomeration trends, new products even reached 41 per cent of the total output value, which showed a significant correlation between FDI and innovation of those regions.

Capital intensity

The ratio of fixed assets to employees, which has been frequently used to measure the capital intensity of a company, indicates that regions where there is strong FDI and industrial agglomeration register the highest score, that is 18.9 as compared to 9.5 for other regions. The ANOVA test confirmed the statistical evidence of this regional difference.

International competitiveness

The ratio of exports to total sales is used to assess the competitiveness of a region in the international market. Regions with agglomeration trends are clearly more competitive as this ratio is twice as high (31%) as compared to regions without industrial clusters (14%). The effect of FDI also has a positive impact on the international competitiveness of a region in terms of exports, although less-pronounced. In regions with strong FDI concentration, the export ratio reached 29 per cent as compared to 21 per cent in the regions without a strong presence of FDI. Yet, the concentration of FDI in the regions with strong agglomeration has certainly enhanced their competitiveness in the international market.

Conclusion

From the above statistical analysis, the following conclusions can be drawn (Table 9.6). First, agglomeration has significantly contributed to the labour productivity of China's electronics industry and industrial growth, especially in the regions where there is a strong concentration of FDI. This evidence confirms the findings of previous studies on the positive impact of industrial clusters on productivity (Blomström, 1986; Cantwell, 1989; Caves, 1974; Kokko, 1992, 1994; Birkinshaw, 2000; Enright, 2000). Yet, the impact of industrial clusters on the productivity and regional growth of China's electronics industry seems closely related to FDI, which has improved the productivity either through the higher productivity of foreign plants or through strategic Original Equipment Manufacturers (OEMs), where foreign partners set up a joint venture in Chinese operations and then improve productivity of its manufacturing operations in order to reduce costs.

Secondly, the agglomeration trends in China's electronics industry are positively related to the regional competitive position in the international

Table 9.6   Summary of estimated effects of FDI and agglomeration economies

Effects	*Agglomeration economies*	*FDI*	*FDI/ Agglomeration*
Capital intensity	+	+ +	+
Industrial growth	+	+	+ +
Labour productivity	+ +	+ +	+ +
Labour quality (human capital)	=	=	+
Innovation capability	+	+	+
International competitiveness	+ +	+	+
Market competition	−	−	=

Note: + + highly positive; + positive; = neutral; − negative; − highly negative.

market. The results show that the regions with stronger agglomeration trends have higher export ratios, meaning that China's electronics manufacturing clusters are strongly integrated into global production networks, especially in the coastal regions where foreign subsidiaries and domestic subcontracting firms are 'clustered' in export processing and technology zones for mostly low-cost outsourcing manufacturing. Although the concentration of foreign-invested firms seems positively related to the export ratio, this correlation is less significant than in the case of agglomeration. This finding can be explained by the fact that on the one hand FIEs have invested in China not only for export-oriented low-cost manufacturing (efficiency-seeking), but also to participate in the local booming market (market-seeking). In fact, while the high concentration of export-oriented OEM companies in the Zhujiang Delta Area can only be explained as a part of the agglomeration trends of China's electronics industry, other industrial clusters in Shanghai and Beijing basically focus on the local market, especially with regard to investment electronics products.

Thirdly, FDI is positively related to the capital intensity of the company, reflecting that FIEs are more relying on capital-intensive technology and production facilities. This certainly contributed to the higher labour productivity of the industrial clusters, where there is a stronger concentration of FIEs.

Fourthly, the findings of this study show that both agglomeration and FDI are negatively related to local competition. This clearly contrasts with the findings of the existing literature, which have assumed that the agglomeration as well as FDI tends to favour local competition. The high competitive pressure in a cluster and its associated push to innovation provide dynamism and advantages to clustered companies. According to Porter's approach, the geographical concentration of rivals enhances competitiveness and stimulates innovative activity, firm entry and growth (Porter, 1990; Feldman, 1994; Baptista, 1998, 1999). Although this observation has been empirically verified in many countries and industries (Glaeser, Kallal *et al.*, 1992; Audretsch and Feldman, 1996; Baptista and Swann, 1996, 1998), it could not be confirmed for China's electronics industry. This might be explained by the industrial policy of China's government, which has strongly supported state-owned enterprises to build up large-sized enterprises without taking the necessary measures to favour competition from small and medium-sized companies and the non-state sector.

Fifthly, as recently pointed out by many authors, the agglomeration effects on innovative activities can be underlined by the increasing role played by global firms as creators of innovation across national boundaries, and, in addition, the advantages of geographical agglomeration may reinforce the existing sectoral pattern of technological specialization of local systems (Cantwell and Iammarino, 1997). The results of this study confirm that both the concentration of FDI and geographical agglomeration are positively related to the innovation capability of China's electronics industry.

This study was designed to determine the correlation between geographical agglomeration of China's electronics industry and FDI on the one hand, and the effect of agglomeration and FDI on the specific characteristics in different regions on the other hand. However, since the data used were based on provincial statistics, they do not allow us to identify agglomeration effects at the sub-regional level. This constraint might substantially limit the theoretical implications of this study.

References

Alderman, N. and Davies, S. (1990) 'Modelling Regional Patterns of Innovation Diffusion in the UK Metalworking Industries', *Regional Studies*, 24: 513–28.

Audretsch, D.B. and Feldman, M.P. (1996) 'R&D Spillovers and the Geography of Innovation and Production', *American Economic Review*, 86: 630–40.

Baptista, R. (1998) 'Clusters, Innovation and Growth: A Survey of the Literature', in G.M.P. Swann, M. Prevezer and D. Stout (eds), *The Dynamics of Industrial Clustering: International Comparisons in Computers and Biotechnology*. Oxford: Oxford University Press.

Baptista, R. (1999) 'The Diffusion of Process Innovations: A Selective Review', *International Journal of the Economics of Business*, 6: 107–29.

Baptista, R. (2000) 'Do Innovations Diffuse Faster Within Geographical Clusters?', *International Journal of Industrial Organization*, 18: 515–35.

Baptista, R. and Swann, P. (1996) *The Dynamics of Industrial Clusters: A Comparative Study of the US and UK Computer Industries*, Working Paper no. 165. London: Centre for Business Strategy, London Business School.

Baptista, R. and Swann, P. (1998) 'Do Firms in Clusters Innovate More?', *Research Policy*, 27: 527–42.

Bartlett, C. and Ghoshal, S. (1986) 'Tap Your Subsidiaries for Global Reach', *Harvard Business Review*, 64: 87–94.

Beckmann, M.J. and Thisse, J.-F. (1986) 'The Location of Production Activities', in P. Nijkamp (ed.), *Handbook of Regional and Urban Economics*, *I*. Amsterdam: North-Holland, pp. 21–95.

Birkinshaw, J. (2000) 'Upgrading of Industrial Clusters and Foreign Direct Investment', *International Studies of Manufacturing and Organisation*, 30: 93–111.

Birkinshaw, J. and Hood, N. (1998) *Roles of Foreign Subsidiaries in Industry Clusters*, Working Paper. Stockholm: Institute of International Business, Stockholm School of Economics.

Birkinshaw, J. and Hood, N. (2000) 'Characteristics of Foreign Subsidiaries in Industry Clusters', *Journal of International Business Studies*, 31: 141–54.

Cantwell, J. and Santangelo, G.D. (1999) 'The Frontier of International Technology Networks: Sourcing Abroad the Most Highly Tacit Capabilities', *Information Economics and Policy*, 11: 103–23.

Cantwell, J.A. and Iammarino, S. (1997) *Regional Systems of Innovation in Europe and the Globalisation of Technology*. University of Reading, mimeo.

Dicken, P. and Lloyd, P. (1990) *Location in Space: Theoretical Perspectives in Economic Geography*. New York: HarperCollins.

Dunning, J.H. (1998) 'Globalisation, Technological Change and Spatial Organisation of Economic Activities', in Chandler *et al.* (eds), *The Dynamic Firm: The Role of Technology, Strategy, Organisation, and Regions*. Oxford: Oxford University Press.

Dunning, J.H. (1998) 'Location and the Multinational Enterprise: A Neglected Factor', *Journal of International Business Studies*, 29: 45–66.

Dunning, J.H. (2000) 'Regions, Globalisation, and the Knowledge Economy: The Issues Stated', in J.H. Dunning (ed.), *Regions, Globalisation, and the Knowledge Economy*. Oxford: Oxford University Press.

Enright, M.J. (1991) 'Geographical Concentration and Industrial Organisations', PhD dissertation, Harvard University.

Enright, M.J. (1996) 'Regional Clusters and Economic Development: A Research Agenda', in U.H. Staeber, N.V. Schaefer and B. Sharma (eds), *Business Networks: Prospects for Regional Development*. Berlin: Walter de Gruyter.

Enright, M.J. (1998) Regional Clusters and Firm Strategy, in A. Chandler *et al.* (eds), *The Dynamic Firm: The Role of Technology, Strategy, Organisation, and Regions*. Oxford: Oxford University Press.

Enright, M.J. (2000) 'Regional Clusters and Multinational Enterprises', *International Journal of Industrial Organization*, 30: 114–38.

Enright, M.J., Frances, A. *et al.* (1996) *Venezuela: The Challenge of Competitiveness*. New York: St Martin's Press.

Feldman, M.P. (1994) *The Geography of Innovation*. Dordrecht: Kluwer Academic Publishers.

Glaeser, E.L., Kallal, H.D. *et al.* (1992) 'Growth in Cities', *Journal of Political Economy*, 100: 1126–52.

Granovetter, M. (1985) 'Economic Action and Social Structure: The Problem of Embeddedness', *American Journal of Sociology*, 91: 481–510.

Hagerstrand, T. (1967) *Innovation Diffusion as a Spatial Process*. Chicago: University of Chicago Press.

Harrison, B. (1992) 'Industrial Districts: Old Wine in New Bottles?', *Regional Studies*, 26: 469–83.

Krugman, P. and Venables, A.J. (1995) 'Globalization and the Inequality of Nations', *Quarterly Journal of Economics*, 60: 857–80.

Krugman, P.R. (1995) *Development, Geography, and Economic Theory*. Cambridge, Mass., MIT Press.

Liu, X., Parker, D. *et al.* (2001) 'The Impact of Foreign Direct Investment on Labour Productivity in the Chinese Electronics Industry', *International Business Review*, 10: 421–39.

Lundvall, B. A. (1988) 'Innovation as an Interactive Process: From User-Producer Interaction to the National Systems of Innovation', in G. Dosi *et al.* (eds), *Technological Change and Economic Theory*. London: Pinter Publishers.

Malmberg, A., Sölvell, Ö. et al. (1996) 'Spatial Clustering, Local Accumulation of Knowledge and Firm Competitiveness', *Geografiska Annaler*, 78B(2): 85–97.

Mariani, M. (1999) *Next to Production or to Technological Clusters? The Economics and Management of R&D Location*, MERIT Research Memorandum, 99–029. Maastricht: MERIT.

Martin, P. and Ottaviano, G.I.P. (1996) *Growth and Agglomeration*. CEPII-Document de travail, 96–14.

Patibandla, M. and Petersen, B. (2002) 'Role of Transnational Corporations in the Evolution of a High-Tech Industry: The Case of India's Software Industry', *World Development*, 9: 1561–77.

Peters, E. and Hood, N. (2000) Implementing the Cluster Approach: Some Lessons from the Scottish Experience, *International Studies of Manufacturing and Organisation*, 2: 68–92.

Porter, M.E. (1990) *The Competitive Advantage of Nations*. New York: Free Press.

Porter, M.E. (1996) 'Competitive Advantage, Agglomeration Economies, and Regional Policy', *International Regional Science Review*, 1–2: 85–94.

Rees, J., Briggs, R. et al. (1984) 'The Adoption of New Technology in the American Machinery Industry', *Regional Studies*, 6: 489–504.

Rugman, A.M. and Verbeke, A. (1993) 'Foreign Subsidiaries and Multinational Strategic Management: An Extension and Correction of Porter's Single Diamond Framework', *Management International Review*, 2: 71–84.

Rugman, A.M. and Verbeke, A. (1993) 'How to Operationalize Porter's Diamond of Competitive Advantage', *International Executive*, 4: 283–99.

Rugman, A.M. and Verbeke, A. (2001) Subsidiary Specific Advantages in Multinational Enterprises, *Strategic Management Journal*, 3: 237–50.

San Diego Association of (SDAOF) (1999) *Understanding Cluster Analysis*. San Diego: San Diego Association of Governments.

Saxenian, A. (1994) *Regional Advantage: Culture and Competition in Silicon Valley and Route 128*. Cambridge: Harvard University Press.

Thwaites, A. (1982) 'Some Evidence of Regional Variations in the Diffusion of New Industrial Products and Processes within the British Manufacturing Industry', *Regional Studies*, 5: 371–81.

Van Den Bulcke, D. and Zhang, H. (1994) 'Belgian Equity Joint Ventures in China', in S. Stewart (ed.), *Joint ventures in the People's Republic of China*. Greenwich: JAI Press, pp. 147–61.

Van Den Bulcke, D. and Zhang, H. (2000) 'The restructuring of the Chinese automotive industry', in C. Millar, R. Grant and C.J. Choi (eds), *International Business Emerging Issues and Emerging Markets*. London: Palgrave Macmillan, pp. 290–312.

Van Den Bulcke, D., Zhang, H. and Esteves, M.D.C. (2003) *European Direct Investment in China*. Cheltenham: Edward Elgar.

Van Den Bulcke, D., Zhang, H. and Li, X. (1999) 'Interaction between the Business Environment and the Corporate Strategic Positioning in the Pharmaceutical Industry. A Study of the Entry and Expansion Path of MNEs into China', *Management International Review*, 4: 353–77.

Westney, E.D. (1990) 'Internal and External Linkages in the MNC: The Case of R&D Subsidiaries in Japan', in C. Barlett, Y. Doz and G. Hedlund (eds), *Managing the Global Firm*. London and New York: Routledge.

Young, S., Hood, N. et al. (1994) 'Multinational Enterprise and Regional Development', *Regional Studies*, 7: 657–77.

Zander, I. and Sölvell, Ö. (2000) 'Cross-Border Innovation in the Multinational Corporation: A Research Agenda', *International Studies of Management and Organisation*, 2: 44–67.

10
FDI Productivity Spillovers in the Andean Region: Econometric Evidence from Colombian Firm-Level Panel Data

Philippe De Lombaerde and Erika B. Pedraza Guevara

Introduction

In recent years, research on FDI spillovers in host countries has undergone substantial qualitative progress as it benefited from the increasing availability of firm-level data. These studies often relied on developing-country data, not only because of the fact that the productivity gap between domestic and foreign companies was expected to be larger there, but also for the (perhaps unexpected) reason that these countries often publish superior statistical data for this kind of research. From an academic point of view, however, the results have been rather deceiving. Whereas the previous cross-section estimations based on aggregate industry-level information tended to show evidence of positive effects of the presence of foreign firms and to confirm mainstream theory on FDI and TNCs in the tradition of Caves and Dunning,[1] more recent econometric studies using firm-level panel data have generally, and unexpectedly, not revealed sufficient evidence that allows us to state that domestic firms in developing countries increase their productivity levels in the presence of foreign firms. In some cases, even negative effects have been shown. This was the case, for example, in the work done by Aitken and Harrison (1999), using data from Venezuelan firms for the 1976–89 period. They found a negative relationship between the presence of FDI at the industry level and total factor productivity of local firms, although positive intra-firm effects were detected.

This is a particularly important result given the historically high degree of scepticism *vis-à-vis* FDI in the region and the current debate on the optimal level of economic openness in the context of globalization, in general, and the Free Trade Area of the Americas, in particular. In the following sections a short overview of the recent empirical research on productivity spillovers in developing countries will be presented, placing it in the context of FDI policies in the Andean region, and presenting new results on productivity spillovers using Colombian manufacturing firm-level panel data for the 1995–2000 period. We will test (1) whether foreign ownership is associated with an increase in productivity at the plant level, and (2) whether foreign ownership in an industrial sector affects the productivity of domestically owned firms in the same industry.

FDI productivity spillovers

The hypothesis of positive productivity spillovers is based on a set of arguments. Caves (1974) argued that domestic firms might benefit from inward FDI because of positive effects (1) from increased competition on resource-allocation efficiency, especially in industries characterized by high barriers-to-entry, (2) on the technical efficiency of local firms through backward or forward linkages with the foreign companies, and (3) on the adoption of new technologies.[2] Blomström and Kokko (1998) considered two broad modalities of spillover effects: (a) those related to factor productivity increases, and (b) those related to accessing third markets.

Productivity spillover effects are transmitted through various channels: (i) the effects generated by backward and forward linkages, (ii) the effects of labour mobility from foreign to domestic firms, (iii) the demonstration effects, and (iv) the competition effect (Blomström and Kokko, 1998).

As an *ex post* rationalization of their findings, Aitken and Harrison (1994) pointed to the possibility for foreign-owned companies to have a negative effect on the productivity levels of domestic firms. They showed that when in imperfect competition, domestic firms are facing fixed production costs; foreign companies can conquer part of the local demand, forcing the local firms to diminish their production and spread their fixed costs over a smaller market. As a result, if the negative effect on the domestic firms' productivity is greater than the benefits of knowledge and technology transfers from the foreign-owned companies, the net effect on productivity will be negative. This is shown in Figure 10.1. With the entrance of foreign companies, the average cost curve of the domestic plants falls from AC_0 to AC_1, because of positive spillovers. But, at the same time, the increased competition forces the domestic firms to reduce the scale of production, thus moving along the AC_1 curve back upwards. The net effect of FDI in the case shown in Figure 10.1, moving from A to B, is an increase in the average output cost.

In general, the more recent studies, using firm-level panel data, seem to suggest that indirect effects of FDI on productivity levels are not important or, at least, that they do not occur in all industries.

Using data from Venezuelan firms for the 1976–89 period, Aitken and Harrison (1999) found a negative relationship between the presence of FDI

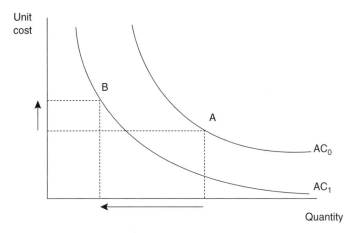

Figure 10.1   Output response of domestic firms to foreign entrants
Source: Aitken and Harrison (1999).

at the industry level and total factor productivity of local firms. However, they concluded that there are positive intra-firm effects given the fact that the productivity of foreign-owned firms seems to increase with the volume of foreign capital. These results varied systematically with plant size, the effect being more robust for small firms.

The research findings in the Venezuelan case are interesting to the extent that the authors controlled for inter-industry productivity differentials. Given the possibility (hypothesis) that foreign firms tend to prefer industries with higher productivity levels, the authors included this correlation in order not to bias the conclusions. In addition, estimations were performed in order to determine whether the effects of FDI were observable at the regional level. Again, they reached the conclusion that no important effects were caused by the presence of foreign firms.

Kokko (1994), using data for the Mexican manufacturing sector for 1970, suggested that the characteristics of the host country and host industry influence the generation of the spillover effects. According to this author, it is important to distinguish between industries where the foreign firms compete directly with the local firms, and those where positive spillovers can be expected, and also industries with enclave characteristics and few linkages with other firms. Kokko found positive spillovers in industries with moderate levels of FDI and moderate technology gaps between foreign and local firms.

In a study on the manufacturing industry in Uruguay, Kokko *et al.* (1996) obtained similar results. In contrast with previous work (Kokko, 1994), the authors established that the technological capacity at the firm-level is crucial for having positive spillovers. Kokko *et al.* (2001) showed further the importance of the trade regime for assessing FDI spillovers and found that productivity spillovers are more likely with FDI in periods of inward-oriented trade policies; whereas export spillovers are more likely with FDI in periods of outward orientation.

Other studies were carried out outside Latin America by Haddad and Harrison (1993), Barrios (2000), Barrios and Strobl (2002) and Sembenelli and Siotis (2002). Haddad and Harrison (1993) analysing manufacturing firms in Morocco over the period 1985–89, concluded that there is no evidence of a positive effect of FDI on productivity growth of domestic firms. However, they found a smaller dispersion of productivity levels *vis-à-vis* the most productive firm in the industries with a greater presence of foreign firms. Sjöholm (1997) examined the manufacturing industries in Indonesia, and demonstrated that local firms benefited from FDI, especially in sectors characterized by high levels of domestic competition. According to this author, it is in these cases that overseas headquarters decide to transfer more technology to their affiliates, which can give rise to more spillovers.

Barrios (2000), using Spanish data for the 1990–94 period, stated that it is not possible to identify positive effects for local firms and that they might even be negative in industries with low levels of R&D activity. Barrios and Strobl (2002) confirm that the absorptive capacity of local firms is crucial for positive spillover effects. Sembenelli and Siotis (2002) however, identifed, positive spillovers in knowledge-intensive industries in Spain.

Summing up, there is neither a consensus (yet) on FDI productivity spillovers to local firms, nor on the driving factors and the channels through which they are transmitted. It is clear that the characteristics of the host economies, the industries and the local firms should be taken into account.

Most of the previous studies have focused on intra-industry effects. An exception has to be made for Katz (1969),[3] who demonstrated that FDI in Argentina provoked technological changes, not only in the industries that received FDI but also in other industries. The reasons behind this were related to the specific quality standards, price and delivery of the products imposed by the transnationals.

More recent studies have also focused on vertical spillovers through vertical (usually backward) linkages. Kugler (2000) showed evidence of positive inter-industry spillovers for Colombia; López-Córdova and Mezquita (2002) identified positive spillovers for Mexico but negative ones for Brazil. Schoors and van der Tol (2001) for Hungary, and Smarzynska (2002) for Lithuania, also found positive inter-industry spillovers.

These studies still leave us, however, with a number of questions: Why is it that significant vertical spillovers can be found in the absence of horizontal spillovers? Is it that the evidence available so far on inter-industry spillovers is biased towards cases with moderate technology gaps and, therefore, relatively high absorption capacity? Are the potential positive effects for the domestic competitor in the case of sourcing from the same industry, not captured by the analysis? Is it because of the use of the productivity measures? Should we use competitiveness indicators instead?[4] Should the institutional arrangements, such as exclusive contracts between related firms, be included in the analysis?[5]

Finally, the ambiguous results of econometric studies based on firm-level data have also been reflected in cross-country estimations of the relationship between FDI and economic growth (Borensztein *et al.*, 1998; Carkovic and Levine, 2000).[6]

The fact that spillovers are not automatic consequences of foreign direct investment, is the main reason why investment incentives focusing exclusively on foreign companies are not to be recommended from a national welfare point of view (Blomström and Kokko, 2003). At least, accompanying measures will be needed, oriented towards strengthening the capacity to absorb technological knowledge and skills.

FDI policies in the Andean region

FDI policies in the Andean region have followed a pendular movement between the open (liberal) and closed (protectionist, nationalist) models. From initially rather restrictive policies there was a move towards more open policies in the first phase of import-substitution policies when FDI was seen as complementary to industrial policy and a source of financial and technological resources to sustain the industrialization processes. This was followed by a more sceptical and nationalist view of FDI policies towards the end of the 1960s. Right from the start of the Andean integration process, the countries involved have opted for a common FDI policy, which adds to the interest of the Andean case (Van Den Bulcke 1977). The common regime was made possible because of a *de facto* convergence of the economic policy models in the different countries. The larger countries of the Latin American subcontinent (Argentina, Brazil, Mexico, Colombia) had adopted inward-looking policies before the smaller countries did. Towards the end of the 1980s, finally, policies moved back in the direction of liberalization.[7]

Both in the protectionist period of the 1970s, as in the liberal period of the 1990s, the region developed regulatory models that influenced and were sometimes copied by other developing countries. The legislation of the Andean Common Market was at the forefront of rule-making in a developing-country context. The Cartagena Agreement was signed in 1969 when the dominating development model followed by the Latin American countries since the end of the 1950s pursued import substitution industrialization (ISI). The agreement sought a common industrialization strategy for the member countries, consisting of a harmonization of trade, exchange rate, monetary, fiscal and foreign investment policies.

Decision 24 of the Council of the Cartagena Agreement of 1971 established a common foreign investment regime,[8] the principal elements of which were the following:

- Obligatory authorization and registration of each investment project by the competent national authority.
- Prohibition of FDI in communications, infrastructure, electricity, public services, waste collection and the financial sector.
- Restrictions on the authorization of FDI in those sectors where foreign firms would enter to compete with the domestic ones.
- Prohibition of takeovers of existing national firms, except for very specific circumstances, like for example a risk of bankruptcy of the domestic company.
- Restriction of access to official long-term credits for foreign companies.
- Compulsory and programmed transformation of foreign companies into national or mixed companies during in a time span of 15 years (the rule) or 20 years (the exception, applying to Bolivia and Ecuador); for existing companies foreign participation had to be brought down to a maximum of 85 per cent within three years, and a maximum of 55 per cent within ten years; new companies should have a minimum 15 per cent of national capital at the moment of their creation (see Figure 10.2).
- Non-application of trade preferences derived from the Agreement to goods produced by foreign companies, for those companies that fail to comply with the programmed ownership transformation plan.
- Free repatriation of utilities up to 14 per cent of the invested capital,[9] and free repatriation of capital.

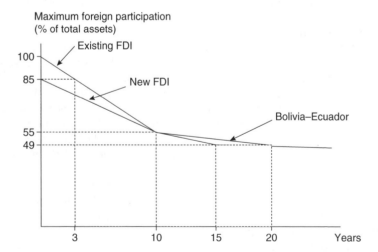

Figure 10.2 Programmed transformation of foreign firms: decision 24 of the Andean Pact

Colombia implemented this Decision through Decree-Law 1900 of 1973, and later complemented it using the "Exchange Statute" as a model (Decree 444 of 1967). The latter decree established strict exchange controls and intervention mechanisms for FDI.

In 1971, a specific regime was also established for Andean transnationals by Decision 48 of the Andean Group. This regime provided for certain benefits for transnational companies with capital from Andean countries, with the objective of supporting the import-substitution process in sectors such as: chemicals, petrochemicals, fertilizers, automobiles, electronics and metallurgy. The Latin American Economic System (SELA) broadened this regime towards Latin American transnationals in 1975. The Andean regime was replaced by the Uniform Regime for Andean Multinational Companies as stated in Decision 292 in the framework of the Cartagena Agreement of 1991. A number of companies have been set up under this regime but its relative benefits were strongly diluted. All in all, these specific regimes have not been all that important for the development of Latin American transnational corporations (Franco and De Lombaerde, 2003).

A confluence of factors in the 1980s led to a reorientation of FDI policies in the region. Countries faced massive capital outflow and sharp foreign exchange restrictions, and in addition it became clear that the integration process, as a development strategy, showed poor results (Reina and Zuluaga, 1998).

Decision 220 of 1987 replaced Decision 24 and its related decisions. It gave each country a certain autonomy in the design of its FDI policies. The requirements, according to which foreign firms could associate themselves with local firms and benefit from the trade-liberalization programme, were made more flexible. The list of restricted industries for FDI was abolished and it was left for the consideration of each member state to take measures related to profit remittances.[10]

By the end of the 1980s and the beginning of the 1990s, the Andean region adopted a new development model based on the opening up (*apertura*) of the economy and the implementation of structural reform programmes. It is in this context that investment regimes, foreign capital markets and exchange markets were liberalized (OECD, 1999; Agosín, 1996; Anzola, 1997).

Decisions 291 and 292 adopted in 1991 by the Andean countries liberalized the FDI regime and eliminated the discrimination between foreign and national investors. Goods produced by foreign firms were entitled to fully benefit from the trade liberalization programme. The new Andean regulatory measures left the individual countries with the possibility to further deepen the liberalization of the FDI regime. Colombia decided to reform its FDI legislation in 1991 in order to attract more investment from abroad (Law 9 of 1991 on the Exchange Regime, further regulated by the Statute of Foreign Investment, Resolution 51 of 1991).

Among the more recent measures, Decree 2080 of 2000 might be mentioned. This decree seeks to further expand FDI, facilitating capital mobility and simplifying administrative procedures, especially in the area of financial investment and the operation of investment funds in Colombia. The general principle of the new Statute is that of equal treatment of foreign and national capital (Cubillos and Navas, 2000; De Lombaerde and Lizarazo, 2001). The decree establishes the possibility to invest in all sectors of the economy, with the exception of defense, national security and toxic wastes. Authorization is only needed in the financial sector, the stockmarket and the oil sector. The only remaining obligation for most of the FDI is to register with the central bank (*Banco de la República*) (DNP, 2001).

The changes in the FDI regime of the region have had a visible impact on FDI inflows from the rest of the world (Table 10.1).[11] If the second half of the 1980s is compared with the second half of the 1990s, FDI inflows as a percentage of GDP almost doubled in the Andean Community. Colombia is the exception here, for two reasons: first, an important rise in FDI was already registered just before 1995, and, second, the negative influence of the continuing internal political conflict in the country. The figure for Chile is relatively high but stable, explained by the fact that Chile had already liberalized its FDI policy in the 1970s. Argentina is a similar case.

Given the depth of the restructuring policies and *apertura* programme, on the one hand, and the particular history of FDI policies in the region, on the other hand, it is timely to further analyse the effects of FDI on economic development. The ambiguous effect of liberalizing trade and investment on industry concentration might represent an additional argument in favour of not neglecting the possibility of negative spillovers (De Lombaerde, 2004).

Table 10.1   FDI inflows in Latin America (% of GDP)

	1985–90	*1995–2000*
Andean Community	1.08	1.96
Bolivia	0.71	4.57
Colombia	2.70	1.61
Ecuador	1.31	1.79
Peru	0.17	2.21
Venezuela	0.28	2.00
CARICOM	0.71	3.16
CACM	1.55	1.22
MERCOSUR	0.73	1.37
Mexico	1.68	1.59
Chile	3.76	3.69

Source: Inter-American Development Bank calculations based on IMF, International Financial Statistics and World Bank, World Development Indicators as cited in Stein *et al.* (2002: 225).

Empirical evidence on FDI spillovers for Colombia, using firm-level data

In this section, new econometric results are presented about the existence of (positive) productivity spillovers in the Colombian manufacturing industries, using firm-level data.

Comparing productivity levels: foreign affiliates versus local firms

As an initial assessment, we compared productivity indicators of foreign and domestic companies using firm-level data from the DANE Annual Manufacturing Survey (AMS) for the 1995–99 period. We calculated labour productivity, capital/labour ratios, unit remuneration, and the unit labour cost.[12]

The results are presented in Table 10.2.[13] They are shown as ratios of the average indicator for the foreign firms over the average for the local firms.[14] A value of 2 for labour productivity, for example, indicates that the foreign affiliates obtained productivity levels twice as high as the competing local firms. The general conclusion is that foreign affiliates are more productive than local ones. Foreign affiliates are also more capital-intensive than local firms, which confirms previous studies on Colombia's manufacturing industry (Misas, 1993; Agudelo and Silva, 1996). Likewise, foreign affiliates show higher average levels of labour productivity. Only for the leather sector do local firms seem to be more productive than their foreign counterparts. Foreign affiliates also exhibit higher unit remuneration, which is consistent with Misas' observations (Misas, 1993). Finally, foreign-owned companies operate with lower unit labour costs than local companies.

This general result of higher productivity levels for foreign affiliates suggests that there might be scope for positive productivity spillovers. This will be tested in the following sections.

Sample

The firm-level data used for the estimations were obtained from the *Superintendencia de Sociedades* (Superintendence of Companies) for the period 1995–2000. The information from this source consisted of accounting information, and consequently made it necessary to first calculate the economic variables to be included in the econometric model.[15]

Starting with an initial sample of about 2,000 firms, due to problems of availability and consistency of the data, 1,533 manufacturing firms were finally selected. Foreign firms are defined as those firms that register any foreign ownership superior to 0 per cent,[16] and this discrimination was based on the same data source. According to this definition, 23 per cent of the firms in the sample were called 'firms with FDI' or 'foreign firms', the remaining 77 per cent 'local firms'.

Table 10.2   Comparison of productivity indicators in Colombia, 1995–99

ISIC	Manufacturing sectors	PL^a	UR^a	K/L^a	ULC^a
311	Food	1.73*	1.22	1.46	0.77*
312	Other food	2.50*	1.39*	3.11*	0.84
313	Beverages	1.49	1.01	1.76*	0.62*
321	Textiles	1.72*	1.22*	1.29	0.71*
322	Garments	1.57*	1.24*	1.74	0.95
323	Leather products	0.68*	1.18	1.10	1.82*
324	Footwear	1.32*	1.41*	1.71*	1.07
331	Wooden products	1.21	1.24*	1.10	1.18
332	Furniture etc.	2.35*	1.49*	2.84*	0.62*
341	Wood pulp, paper and cardboard	1.40*	1.28*	1.60	0.94
342	Printing and editorials	1.51*	1.10	1.13	0.80*
351	Industrial chemical substances	2.66*	1.38*	2.98*	0.58*
352	Pharmaceuticals, soaps	2.27*	1.68*	2.80*	0.84
354	Derivatives of oil and coal	1.66	2.02*	2.36*	1.37
355	Rubber products	2.00*	1.54	3.23	0.74*
356	Plastic products	1.94*	1.31	2.65*	0.69*
361	Objects of clay, porcelain, etc.	1.23	1.08	1.77*	0.63
362	Glass	3.37*	1.85*	4.54*	0.55*
369	Non-metal mineral products	1.89*	1.30*	2.24*	0.59*
371	Basic iron and steel industry	2.65*	1.63*	3.69*	0.57*
372	Basic manufacturing of non-ferrous metals	1.07	1.27*	1.52	0.92
381	Metal products, except machines and equipment	2.01*	1.37*	1.91*	0.74*
382	Machines, except electrical	1.62*	1.31*	1.93*	0.87
383	Electrical machines and equipment	2.23*	1.87*	2.42*	0.93
384	Transportation material	2.76*	1.44*	1.66*	0.47*
385	Professional and scientific material	3.71*	1.49*	2.22*	0.51*
390	Other manufacturing industries	1.60*	1.47*	1.19	0.99

Notes: [a] PL = productivity of labour, UR = unit remuneration, K/L = capital/labour ratio, ULC = unit labour cost. Ratios are of average performance of foreign affiliates over average performance of local firms.
* indicate that differences between averages are statistically significant at the 5% level.

Source: Authors' calculations based on Annual Manufacturing Survey, DANE.

The sample of the *Superintendencia de Sociedades* has certain particularities. First, the companies included are mostly large, given the fact that the Superintendencia has a controlling function over large companies.[17] Second, those companies included have mainly the legal status of 'sociedad limitada' or 'sociedad anónima'. Companies with financial activities are excluded.

Using the AMS criteria to classify the companies by size, 19 per cent are classified as large companies (≥200 employees), 47 per cent as medium-sized (51–199 employees), and 34 per cent as small (10–50 employed). The most important subsectors (ISIC Rev 2) represented in the sample, were pharmaceuticals (18.44 per cent of the total number of companies), industrial chemical substances (8.07 per cent), food (7.49 per cent), plastic products (7.49 per cent), and metal products, except machines and equipment (6.34 per cent). Of the 346 firms with FDI, two thirds (65.5 per cent) have a majority foreign capital stake (>50 per cent of assets).[18]

The sample is representative of the survey population. The 1533 firms represent on average 65 per cent of total sales registered in the AMS for the 1995–99 period.

Model estimation

The econometric model that we estimated is similar to those used by Haddad and Harrison (1993), Aitken and Harrison (1999) and Barrios (2000). A log-linear production function was estimated, in which the production level is modelled as a function of its inputs (capital and labour) and variables that measure the presence of FDI within the firm and in each manufacturing subsector. Answers to two questions are sought: (1) Is foreign ownership of a firm positively associated with its productivity?, and (2) Is foreign ownership in a sector related to productivity levels of local firms competing in the same sector through positive spillover effects? Both hypotheses can be tested estimating the following equation with balanced panel data:[19]

$$Y_{ijt} = C + B_1 \, FDI\_Firm_{ijt} + B_2 \, FDI\_Sector_{jt} + B_3 \, L_{ijt} + B_4 \, K_{ijt} + e_{ijt} \qquad (10.1)$$

where, Y_{ijt} = (logarithm) production (sales + change in stocks,) of firm i in sector j in year t; FDI_Firm_{ijt} = foreign participation in total assets of firm i in sector j in year t; FDI_Sector_{jt} = foreign participation in sector j; K_{ijt} = stock of fixed assets of firm i in sector j in year t; and L_{ijt} = number of employed, both permanent and temporal, in firm i in sector j in year t.

FDI_Sector was calculated as the level of foreign direct investment in total fixed assets of the sector:

$$FDI\_Sector_{jt} = \frac{\sum_i FDI\_Firm_{ijt} \times Fixed\_Assets_{ijt}}{\sum_i Fixed\_Assets_{ijt}} \qquad (10.2)$$

The use of alternative variables to measure the presence of FDI at the sectoral level did not reveal important changes in the estimation results.[20] All nominal values were deflated by the sectoral 3-digit PPI (base year = 2000). In addition, all estimations with panel data included time dummies to capture business-cycle effects.

Confirmation of our hypotheses would require significant positive coefficients for variables *FDI_Firm* and *FDI_Sector* in equation [10.1]. The results of the estimations with the fixed-effects model are presented in Table 10.3. The

Table 10.3 Impact of FDI on total productivity

	Fixed effects			
	All firms		All local firms	
	FDI_Sector with Assets variable	FDI_Sector with Sales variable	FDI_Sector with Assets variable	FDI_Sector with Sales variable
FDI_Firm	0.0003049	0.0003411		
	(0.0007259)	(0.0007163)		
FDI_Sector	0.0044238*	0.0041646*	0.0047066*	0.0022916
	(0.0010281)	(0.0013347)	(0.0012399)	(0.001616)
Log_L	0.5418639*	0.5432312*	0.5561922*	0.5567935*
	(0.0180778)	(0.0180934)	(0.020538)	(0.0206077)
Log_K	0.118925*	0.1189663*	0.1101904*	0.1110921*
	(0.0143952)	(0.0145093)	(0.0179037)	(0.0180986)
R^2	0.66	0.65	0.60	0.60
F-test for firm-specific effects	33.27	33.15	30.98	30.93
	(0.0000)	(0.0000)	(0.0000)	(0.0000)
Hausman test	423.67	448.92	230.40	241.66
	(0.0000)	(0.0000)	(0.0000)	(0.0000)
Number of observations	9,198	9,198	7,122	7,122

Notes: Estimation period was 1995–2000. All estimations included time dummies and intercept terms, not reported here. Standard errors (between brackets) are corrected for heteroscedasticity. * = significant at 1% level. The *F*-test suggests that specific firm-level effects exist. The Hausman test compares the fixed effects model with the variable effects model.

table contains results for the totality of the firms and for the subgroup of local firms.[21]

The coefficient for *FDI_Firm* suggests that an increase of foreign ownership in a firm, from 0 to 100 per cent, increases its production by 0.03 per cent. However, the coefficient is not statistically significant so that there is very weak evidence that firms that receive FDI benefit from it.

On the other hand, the coefficient for *FDI_Sector* is positive and statistically significant, although very small. An increase of 10 per cent in foreign participation in a sector would augment the production of local firms by 0.04 per cent, *ceteris paribus*.

The coefficients for the variables *Log_L* and *Log_K* have the expected positive signs and are statistically significant. The effects of *FDI_Sector* continue to be positive and small if we limit the estimation to local firms without FDI. The value of the coefficients is very similar although it is only statistically significant when the assets variable is used for the measurement of the sectoral FDI presence.

The low value and lack of statistical significance of the *FDI_Firm* variable is surprising, given the evidence of superior productivity of foreign affiliates (see above). Nevertheless, other empirical studies also revealed mixed and unclear results. For example, whereas the value for this coefficient was 10.5 per cent and statistically significant for Venezuela, in Spain it was 0.1 per cent and not significant.[22]

One possible explanation for these differences in the results might be related to the different types of samples that were used. As was mentioned before, the sample of firms controlled by the *Superintendencia de Sociedades* is biased in terms of scale and legal type of company. The results might also be explained by the way in which foreign involvement is measured. Instead of using foreign ownership (expressed as a percentage of total assets), it might be necessary to directly measure foreign involvement in the management of the affiliate (flows of knowledge and experience), and the type and intensity of institutional arrangements and/or technological dependence between affiliates and headquarters. Finally, it might also be necessary to consider longer periods of time so that learning curve effects may be measured.

As far as the FDI spillover effects are concerned, the studies performed with aggregate data and cross-section estimations found evidence that the presence of foreign companies is beneficial for the domestic firms. On the other hand, the estimations with firm-level panel data revealed less positive conclusions. The study on Venezuela found a significant negative coefficient for the FDI_Sector variable (-2.67 per cent), the one on Morocco a negative but not significant coefficient (-0.3 per cent), whereas the study on Spain revealed a small but insignificant effect, with changing signs according to the model specification (around 0.001 per cent in absolute terms). Our results thus seem to confirm the weak evidence of positive productivity spillovers from FDI.

These results were also confirmed by the separate estimates for subsamples of firms, classified according to size. These estimates, which will not be presented in detail here, did not result in statistically significant coefficients for the FDI_Firm variable; they were positive for large and medium-sized firms, but negative for small firms.

The coefficients showing the spillover effects (FDI_Sector) continued to be significant in most cases, although they were not important in magnitude. Certain variations were observed with varying measurements of foreign participation (assets *versus* sales).[23]

'Better' results with the sales variable suggest that the effect of FDI on competition levels might be crucial for explaining positive spillovers. Further research, involving direct measurements of the effect of FDI policies on the level and nature of competition, would be needed on this point.[24]

A number of authors have pointed out that positive FDI spillovers are more likely when local firms have the management and production capacity to absorb them, and/or when the technological knowledge gap is not too important (Kokko, 1994; Kokko *et al.*, 1996; Barrios, 2000). In order to check these results, separate estimates were performed for subsamples with high and low labour productivity levels. We found that the existence of significant positive spillovers is limited to the case of sectors with higher productivity levels. The value of the coefficient for FDI_Sector (0.006) was close to the value in Table 10.3 and appeared to be statistically significant.

Finally, our results showing the small magnitude of the spillovers are consistent with the conclusions obtained by Steiner and Giedion (1995) in their qualitative assessment of FDI in Colombian manufacturing industries.[25] They found that the manufacturing firms with foreign participation make apparently little effort to transfer and diffuse technology, not even internally, in spite of the fact that foreign affiliates consider that one of their principle advantages *vis-à-vis* local firms is the possession of technological resources.

Conclusions

FDI policies have been much debated in the Andean region. The postwar period shows a pendular movement of FDI policies between the open liberal model, on the one hand, and the inward-looking nationalist model, on the other. The deregulation of the FDI policy regime in the Andean countries in the beginning of the 1990s has had a clear positive impact on the volume of incoming FDI flows in the region. And although there are good theoretical reasons to believe that FDI generates positive spillover effects for domestic firms, estimates using firm-level panel data do not necessarily reveal their existence. As a result this, in turn, might again foster a more critical stance towards FDI and capital flows in the region. This is of particular importance in the light of the ongoing negotiations of the Free Trade Area of the Americas.

As previous estimates with Venezuelan data have suggested, negative spillovers are not impossible. When Colombian data are used, the econometric results show no or very weak (and insignificant) spillover effects. If positive effects on the productivity of domestic firms are found at all, they are apparently completely absorbed by the most productive domestic firms.

Positive productivity spillovers should thus not be taken for granted, or at least not be overestimated. Based on the evidence presented here, including the estimates with sub-samples, the following conclusions can be drawn:

- The informative and explanatory capacity of other measures of the importance of FDI at the firm or industry level, instead of stakeholder participation, should be explored.
- Both the empirical and theoretical work on inter-industry spillovers in the supply chain should be continued and refined.
- Related to this, international (border-crossing) supply chains and international spillovers deserve specific attention.[26]

- Further analysis is required about the determinants of the absorptive capacity of (local) firms.
- Further analysis about the macro-institutional context of spillovers: contractual relations between companies, intellectual-property-rights regimes, and financial markets.
- The same holds for the micro-institutional context: implications of new organization principles and the tendency towards more flexible production networks working on a project basis with short time horizons.
- Qualitative variables might be used to capture institutional characteristics in the econometric models.
- A more thorough analysis is still required on the policy context: trade and FDI policy regimes at the national, regional and multilateral levels.
- Cross-section and panel-data approaches should be combined with approaches based on longer time series, so that learning effects can be detected.
- Although little attention was devoted to the policy implications of the findings, there are important implications: Should/can measures be taken to maximize positive spillovers? Given the fact that FDI spillovers are apparently mostly absorbed by the most productive domestic firms, should policies that seek to close the widening gap between high and low technology-intensive firms (and sectors) be considered?
- Finally, the future role of the macro-regional level in governing capital flows, in general, and FDI, in particular, should be discussed. This is of particular interest to the Andean region where different strategic options in terms of regional integration, all of which have implications for the FDI regime, are still open to discussion (CAN, CAN-Mercosur, G-3, FTAA, CAN-EU, ...).

Notes

1 These studies include: Caves (1974), with data for Australia's manufacturing sector in 1966; Globerman (1979), with Canadian data for 1972; Blomström and Persson (1983) and Blomström and Wolff (1994), with data on the Mexican manufacturing sector for the 1970–75 period; and Nadiri (1991), with data on North-American investment in France, Germany, Japan and the UK (see also Blomström and Kokko, 1996).
2 On the latter point, see also Blomström and Wolf (1994).
3 See also Blomström and Kokko (1996).
4 Using competitiveness indicators would allow us to consider and capture situations in which domestic competitors indirectly benefit from vertical spillovers through backward linkages of the foreign firm, improving their competitiveness (lower prices thanks to cheaper inputs), while leaving their productivity levels unchanged or even worse off (because of the combination of lower prices and unchanged factor costs and technologies).
5 On the role of financial institutions as catalysts of knowledge spillovers for FDI, see Alfaro *et al.* (2003).

 6   Borensztein *et al.* (1998) point also to the crucial role of the absorption capacity in the host countries.
 7   See e.g. Bulmer-Thomas (1998: chapter IX). See also Van Den Bulcke (1988) for a general perspective.
 8   Foreign firms were defined as firms with foreign ownership of total capital of more than 49%. Mixed companies were defined as companies with a participation of foreign shareholders between 20 and 49%, and national companies as those with 20% or less of foreign participation. For an early discussion of the common FDI regime incorporated in Decision 24, see Tironi (1978).
 9   Later, this percentage has been raised to 20% by Decision 103.
10   In Colombia, this Decision was adopted through Resolution 49 of 1989.
11   See also Agosín (1996).
12   The indicators were calculated by manufacturing establishment, but because of the statistical secrecy obligation, we were not given access to the results at that level. It was necessary to aggregate the results by industrial sector at the 3-digit level ISIC Rev. 2.
13   For a discrimination of the comparisons by firm size, see Pedraza (2003).
14   Foreign firms were defined here as companies with a positive (>0%) ratio of foreign capital.
15   The firm-level data from the Annual Manufacturing Survey (DANE) are not available for the public, only on an aggregated level. This would however be an interesting alternative source of information on firms, and would also permit analysis of spillover effects via vertical linkages. A disclosure of the information by the authorities is a necessary prerequisite.
16   This definition of foreign firms was also used in Aitken and Harrison (1999) for Venezuela. However, other criteria of more than 0% of foreign ownership have also been used (>5% or >10% of total assets), without altering the conclusions; see Pedraza (2002).
17   See Decree 3100 of 1997.
18   See also Misas (1993) and Steiner and Giedion (1995).
19   The principal advantage of panel estimation is its capacity to control for the presence of specific (individual or group) effects, which is not the case in cross-section estimations. In all estimations that were performed here, specific firm effects were detected.
20   In the empirical literature there does not seem to exist a consensus on which is the 'right' variable to measure sectoral foreign participation. Assets, value added, production, sales and employment have all been used. We also performed estimations with assets and employment.
21   Fixed-effects models assume that specific effects for each group can be modelled as a specific constant term for each group in the regression model. The variable-effects approach considers specific error terms per group (Green, 1999). Equation [10.1] has been estimated with the two approaches (fixed and variable effects). Hausman tests revealed that all estimations with the variable-effects model were statistically inconsistent (evidence of correlation between explanatory variables and specific firm-level effects); consequently, estimations with the fixed effects model were preferred.
22   Blömstrom and Sjöholm (1999), and Haddad and Harrison (1993) also failed to find significant positive coefficients for the *FDI_Firm* variable.
23   See Pedraza (2002).
24   On the nexus between *apertura* and industrial concentration in Colombia, see De Lombaerde (2004).

25 Steiner and Giedion (1995) report on the results of a questionnaire among foreign-owned firms based in Colombia; they analysed the determinants of FDI and the contribution of foreign firms to development and the transfer of technology.
26 Lall (1995: 17) suggests that spillover effects might be reduced by the expansion of globally integrated production patterns.

References

Agosín, M.R. (1996) 'El retorno de la inversión extranjera a América Latina', in M.R. Agosín (ed.), *Foreign Direct Investment in Latin America*, BID y Universidad de Chile, Washington, DC, pp. 1–45.

Agudelo, M.I. and Silva, J.M. (1996) 'Inversión Extranjera y Desempeño de la Industria Colombiana', Masters thesis. Bogotá: Universidad Nacional de Colombia.

Aitken, B. and Harrison, A. (1994) 'Do Domestic Firms Benefit from Foreign Direct Investment? Evidence from Panel Data', *Policy Research Working Paper* No. 1248. Washington, DC: The World Bank.

Aitken, B. and Harrison, A. (1999) 'Do Domestic Firms Benefit from Direct Foreign Investment? Evidence from Venezuela', *American Economic Review*, 89(3): 605–18.

Alfaro, L., Chanda, A., Kalemli-Özcan, Ş and Sayek, S. (2003) '*FDI Spillovers, Financial Markets, and Economic Development*', *IMF Working Paper* No. WP/03/186. Washington, DC: IMF.

Anzola, M. (1997) 'Las normas de inversión en el marco de la Comunidad Andina y G-3', in P. De Lombaerde (ed.), *La Inversión Extranjera en Colombia. Régimen Jurídico y Análisis Económico*. Bogotá: Universidad Sergio Arboleda, pp. 47–91.

Barrios, S. (2000) 'Foreign Direct Investment and Productivity Spillovers, Evidence from the Spanish Experience', *Working paper* 86. Madrid: Fundación de Estudios de Economía Aplicada (FEDEA).

Barrios, S. and Strobl, E. (2002) 'Foreign Direct Investment and Productivity Spillovers: Evidence from the Spanish Experience', *Weltwirtschaftliches Archiv*, 138(3): 459–81.

Blomström, M. and Persson, H. (1983) 'Foreign Investment and Spillover Efficiency in an Underdeveloped Economy: Evidence from the Mexican Manufacturing Industry', *World Development*, 11(6): 493–501.

Blomström, M. and Kokko, A. (1996) 'The Impact of Foreign Investment on Host Countries: A Review of Empirical Evidence', *World Bank Working Papers*. Washington, DC: The World Bank.

Blomström, M. and Kokko, A. (1998) 'Multinational Corporations and Spillovers', *Journal of Economic Surveys*, 12(2): 1–31.

Blomström, M. and Kokko, A. (2003) 'The Economics of Foreign Direct Investment Incentives', *CEPR Discussion Papers* No. 3775. London: Centre for Economic Policy Research.

Blomström, M. and Sjöholm, F. (1999) 'Technology Transfer and Pullovers: Does Local Participation in Multinationals Matter?', *European Economic Review*, 43(4/6): 915–23.

Blomström, M. and Wolff, E. (1994) 'Multinational Corporations and Productivity Convergence in Mexico', in W. Baumol, R. Nelson and E. Wolff (eds), *Convergence of Productivity: Cross-National Studies and Historical Evidence*. Oxford: Oxford University Press.

Borensztein, E., De Gregorio, J. and Lee, J.-W. (1998) 'How Does Foreign Direct Investment Affect Economic Growth?', *Journal of International Economics*, 45: 115–35.

Bulmer-Thomas, V. (1998) *La historia económica de América Latina desde la independencia*. Mexico: Fondo Económico de Cultura.

Carkovic, M. and Levine, R. (2000) 'Does Foreign Direct Investment Accelerate Economic Growth?', *Working Paper*, University of Minnesota.

Caves, R.E. (1974) 'Multinational Firms, Competition, and Productivity in Host Country Markets', *Economica*, 41(162): 176–93.

Cubillos, M. and Navas, V. (2000) *Inversión Extranjera Directa en Colombia: Características y Tendencias*. Bogotá: Departamento Nacional de Planeación.

De Lombaerde, P. and Lizarazo, C. (2001) 'Comercio Exterior e Inversión Extranjera', in L.A. Restrepo Moreno (ed.), *Síntesis 2001. Anuario Social, Político y Económico de Colombia*, IEPRI, Tercer Mundo Editores, Bogotá.

De Lombaerde, P. (2004) 'Liberación comercial, concentración industrial y política de competencia en Colombia', in M. Anzola and C.L. Lizarazo (eds), *Regulación Económica: Tendencias y Desafíos*, Universidad del Rosario-Temis, Bogotá.

Franco, A. and De Lombaerde, P. (2003) 'Latin American Multinationals: A Historical and Theoretical Approach', *Global Economic Review*, 32(1): 81–102.

Globerman, S. (1979) 'Foreign Direct Investment and Spillover Efficiency Benefits in Canadian Manufacturing Industries', *Canadian Journal of Economics*, 12(1): 42–56.

Greene, W. (1999) *Análisis Econométrico*. Madrid: Prentice-Hall Iberia.

Haddad, M. and Harrison, A.E. (1993) 'Are There Positive Spillovers from Direct Foreign Investment? Evidence from Panel Data for Morocco', *Journal of Development Economics*, 42: 51–74.

Katz, J.M. (1969) *Production Functions, Foreign Investment and Growth*. Amsterdam: North Holland.

Kokko, A. (1994) 'Technology, Market Characteristics and Pullovers', *Journal of Development Economics*, 43(2): 279–93.

Kokko, A., Tansini, R. and Zejan, M. (1996) 'Local Technological Capability and Spillovers from FDI in the Uruguayan Manufacturing Sector', *Journal of Development Studies*, 34(4): 602–11.

Kokko, A., Tansini, R. and Zejan, M. (2001) 'Trade Regimes and Spillover Effects of FDI: Evidence from Uruguay', *Weltwirtschaftliches Archiv*, 137(1): 124–49.

Kugler, M. (2000) 'The Diffusion of Externalities from Foreign Direct Investment', *Discussion Papers in Economics and Econometrics*, University of Southhampton, November.

Lall, S. (1995) 'Changing Perceptions of Direct Foreign Investment in Developing Countries', *CIMDA Discussion Papers* E/19. Antwerp: Centre for International Management and Development, University of Antwerp.

López-Córdova, E. and Mezsquita Moreira, M. (2002) 'Regional Integration and Productivity', in IADB, *Beyond Borders. The New Regionalism in Latin America*. Washington DC: Inter-American Development Bank, pp. 245–68.

Misas, G. (1993) 'El Papel de las Empresas Trasnacionales en la Reestructuración Industrial de Colombia: Una Síntesis', *Estudios e Informes de la CEPAL* 90. Santiago de Chile: CEPAL.

Nadiri, M. (1991) *U.S. Direct Investment and the Production Structure of the Manufacturing Sector in France, Germany, Japan and the U.K.* Washington, DC: NBER.

Organization for Economic Cooperation and Development (1999) *Política y promoción de la inversión extranjera directa en América Latina*, Proceedings. Paris: OECD.

Pedraza, E.B. (2002) *Efectos indirectos de la inversión extranjera directa: evidencia para la economía colombiana*, Master thesis. Bogotá: Faculty of Economics, Universidad Nacional de Colombia.

Pedraza, E.B. (2003) 'Desempeño económico por tipo de firma: Empresas nacionales vs. grandes y pequeñas receptoras de inversión extranjera', *Archivos de Economía*, (225).

Reina, M. and Zuluaga, S. (1998) *Colombia: siete años de apertura a la inversión extranjera 1991–1997*, Bogotá: Coinvertir-Fedesarrollo.

Schoors, K. and van der Tol, B. (2001) 'The Productivity Effect of Foreign Ownership on Domestic Firms in Hungary', *Working Paper*. Ghent: University of Ghent.

Sembenelli, A. and Siotis, G. (2002) 'Foreign Direct Investment, Competitive Pressure and Spillovers: An Empirical Analysis on Spanish Firm Level Data', *Working Paper* 169. Milano: Centro Studi Luca d'Agliano Development Studies (169).

Sjöholm, F. (1997) 'Technology Gap, Competition and Spillovers from Direct Foreign Investment: Evidence from Establishment Data', *Working Paper Series in Economics and Finance*, no. 211.

Smarzynska, B.K. (2002) 'Does Foreign Direct Investment Increase the Productivity of Domestic Firms? In Search of Spillovers through Backward Linkages', *Working Paper*. Washington, DC: The World Bank.

Stein, E., Daude, C., Meardon, S. and Levy Yeyati, E. (2002) 'Regional Integration and Foreign Direct Investment', in IADB, *Beyond Borders. The New Regionalism in Latin America*. Washington, DC: Inter-American Development Bank, pp. 223–44.

Steiner, R., and Giedion, U. (1995) 'Characteristics, Determinants and Effects of Foreign Direct Investment in Colombia', in M.R. Agosin (ed.) *Foreign Direct Investment in Latin America*. Washington, DC: BID – Universidad de Chile.

Tironi, E. (1978) 'Políticas frente al capital extranjero: la Decisión 24', in E. Tironi (ed.), *Pacto Andino. Carácter y Perspectivas*, Lima: Instituto de Estudios Peruanos, pp. 71–110.

Van Den Bulcke, D. (1977) 'Rol van de Buitenlandse Directe Investeringen in de Economische Integratieprojecten van de Ontwikkelingslanden', in K. Steel, D. Van Den Bulcke and C. Van Der Vaeren (eds), *Buitenlandse Handel, Hulp, Investeringen en Regionale Integratie in de Derde Wereld*, Ghent: UVOS, pp. 295–360.

Van Den Bulcke, D. (1988) 'Entreprises multinationales et pays en voie de développement: vers une déréglementation?', *Revue Tiers Monde*, XXIX (113): 27–51.

11
The Multinationalization of Privatized Firms: The Case of the Main Spanish Multinationals in Latin America

Juan J. Durán

Introduction

Foreign direct investment (FDI) differs, not only from the point of view of sectors of activity but also from the geographical areas of origin and destination of such investments. These processes are related, among others, to technological progress, to institutional changes and to cultural distance between home and host countries. The internationalization of sectors has taken place gradually: first natural resources and infrastructure, later manufacturing and commerce, followed by business services (financial, accounting, advertising, ...), construction and tourism, and finally so-called public utilities (energy, telecommunication, water). The developed countries were the main actors leading the process (not only from the point of view of outward direct investment but also from the inward perspective), in particular the Triad countries and to a lesser extent the less developed countries (mostly emerging countries).

The existence of a systematic relationship between the degree of internationalization of firms in an economy (as measured by influx and outflow of direct investment) and its degree of economic development was first observed by Dunning (Dunning, 1993; Dunning and Narula, 1996). This so-called investment development path (IDP) is made up of five stages: the first three cover less-developed countries (LDCs), while the final two stages consists of more advanced countries. The first group is a net recipient of direct investment, and the type of investment received is associated with each country's specific location factors. Typical entry sectors for direct investment in countries of the first three stages are natural resources, capital-intensive sectors and other differentiated sectors (Ozawa, 1996; Narula and Dunning, 1998); while in the 1990s public services and information technologies were also affected. Third-stage countries are those known as 'emerging economies', whose foreign direct investment levels are significant and sometimes attain consistent rates of growth that bring them closer to countries in the fourth stage of the international cycle of direct investment. Van Den Bulcke and Zhang (1996) placed China in this stage.

Fourth-stage countries are characterized, as from a given level of GDP per capita, by having produced exponential growth in the outflow of direct investment. Such countries mostly behave heterogeneously with regard to inflows of foreign direct investment. Therefore, their net position (difference between outward and inward investment) may be either positive or negative (Durán and Úbeda, 2001). Finally, fifth-stage countries fluctuate around zero. There is no statistically significant difference between inward direct investment positions in fourth- and fifth-stage countries. Fourth-stage countries have less knowledge-intensive assets, and subsequently have a lower capability for engaging in foreign investment (Narula, 1996; Durán and Úbeda, 2001).

In this chapter the potential of privatizations for the internationalization of companies is researched. Also the impact of privatizations on foreign direct investment is examined, and in particular, the relation between the acquisitions of privatized firms by foreign companies on the level of development of countries according to the investment development path. Furthermore, this chapter outlines new scenarios that have emerged over the last two decades and describes the relationship between privatizations and corporate internationalization.

The privatization of state-owned firms: determinant factors

The privatization of public utilities may, *prima facie*, be viewed as an issue of ownership rather than one of control, because their operation is governed by a given system of rules (service quality and safety requirements). Control of public utilities may be exercised politically, either directly through State-ownership or indirectly by regulation. Privatization and liberalization in a context of market competition may improve efficiency, while requiring effective regulation (Vickers and Yarrow, 1991). However, it may be that privatization is a necessary but not a sufficient condition of efficiency (Newbery, 1997), because the degree of efficiency is determined, more by the extent and quality of market competition, than by company ownership.

Public companies (owned by the state and managed and controlled by government) are created for a wide variety of reasons: shortage of private capital in phases of autarky or relative closure to the outside; in order to set in place activities in aid of the private economy; to work out economic crises (at the large company or industry-wide scale); or for ideological or political reasons (expropriations and nationalizations).

It used to be common that the State should own (or closely control) certain activities, in particular telecommunications and postal services, electricity and gas, air and rail carriers, industries relating to national defence, and steel.[1] Economies of scale and scope, externalities and entry barriers (for example political or legal impediments) may, it has been argued, make state-ownership preferable to private ownership (Vickers and Yarrow, 1991). In open, competitive economies, however, technological progress provides grounds for a contrary argument. Thus, the effects of regulation and ownership on the efficiency of an enterprise depend on whether or not the firm operates in a competitive sector (Vickers and Yarrow, 1991).

The ownership structure of a firm is important insofar as it influences its objectives, decision-making process and corporate governance. Privatization transfers ownership of corporations from the state to the private sector, which may change the structure of incentives and the nature of the agency relationships.

In a public company, the principal (the government) may give priority to aims other than making the largest possible profit, which is what a private firm must pursue over the long term in its shareholders' interests. It is generally accepted that a private company is more efficient than a state-owned company (Megginson and Netter, 2001), because it brings forth better operating and financial performance indicators (Dewenter and Malatesta, 2001; D'Souza and Megginson, 1999).

There is no financial market for state-owned companies, which aids the alignment of executives' interests with those of the government. Instead, control is in the hands of the government. Indebtedness, financial risk, financial solvency and the likelihood of going bankrupt are perceived differently by the management of public and private firms.

Privatization by a public offering of shares can be regarded as a transparent and competitive process, because it enables the market to assess the value of the company. This method is also appropriate for privatizing large corporations that require some restructuring after privatization. However, the procedure may not be suitable for underdeveloped financial markets. This drawback may be partly made up for if a tranche of shares or equivalent securities (for example share depositary receipts) is allocated to liquid, efficient foreign markets able to provide a market value. Subscription of these securities lends credibility to the process. But obviously not all privatized companies are able to internationalize their shareholder composition in this way.

The international privatization process is associated in significant ways with countries' public deficit, with how developed (and liquid) domestic capital markets are, with government ideology and with institutional development (Bortolotti *et al.*, 2003). The high uptake capacity of highly developed, liquid financial markets makes it easier for privatization proceeds to match the total value of a privatized company, as there will be no need to discount stock, as tends to be the norm in shallower, less liquid markets. Privatizations are fewer in less-advanced democracies and less-developed economies. A paper by Jones *et al.* (1999) examined 137 privatizations in 34 countries that were underpriced with respect to their estimated value, and found that this move was associated with government's need to obtain domestic political support for its decisions.

The process of privatization, in progress worldwide since the mid-1980s, is to be viewed against a backdrop of economic liberalization (deregulation of markets and encouragement of competition). One of the distinctive features of the period is the privatization of enterprises operating in regulated sectors: telecommunications, air carriers, gas, water and electricity. The deregulation of other sectors such as banking and insurance has also fostered internationalization, especially through foreign direct investment. Therefore, taking a gradualist view, it can be said that one of the key features of the 1990s was the multinationalization of public utilities.

As a forerunner of the current privatization process, one could point to the decisions to 'denationalize' in Germany in 1961 (Nool, 2000) through the sale of shares in state-owned companies (Volkswagen, among others) to small investors. Later came the Chilean privatizations of 1974–75 following the Pinochet coup d'état, as a reversal of the nationalizations of 1970–73 under President Allende. Another forerunner was the United Kingdom; with its privatizations of 1979 the privatization process began to spread to the rest of the world. Currently, privatizations have been carried out in over 120 countries (Megginson and Netter, 2001; Mahboobi, 2000).

Some of the empirical evidence on the role of privatizations in the internationalization of business – on foreign direct investment, specifically – can be found in the data about the sale of privatized companies to foreign investors in the annual world investment reports and, for Latin America, in CEPAL (2001). For Central and Eastern European countries, the journal *Transnational Corporations* has devoted two issues to the subject (UNCTAD, 2000, 2001). Van Den Bulcke and Zhang (1998, 2000) studied the relationship between state owned enterprises and transnational firms in the Chinese context.

International privatizations and micro country risk

Country risk may take the form of events (expropriations, strikes and so on) or stem from ongoing processes (for example effects of a given economic policy, currency devaluation ...). Country risk can operate at the macro level, affecting foreign investors as a whole, or at the micro level, being influenced even by individual companies. Generally, the most common instances of country risk are administrative action, government intervention, legal uncertainty, and so on.

Popular sensibilities and nationalist sentiment are more marked with regard to public utilities than in connection with other sectors penetrated by foreign capital such as, for instance, automobile parts manufacturing or furniture. Cases in point range from the demonstrations in Peru against privatization of power plants by Belgian companies, to tariff- and rate-freezing for telecommunications, water, gas and electricity companies in Argentina. Therefore, nationalist sentiment, laws, their frequency of change, the extent to which they are enforced, how they are interpreted by the judiciary, corruption and, in general, the quality of public institutions are key factors of country risk that influence a firm's decision-making.

Political (and thus social) acceptance of and support for privatizations in a competitive, transparent and independent context facilitate efficient allocation of resources. This is especially necessary for the sale to foreign investors of large corporations and companies in sensitive sectors of the economy. If the privatization process is accepted by public opinion, therefore, the multinational acquiring a local privatized firm will find it easier to manage micro country risk.

Country risk may also be exacerbated by structural risk (UNCTAD, 2004) or the creation of private monopolies as a result of privatizations, due to the appearance of corruption that surrounds such a development, increased prices and tariffs, inadequately explained staff lay-off processes, and so on. Likewise, difficulties in the supply of public services that are *prima facie* beyond the control of a foreign-owned privatized company may be used in an election campaign as a cudgel with which to beat the government and its privatizations policy, thus bringing about a negative reaction of public opinion against the company in question. A government might also blame previous incumbents for supposedly tolerating opportunistic behaviour by foreign firms providing public services, without proper reference to the quality and productivity of those services. But consistent ongoing privatization programmes may remove uncertainty about a country's political commitment to market-orientated policy in a context of respect for the right to property. Successful privatization programmes have not only favoured the growth of securities markets in general and of emerging economies in particular (Boutchkova and Megginson, 2000), but also reduce public deficit and have a beneficial indirect effect on the macro political risk perceived by investors by improving credibility and credit ratings (Perotti and Van Oijen, 2001). In any event, country risk management is a key consideration for a company. Micro country risk should be managed, as far as possible, in cooperation with government, thus enhancing the company's 'relational capital'.

Expropriations and privatizations: two sides of the same coin

Figure 11.1 shows the behaviour to date of expropriations, defined as takeover by the state of a foreign-owned subsidiary (foreign direct investment).

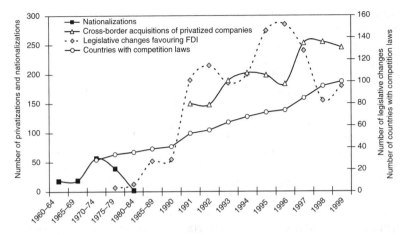

Figure 11.1 Nationalizations, international privatizations and legislative (favourable) changes on direct investment

Source: Based on Kobrin (1982), Kennedy (1992), UNCTAD (1993, 1998, 2003).

Table 11.1 Number of expropriated firms by type and sector, 1960–80

Sector	Mass expropriation 28 countries	Selective expropriation 95 countries
Oil	49	129
Ore and mineral extraction	39	53
Energy	16	22
Communications	7	10
Transport	15	16
Banking	260	27
Insurance	71	17
Trade	95	8
Manufacturing	248	36

Source: Adapted from Kennedy (1992).

The process was especially significant from the late 1960s to the early 1980s. Most expropriating countries were states created by decolonization. Selective expropriation affected one or more sectors chosen by government, while mass expropriation affected the virtual entirety of foreign direct investment in the country. Twenty-eight less-developed countries accounted for two-thirds of total expropriations (Kobrin, 1982) and, as a whole, covered a wide range of sectors (see Table 11.1).

In Europe, a number of key companies were nationalized after the Second World War. Hence, the same sectors that were nationalized in the 1940s to promote efficiency, were privatized starting in the 1980s in pursuit of that same goal.[2] In both cases, most of the expropriated sectors became the target of foreign direct investment and privatizations in the 1990s: energy, telecommunications, banking and insurance, transport, and so on.

Figure 11.1 also shows increasing convergence among countries with laws favouring foreign direct investment. Convergence is reinforced by a wide range of agreements to avoid international double taxation and bilateral agreements for promotion and reciprocal protection of investments: 2,256 and 2,181, respectively, were signed in 2002 (UNCTAD, 2003). Increasing numbers of less-developed countries have set up competition watchdogs – such are now present in 93 countries, almost 50 per cent of all countries in existence. Likewise, 154 countries have agencies for the promotion of investment or equivalent bodies (UNCTAD, 2003: 29). In addition to this system – made up of national laws, bilateral treaties and regional and multilateral agreements – a particular highlight is that many countries now accept that disputes about foreign direct investment should be decided by international arbitration. Institutions operating in this field include the Arbitration Court of the International Chamber of Commerce and the International Centre for Settlement of Investment Disputes (ICSID) attached to the World Bank. The aim of this institution is to 'provide a forum to settle disputes in a context that aims expressly to de-politicize investment disputes'. Today, about 130 countries are signatories to the ICSID convention. It can now be said that the salient risk faced by multinational firms is the risk of legislative changes or discriminatory application of the law based on a company's sector or nationality.

Technological progress destroys the alleged 'natural monopoly' of certain businesses, transforms whole sectors and creates new areas of activity. Institutional change (deregulation of domestic markets, proliferation of bilateral, regional and multilateral agreements) and greater international interdependence are also arguments in favour of privatizing state-owned companies. Many privatized firms operate in sectors that have now become strategic and are, precisely, the driving force of internationalization; it is of note that some were formerly not of that nature at all. A further consideration is the impact on expectations (and on corporate morale) of the triumph of the decentralized or market economy in the wake of the fall of the Berlin Wall and the subsequent dismantling of the Soviet Union. These events gave rise to processes of privatization in the so-called 'transitional economies'. In addition, there has been a direct relationship between privatizations and the prime goals that governments have pursued to some extent or another: to improve the state of public finance, increase investment, achieve higher service quality, and obtain a better economic balance with the outside world (improve foreign trade, attract foreign investment, and so on).

The key privatized sectors as from the late 1980s and, especially, in the 1990s were also the fastest to become internationalized, basically through foreign direct investment and strategic alliances (joint ventures, cooperation and partnership agreements). Again, the following industries took the lead: telecommunications, electricity, gas, water, air carriers and banking. Other relevant fields were natural resources, oil and mining. These were the sectors that had mostly been nationalized in earlier phases, and subjected to tough restrictions and prohibitions on foreign ownership.

Privatizations are carried out in several different ways: private sale of shares (to domestic or foreign investors), public offerings of shares (domestic and foreign markets), sale to employees and executives, and winding-up and subsequent sale of assets. The degree of transparency, independence and competitiveness of a privatization process tends to be associated with negotiation costs, the potential for corruption and, taken as a whole, efficiency.

In the period 1977–99 there were 2,459 privatizations in 121 countries for a total value of about $1,100 billion (Megginson and Netter, 2001). Only rarely, however, did government completely transfer ownership and control of a public corporation. In that period (1977–99), of a total of 617 privatized companies studied (Bertolli *et al.*, 2003), a shareholding majority was sold only 30 per cent of the time, and this was never the case in 11 of the 76 privatizing countries under study. In some countries (Spain, Belgium, France and others) where a majority of stock was privatized in public utilities regarded as strategic, government held on to a 'golden share', carrying a right of veto in certain circumstances. The empirical evidence, therefore, shows that privatizations have mostly been partial or incomplete so as to let government hold on to some measure of direct or indirect power. Such power may take the form of influence on company management appointments and on decisions about future transfers of ownership (for example to foreign investors).

From a financial standpoint it has been observed (Boutchkova and Megginson, 2000; Henry, 2000; Perotti and Van Oijen, 2000) that privatizations have increased market liquidity and the number of both minority and institutional shareholders in several countries. Privatized firms – mostly utilities (telecom, electricity, water and gas) and oil companies – are among the largest and most highly valued in both developed and emerging economies. Moreover, 30 of the 34 largest public offerings of shares in history were privatizations (Boutchkova and Megginson, 2000).

In countries of the civil law tradition (as opposed to common law countries), investor protection is lower (while creditor protection is higher), and capital markets carry less weight than credit institutions (La Porta *et al.*, 1997). This may explain why there have been fewer privatizations in civil law countries (Bertolli *et al.*, 2001).

At the end of 2003, there were 64 cases (eight of which were Spanish) being disputed before the International Centre for Settlement of Investment

Disputes (ICSID) of the World Bank group; 37 related to Latin America (Argentina was concerned with 25 of those cases, six of which involved Spanish companies), 13 to Africa and 16 to transitional economies. The vast majority of cases pending arbitral award concerned electricity, water, gas, oil (30) and construction (7), followed by financial services (4) and mining (3).

The impact of privatizations on the development of foreign direct investment

Cross-border acquisitions through privatizations in the period 1987–99, have strongly accelerated in the second half of the 1990s. The distribution of the value of international acquisitions of privatized firms, by vendor country and divided into two sub-periods (1987–95 and 1996–99), is shown in Table 11.2. Thus, from 1987 to 1995 Australia and Sweden led the field, followed by Argentina and Peru, while from 1996 to 1999 the largest vendors of privatized firms to foreign investors were Brazil, Argentina, Australia and Germany. In fact, the weight of privatizations in the second sub-period determines the order of vendor countries for the entire period from 1987 to 1999. Spain was ranked as the 12th-largest seller for the whole period, being 16th from 1987 to 1995 and 10th from 1996 to 1999.

Table 11.2 illustrates the importance of the sale of privatized firms to foreign investors. In the period 1987–90, privatizations accounted for about 4 per cent of FDI, while from 1991–99 they took up 96 per cent. On a classification by stages of investment development (Durán and Úbeda, 2001), the more advanced countries sold 47.13 per cent and 39.11 per cent of the privatized firms acquired to TNCs in the periods 1987–90 and 1991–99, respectively.

Privatized firms in LDCs, acquired by foreign investors, which represented about 60 per cent of the world total in the 1990s have had a highly diversified impact on the IDP of those countries. Table 11.2 shows that countries moving from stage two to stage three account for over 42 per cent of privatized firms acquired by transnationals that are based in developed countries. But some second-stage countries that entrained large privatization programmes (Venezuela, Peru, Colombia and Romania) remain at the same stage of development; privatization has not enabled them to advance to the next stage. In a considerable number of countries, moreover, privatizations make up over 40 per cent of foreign direct investment, and occasionally account for most of it (83 per cent in Bulgaria, for instance). In some cases, privatization explains progress in the IDP, moving from stage two to stage three (Argentina, Brazil, Poland, the Philippines, Hungary and the Czech Republic). Privatizations have also been highly significant in Australia. In countries at stages one and two, however, although privatizations accounted for a high proportion of incoming foreign direct investment, this has not boosted growth sufficiently to move the economy ahead to a more advanced stage in the IDP cycle.

Table 11.2 Value of privatizations acquired by foreign investors, classified by country and IDP stage, 1987–99

	1987–90			1991–99			
	US$ billions	% of total	Privatization/ FDI inflow (%)	US$ billions	% of total	Privatization/ FDI inflow (%)	Total
Stage 1	**0**	**0.00**		**3.4**	**1.60**		**3.4**
Pakistan	0	0.00	0.0	1.1	0.52	23.4	1.1
El Salvador	0	0.00	0.0	0.9	0.42	61.2	0.9
Stage 2	**0.3**	**3.45**		**20**	**9.39**		**20.3**
Venezuela	0	0.00	0.0	5.4	2.54	26.7	5.4
Peru	0	0.00	0.0	5.2	2.44	34.6	5.1
Colombia	0.3	3.45	18.8	3.3	1.55	18.8	3.8
Romania	0	0.00	0.0	2.4	1.13	43.5	2.4
Bolivia	0	0.00	0.0	1.7	0.80	40.6	1.7
Stages 2 to 3	**2.8**	**32.18**		**89.9**	**42.21**		**92.7**
Brazil	0.1	1.15	1.6	31.7	14.88	32.3	31.9
Argentina	0.6	6.90	15.0	25.7	12.07	38.8	26.4
Poland	0	0.00	0.0	7.5	3.52	24.0	7.5
Philippines	0	0.00	0.0	5.2	2.44	43.1	5.3
Hungary	0.2	2.30	38.9	4.2	1.97	21.6	4.3
Mexico	1.8	20.69	20.9	2.8	1.31	4.0	4.6
Czech Republic	0	0.00		3.7	1.74	22.0	3.7
Russia	0	0.00	–	2.3	1.08	12.7	2.3
Chile	0.1	1.15	3.3	2.2	1.03	6.9	2.2
Thailand	0	0.00	0.0	2.1	0.99	7.2	2
South Africa	0	0.00	0.0	1.7	0.80	19.8	1.7
Stages 3 to 4	**1.8**	**20.69**		**17.3**	**8.12**		**19.1**
Spain	0.2	2.30	0.6	4.4	2.07	4.8	4.7
Italy	0.4	4.60	2.0	4.2	1.97	12.7	4.6
Austria	0.2	2.30	0.4	3.2	1.50	14.9	3.5
New Zealand	1	11.49	13.1	1.6	0.75	8.3	2.7
Ireland	0	0.00	0.0	2.1	0.99	5.4	2.2
Stage 5	**2.3**	**26.44**		**66**	**30.99**		**68.3**
Australia	0.4	4.60	19.3	24	11.27	38.6	24.3
Germany	0.6	6.90	4.6	8.4	3.94	6.9	9
Belgium	0.1	1.15	0.4	8.6	4.04	3.9	8.7
Sweden	0	0.00	0.0	8.4	3.94	6.9	8.3
France	0.4	4.60	1.1	5.6	2.63	2.6	5.9
United Kingdom	0.2	2.30	0.2	4.3	2.02	1.5	4.5
Netherlands	0	0.00	0.0	4.4	2.07	3.1	4.3
Finland	0.1	1.15	4.8	1.7	0.80	12.6	1.8
Canada	0.5	5.75	1.8	0.6	0.28	0.6	1.2
Unclassified	**1**	**11.49**		**11.6**	**5.45**		**12.6**
Kazakhstan	0	0.00	–	4.7	2.21	58.2	4.6
Bulgaria	0	0.00	0.0	1.9	0.89	82.5	1.8
Total	**8.2**	**100.00**		**208.2**	**100.00**		**216.4**

Source: Author's calculations based on UNCTAD (2000) and online UNCTAD database.

The internationalization of privatized Spanish firms in Latin America

Spanish direct investment abroad during the period 1993–2003 amounted to over €265 billion of which about 38 per cent went to Latin American countries and 46 per cent to EU countries. The investment made in energy, water, telecommunications, transportation and financial services (banking and insurance) represented about 54 per cent of the total. The direct investment in Latin America in the above-mentioned sectors, for the same period, was 80 per cent of the total investment in the region and 54 per cent, barring the finance sector. Overall privatization in Latin America was the dominant form of investment (World Bank, 2004; UNCTAD, 2004).

Also for the period 1988–92 (Treviño, Daniels, Arbelaez and Upadhyaya, 2002) it has been found that liberalization of capital markets and privatizations in Latin America (Argentina, Brazil, Chile, Colombia, Mexico, Peru and Venezuela) were closely associated with the entry of direct investment into the region. Privatizations may be viewed not only as an option for FDI, but also as a signal of improvement of the environment in which businesses operate. In less-developed countries, over two-thirds of privatizations involve foreign investors (Megginson, 1999).

In the case of Spain, a considerable volume of foreign direct investment has been carried out by previously privatized Spanish state-owned firms, that are now among the country's main transnationals (for example, Telefónica, Repsol-YPF, Endesa). National laws may require that state-owned transnationals must be granted prior authorization. Such requirements may be either of a general nature or more specific with regard to certain levels or sectors of investment. Private enterprises, being free from the political implications of state ownership, may therefore enjoy wider options and lower entry costs in foreign markets. The degree of concentration of Spanish direct investment overseas, especially in Brazil, Argentina, Peru, Mexico and so on, confirms that this phenomenon has helped Spain to attain the fourth stage of the IDP; that is, the process of privatization and of internationalization of privatized public utilities explains the improved level of economic development achieved by the Spanish economy. These enterprises have demonstrated ownership-related competitive advantages which have been transferred to Latin American countries offering location advantages (Durán, 1999).

It should come as no surprise that Spain is one of the main investors in Latin America, and actually is the largest or second-largest foreign investor in most countries of the region, especially since the late 1980s. The main Spanish TNCs in Latin America are situated in the utilities and oil industry (after being privatized) and financial services such as banking and insurance, along with hotels. These businesses mostly built up their competitive advantages during the 1980s, particularly through accession to the European Economic Community. It may even be said that these Spanish companies were able to finance the creation of competitive advantages through monopolistic competition in a sheltered domestic market. Given their newly developed firm-specific advantages, they perceived attractive location advantages in Latin America. This led during the 1990s to a new model of outward expansion. This Latin American option offered a wealth of strategic assets for Spanish business (Durán, 1999).

Spanish privatized public utilities (at various stages of development) made direct investments in Latin American utilities that were likewise being privatized. Spanish direct investment also targeted privatized firms in other fields of business in Latin America and elsewhere (such as Morocco), sometimes through programmes of conversion of debt into equity. The three most prolific Spanish TNCs are Telefónica, Repsol-YPF and Endesa,[3] which together have been involved in nine of the largest privatizations in the period 1987–99. Of the other nine largest privatizations that took place in Latin America; seven were acquired by US companies, one by an Italian firm and another by a Portuguese enterprise. In addition, 21 of these 50 largest privatizations occurred in developed countries, while six firms were privatized in transitional economies.

These Spanish firms were among the 100 largest multinationals present in Latin America, according to consolidated turnover figures. By way of example, Telefónica since 1998 and Repsol-YPF and Endesa since 1999 are on the list of the 100 largest transnationals by overseas assets according to the UNCTAD transnationality index. Similarly, Telefónica is among the 25 privatized companies with the highest market value, according to data from Morgan Stanley Capital International published by *Business Week* and Endesa was among the 35 largest international public offerings of shares of the period 1987–2000.

The privatization in the sector of telecommunications has been a variegated process in Latin America, at either extreme of which one might place Argentina and Brazil. Thus, in 1989 Argentina privatized in favour of two foreign consortia, one led by Telefónica and another by France Telecom. During the following decade the firms made large investments, enabling the sector to grow strongly. The absence of competition, however, made prices remain relatively high and allowed for huge profits, because the consortia retained their dominant positions. Brazil, on the other hand, went through a slower process as from 1995. When it finally started privatization in 1998 it opted for a universalization of services through competition: six segments were created in which several companies were to compete within an appropriate regulatory framework (CEPAL, 2001: 208–10).

Throughout this entire period, Telefónica has gradually penetrated Latin America and exercised a range of real options. The company was also affected by the stock-exchange bubble which caused a process of debt reduction (as in other sectors) and a change of strategy in the rest of the world (disinvestments in Europe) and consolidation of its presence in Latin America.

Telefónica has opted for concentric and international diversification and internationalization of its financial structure. In parallel, Repsol-YPF and Endesa are present in almost all Latin American countries, contributing strategically to greater energy integration in the region.

The ownership structure of a company obviously changes on privatization, by definition. But the nature of this structural change may vary significantly in accordance with the stratification of the new ownership (atomized shareholder structure, institutional investors, controlling shareholders, listing of shares on efficient or inefficient markets, and so on). In this regard, the presence or absence of foreign shareholders (institutional and small investors) is a key consequence of the privatization process. Hence privatizations and their articulation with a company's multinationality (privatized companies making direct investments in other privatized companies in host countries) may influence financial structure, which may also be affected by institutional and sectoral factors.

We shall not examine here the financial internationalization of Spanish TNCs as they have undergone a privatization process in two directions. But as an illustration of the internationalization of the sources of capital of these companies, a number of estimates regarding Repsol-YPF, Endesa and Telefónica will be set out. Table 11.3 shows that the foreign shareholders of Endesa and Telefónica hold over 50 per cent of the equity capital; and that foreigners hold 44.5 per cent of Repsol-YPF. Holdings of foreign institutional investors are significant.[4] Similarly, in Repsol-YPF stable holdings account for about 32 per cent with 68 per cent thus being 'floating' capital. Telefónica was first listed on the New York Stock Exchange in 1987, almost at the same time as its first round of privatization. It currently lists on the London, Tokyo, Paris, Frankfurt, São Paulo, Lima and Buenos Aires exchanges. Repsol-YPF listed on the Madrid, New York and Buenos Aires

Table 11.3 Shareholder structure and debt currency of Repsol-YPF, Endesa and Telefónica: percentages, 2003

	REPSOL-YPF	Endesa	Telefónica
Spanish shareholders	54.5	48	<50%
Individual	27.2	25	
Institutional	27.3	20	
Foreign shareholders	44.5	52	>50%
United States	20.1	18	
Rest of the world (chiefly Europe)	24.4	34	
DEBT			
Foreign currencies	50	35	35
Euros	50	65	65

Source: Based on data released by the companies.

markets. Endesa is present on the Madrid, New York and Santiago de Chile markets.

With regard to these companies's debt, there is a measure of currency diversification. The US dollar predominates, supplemented by the currencies of the countries in which the firms' main direct investments are located. The firms use currency swaps (for example, euro for dollar), among other instruments, to restructure their debt and hedge their foreign exchange risk. Currently, many transnationals, given the internationalization of their financial structure, have become important channels for international savings.

Conclusions

The wave of privatizations worldwide, increasing in the 1990s and very especially in the second half of the decade, has come about in a context of liberalization and opening-out of national economies. Recognition of the importance of foreign direct investment for economic growth and development has significantly reduced the likelihood of expropriation.

The privatization process in connection with the sale of domestic corporations to foreign investors has varied widely in different countries. Less-developed countries account for a majority of sales of privatized companies to multinational firms, while some countries have facilitated their economic development by following the foreign direct investment path. Privatization of public utilities in less-developed countries requires a special emphasis on managing micro country risk.

In the late 1980s, and especially in the 1990s, Spain privatized the main public operators in telecommunications, electricity, fuel, gas, air transport and banking. These companies enjoyed competitive advantages and high availability of funds. They opted strategically for direct investment in Latin America, to a large extent by acquiring companies that had themselves been privatized. In addition to geographic diversification in other areas (chiefly Europe through strategic alliances and, to a lesser extent, through direct investment), these firms have internationalized their borrowings and shareholding structures, and are now international channels for savings from various domestic financial systems.

Notes

1 Many companies have come under government ownership for ideological reasons through expropriation from the private sector or through creation from scratch. They have also been used as instruments of industrial development or to face social (employment) and economic difficulties. On occasion, large interest groups owning distressed businesses have exerted pressure to have ownership transferred to the public sector.

2   An important expropriation was that of the Mexican oilfields in 1938. Also significant were the nationalizations and expropriations of the former Soviet Union and its satellites.
3   The US company ITT operated telecommunications in several European countries (Germany, Spain and Eastern European countries) and was expropriated in the 1940s. Repsol was created in the 1980s on the basis of the State oil monopoly. Endesa was also state-owned, although in general the Spanish electricity industry, unlike the rest of Europe, was not expropriated, albeit heavily regulated.
4   Comparable situations came about in the Spanish banking industry (Durán, 2002).

References

Bortolotti, B., Fantini, M. and Siniscalo, D. (2001) 'Privatization: Politics, Institutions, and Financial Markets', *Emerging Markets Review*, 2: 109–37.

Bortolotti, B., Fantini, M. and Siniscalo, D. (2003) 'Privatization Around the World: Evidence from Panel Data', *Journal of Public Economics*, 88: 305–32.

Boutchkova, M. and Megginson, W. (2000) 'Privatization and the Rise of Global Capital Markets', *Financial Management*, 29(4): 31–76.

CEPAL (2001) *La inversión extranjera en América Latina y el Caribe*. Santiago de Chile: United Nations.

Dewenter, K. and Malatesta, P.H. (2001) 'State-Owned and Privately-Owned Enterprises: An Emprirical Ananlysis of Profitability, Leverage, and Labor Intensity', *American Economic Review*, 91: 320–34.

D'Souza, J. and Megginson, W.L. (1999) 'The Financial and Operating Performance of Privatized Firms during the 1990s', *Journal of Finance*, 54: 1397–438.

Durán, J.J. (1999) *Multinacionales españolas en Iberoamérica. Valor estratégico*. Madrid: Ediciones Pirámide.

Durán, J.J. (2001) *Estrategia y Economía de la Empresa Multinacional*. Madrid: Ediciones Piramide.

Durán, J.J. (2002) 'La expansión multinacional de la banca española. Santander Central Hispano S.A. (SCH) y Banco Bilbao Vizcaya Argentaria S.A. (BBVA)', in M. García Olalla and C.J. Vázquez Ordas (eds), *Estrategias y Operaciones empresariales en los nuevos mercados. 20 casos a estudio*. Madrid: Civitas.

Durán, J.J. and Úbeda F. (2001) 'The International Development Path: A New Empirical Approach and Some Theoretical Issues', *Transnational Corporations*, 10: 1–34.

Henry, P. (2000) 'Stock Market Liberalization, Economic Reform, and Emerging Market Equity Prices', *Journal of Finance*, 55: 529–64.

International Centre for Settlement of Investment Disputes. 'ICSID Cases'. www.worldbank.org/icsid/cases/main.htm

Jones, S., Megginson, W., Nash, R. and Netter, J. (1999) 'Share Issue Privatizations as Financial Means to Political and Economics Ends', *Journal of Financial Economics*, 53: 217–53.

Kennedy, C.R. (1992) 'Relations between Transnational Corporations and Governments of Host Countries. A Look to the Future', *Transnational Corporations*, 1(1).

Kobrin, S.J. (1982) *Managing Political Risk Assessment*. Los Angeles: University of California Press.

La Porta, R., Lopez-De-Silanes, F., Shleifer, A. and Vishny, R. (1997) 'Legal Determinants of External Finance', *Journal of Finance*, 52: 1131–50.

López de Silanes, F. (1997) 'Determinants of Privatizations Process', *Quarterly Journal of Economics*, 112: 965–1025.

Mahboobi, L. (2000) 'Recent Privatisation Trends', *OECD Financial Market Trends*, 76: 43–64.

Megginson, W.L., Netter, J. (2001) 'From the State to Market: A Survey of Empirical Studies on Privatization', *Journal of Economic Literature*, xxxix: 321–89.

Minor, J. (1994) 'The Demise of Expropriation as an Instrument of LDC Policy, 1980/1992', *Journal of International Business Studies*, 25(1): 177–88.

Myro, R. (1988) 'Las empresas públicas' in J.L. García Delgadoi (ed.), *España, Economía*. Madrid: Espasa Calpe.

Narula, R. and Dunning, J.H. (1998) 'Globalization and New Realities for Multinational Enterprise Developing Host Country Interaction'. Unpublished paper.

Newbery, D.M. (1997) 'Privatization and Liberalization of Network Utilities', *European Economic Review*, 41: 357–83.

Nool, R. (2000) 'Telecommunications Reform in Developing Countries', in Krueger, A.O. (ed.), *Economic Policy Reform: The Second Stage*. University of Chicago Press.

Ozawa, T. (1996) 'Japan: The Macro-IDP, Meso-IDPs and the Technology and the Technology Development Path (TDP)', in J.H. Dunning and R. Narula (eds), *Foreign Direct Investment and Governments*. London and New York: Routledge.

Perotti, E.C. and Van Oijen, P. (2000) 'Privatization Political Risk and Stock Market Development in Emerging Economies', *Journal of International Money and Finance*, 20: 43–69.

Toninelli, P.A. (ed.) (2000) *The Rise and Fall of State-Owned Enterprise in the Western World*. Cambridge: CUP.

Treviño, L., Daniels, J.D., Arbelaez, H.A. and Upadhyaya, K.P. (2002) 'Market Reform and Foreign Direct Investment in Latin America', *The International Trade Journal*, xvi(4): 367–92.

UNCTAD (1993) *World Investment Report. Transnational Corporations and Integrated International Production*. New York: United Nations.

UNCTAD (2000) *World Investment Report. Cross-border Mergers and Acquisitions and Development*. New York: United Nations.

UNCTAD (2002) *World Investment Report. Transnational Corporations and Export Competitiveness*. New York: United Nations.

UNCTAD (2003) *World Investment Report. FDI Policies for Development: National and International Perspectives*. Geneva: United Nations.

UNCTAD (2004) *World Investment Report. The Shift Towards Services*. Geneva: United Nations.

Van Den Bulcke, D. and Zhang, H. (1996) 'Rapid Changes in the Investment Development Path of China', in J.H. Dunning and R. Narula (eds), *Foreign Direct Investment and Governments: Catalysts for Economic Restructuring*. London: Palgrave Macmillan, pp. 380–422.

Van Den Bulcke, D. and Zhang, H. (1998) *Joint Ventures between Multinational Corporations and State-Owned Enterprises in the Context of the Chinese Reform Process*. Antwerp: China Europe Management Center.

Van Den Bulcke, D. and Zhang, H. (2000) 'China's New Initiatives Towards the Reform of State-Owned Enterprises', in N. Vrijens and T. Nooteboom (eds), *Beleid en Beheer in een Imperfecte Wereld*. Brussel: Politeia.

Vickers, J. and Yarrow, G. (1991) 'Economic Perspectives on Privatisation', *Journal of Economic Perspectives*, 5: 111–32.

World Bank (2004) The Private Participation in Infrastructure (PPI). Project Database *http://rru.worldbank.org/PPI/*

12
The Research Agenda in International Business: Back to the Future

Peter J. Buckley and Filip De Beule

Introduction

This chapter is intended to celebrate the achievements of international business researchers and to point the way forward for further developments. In part, it is a response to the challenge laid down by Buckley (2002) in the piece 'Is the international business research agenda running out of steam?' Others have risen to this challenge as we will see (Buckley, 2004a, 2004b).

Received theory: the contribution of international business theorists

Until the 1960s, mainstream economists treated transnational corporations (TNCs) as simply investors of capital, moving equity from countries where returns were low to those where it was higher (Jones, 1996). A major theoretical breakthrough came in 1960, when Stephen Hymer expressed his dissatisfaction with the theory of portfolio capital transfers to explain the international operations of firms. Hymer stated that many of the predictions became invalidated once risk and uncertainty, volatile exchange rates and the cost of acquiring information and making transactions were incorporated into classical portfolio theory. This was because market imperfections altered the performance of firms and their strategy in servicing foreign markets (Dunning, 1993). Although Hymer had written his thesis in 1960, it was only – posthumously – published in 1976, because his work was largely ignored until Kindleberger (1969) took it up. Follow-up developments to refine and test the Hymer–Kindleberger hypotheses were only carried out in the early 1970s.

Hymer was also the first to recognize that FDI involved the transfer of a package of resources, such as technology, management skills and entrepreneurship, and not just capital. The most fundamental characteristic of FDI was that it involved no change in the ownership of resources, whereas indirect investment was transacted through the market. Hymer's identification of the international firm as a firm that internalizes and supersedes the market provided a useful prologue to the theory of internalization (see below) as a means for transferring knowledge, business techniques and skilled personnel (Hymer, 1976).

However, Hymer's work is best-known for its application of an industrial organization approach to the theory of international production. Local firms were assumed to possess superior knowledge about the host country markets, resources, legal and political system, language and culture, and all the many other things which distinguish one country from another. As far as this is true, foreign firms would have no incentive to locate in that market or have the ability to survive in it without an advantage. Hymer extended Bain's work (1956) on the barriers to competition in domestic markets to explain the international activities of firms. He argued that such firms had to possess some kind of proprietary advantage. This reasoning led to the view that a foreign firm required competitive advantages over its local rivals to overcome the liability of foreignness (Hymer, 1976). These firm-specific advantages, or ownership advantages, because they are exclusive to the firm owning them, imply the existence of some kind of structural market failure.

Hymer examined the kind of ownership advantages that firms might possess or acquire, as well as the kind of industrial sectors and market structures in which foreign production was likely to be concentrated. Firms can possess any number of ownership advantages when they operate in a foreign market and the type of ownership advantage will differ considerably according to the products and industries. Within manufacturing, superior technology and innovative capacity are especially important in the case of production goods, while product differentiation will often be more relevant for consumer goods (Jones, 1996). Ownership advantages can be generated internally within the firm, or acquired by licensing a technology from a foreign competitor or buying a foreign firm. Transnationals could not only exploit perceived market imperfections, but could use their ownership advantages to create market imperfections themselves (Caves, 1971).

Hymer himself was also interested in the international expansion of firms as a means of fostering their monopoly power, rather than of reducing costs, improving product quality or fostering innovations. In his later publications, Hymer (1968, 1970) did appear to acknowledge that TNCs might help to improve international resource-allocation by circumventing market failure. As such, Hymer's work was a point of departure for the more rigorous work of the internalization economists in the following decade.

Despite the invaluable contributions of Hymer, Kindleberger and Caves, the credit for transforming internalization into a theory of international production is usually attributed to Buckley and Casson (1976). They placed the work of Coase (1937) on the multi-plant firm in an international context. Parallel to the internalization theory, Oliver Williamson developed transaction-cost analysis (Williamson, 1975, 1979, 1985), which was later applied in an international context by Teece (1981, 1982, 1985) and Hennart (1982). While traditional economic reasoning concentrates on the consequences of changes in sales revenues and production costs, transaction-cost economics focuses on factors that influence the choice of foreign operation methods – which are mainly regarded as a question of the degree of control the firm should have over a foreign operation (Anderson and Gatignon, 1986). The underlying logic and analysis of the two approaches is characterized more by similarity than any substantial differences (Rugman, 1980).

Transaction-cost theory provided a different perspective on the reasons for the growth of TNCs. The fundamental insight is derived from the pioneering article by Coase (1937) on the boundaries of the firm. He argued that firms and markets represent alternative methods of organizing production. This theory suggested that the market is costly and inefficient for undertaking certain types of transactions. For instance the costs of discovering relevant prices and in arranging contracts for each market transaction constitute the transaction costs of the market. Firms will internalise transactions whenever they can be organized and carried out at a lower cost within the firm than through the market.

This theory attracted little attention from economists until the 1970s, when it was extended and refined by Oliver Williamson (1975, 1979, 1985). Williamson suggested that transaction costs could be examined systematically in relation to three factors, namely bounded rationality, opportunism, and asset-specificity. Bounded rationality means that people invariably make less than fully rational decisions. Opportunism refers to the possibility of people to cheat or engage in misrepresentations. Asset-specificity reflects the extent to which certain types of transactions, necessitate investments in material and intangible assets such as knowledge. If it is difficult to measure the value of goods and services, and if the opportunities for bargaining and dishonesty are therefore high, there is an incentive to replace the market by hierarchy. The combination of bounded rationality, opportunism and asset-specificity produces the strongest incentive to internalize a transaction rather than to use arm's length market contracts.

Internalization is concerned with imperfections in the markets for intermediate products, including technology, organizational know-how and marketing skills. The theory proposes that firms invest abroad because the transaction costs incurred in international intermediate product markets can be reduced by internalizing these markets within the firm. Internalization theory can be used to explain patterns of both vertical and horizontal integration across borders (Casson, 1987b). The internalization of tangible intermediate product flows between upstream and downstream production explains vertical integration between mining and manufacture, agriculture and food processing, component production and final assembly (Hennart, 1991). The internalization of intangibles such as knowledge and reputation can explain patterns of cross-border horizontal integration. Internalization also avoids the difficulties of determining market prices and the proprietary problems associated with arm's-length transactions. Moreover, internalization may allow the company to circumvent government-created market imperfections including trade barriers, differences in tax systems and levels, and restrictions on capital movements.

Although internalization is a deviation from perfect markets, the internalization of firm-specific advantages constitutes an internal transfer of intangible assets that might not take place otherwise. By replacing inefficient or non-existent external markets with internal ones, or by overcoming government-created market distortions such as tariffs, taxes or exchange rates, TNCs produce a more efficient allocation of resources globally (Casson, 1987a). Thus, to the internalization theory, TNCs represent an integrating and welfare-enhancing force in the world economy rather than a source of collusion, monopoly and dependence as argued by for instance, the global-reach school.

By the late 1970s, the global-reach school (Barnet and Müller, 1974; Lall and Streeten, 1977) was increasingly challenged from the more liberal economic perspective of the internalization school, which believed that TNCs benefit developing countries especially because market imperfections can be expected to be more widespread in developing countries than in industrialized countries. In particular, markets for intermediate products such as technology, capital and supporting services do not function well in many developing countries. More specifically, in internalization logic, FDI may assist developing countries through the provision of capital, through the inflow of technology, and managerial know-how, and, finally, through their impact on the creation of efficient markets (Buckley, 1985). All these effects derive essentially from the fact that TNCs provide resources that would not otherwise be available in developing host countries (Blomström, 1991; Blomström and Kokko, 1996a); for example, TNCs often have privileged access to capital from the international banking sector (Lipsey, 1999), so that the presence of TNCs thereby gives developing countries access to capital that would not otherwise have been available. By providing developing countries with an inflow of investment capital and foreign exchange, TNCs may help in adjusting some of the macro economic imbalances that frequently are major impediments to growth in developing countries.

One of the most frequently cited intangible competencies transferred through FDI is technology (Blomström *et al.*, 1992; Blomström and Kokko, 1996b). Technology transfer can trigger and speed up economic development; for instance, by facilitating the production of goods with higher value-added content, by increasing exports and improving efficiency. TNCs possess the bulk of all patents worldwide, most of the world's R&D takes place within TNCs, and TNCs own many of the technologies that are pivotal to economic and industrial development (Hansen, 1998). Often these technological competencies cannot be obtained in the marketplace (for example via licensing), and FDI may therefore be the fastest, most efficient, and sometimes only way for developing countries to get access to these competencies. TNCs can also play a central role in the transfer of know-how, knowledge and experience to the local workforce through its employment of indigenous professionals and managers (Blomström *et al.*, 1994).

TNCs provide highly efficient organizations that are characterized by a high degree of managerial efficiency arising from training, higher standards of recruitment, effective communication with the parent company and other subsidiaries, and a more global outlook. By virtue of these characteristics, they are able to think strategically on a global scale and to organize complex integrated production networks (Hansen, 1998). The integration into this transnational production network can give developing countries advantages (Blomström *et al.*, 2000). TNCs bring with them improvements in storage, transport and marketing arrangements leading to cheaper delivery, better quality of products, and better information about products to consumers. More importantly, developing countries will be able to use the worldwide marketing outlets of TNCs, selling products where huge marketing investments would otherwise have been required. Hence, the presence of TNCs may assist developing countries in penetrating foreign markets.

At the macro level, the internalization logic would imply that FDI by TNCs may encourage governments to adopt more rational and competitiveness-oriented economic policies (Dunning and Narula, 1996). At the micro level, TNCs may produce various spillovers on the host economy. Two types of spillovers from MNE activity in developing countries have been identified, namely intra-industry spillovers and inter-industry spillovers (Blomström and Kokko, 1996). Intra-industry spillovers are effects such as those that improve the competitiveness of national industries by forcing inefficient companies to adopt more efficient methods and invest in improvements of their assets. The presence of TNCs may force local companies to become more efficient and introduce new technologies earlier than they would otherwise have done (Kokko, 1994). They diffuse competencies when trained employees move to local companies where those skills are in short supply, and speed up technology transfer by forcing local companies to get hold of those technologies. Inter-industry spillovers are effects on suppliers and customers, as the growing use of subcontractors and suppliers by TNCs encourage backward spillovers in terms of diffusion of the standards, know-how and technology of TNCs. The entrance of TNCs may improve the technology and productivity of local firms, as they demonstrate new technologies, provide technical assistance to their local suppliers and customers and train managers and workers (Hansen, 1998).

Stephen Magee (1977a, 1977b), in a more detailed examination of technology as a valuable intangible asset, was primarily interested in the internalization of the market for technology. According to Magee, TNCs distinguish themselves as specialists in the production of advanced and complex products and are better equipped to appropriate the revenues of sophisticated information and knowledge (Calvet, 1981). Magee argued that the incentive for firms to internalize the market for technology varies over time. As such, firms were unlikely to sell their rights to new and idiosyncratic technology because the buying firm was unlikely to pay the selling firm a price that would yield at least as much economic rent as it could earn using the technology itself, and because the licensee might use the technology to the disadvantage of the licensor, and even become a competitor. As the technology matured, however, and lost some of its uniqueness, the need to internalize (or 'appropriate' in Magee's parlance) its use decreased and the firm would consider switching its modality of transfer from FDI to licensing (Dunning, 1993).

In a similar yet contradictory vein, the process of gradually increasing involvement in foreign markets has been a widely noted phenomenon especially in Scandinavian (mostly Swedish) studies (Johanson and Wiedersheim-Paul, 1975; Johanson and Vahlne, 1977; Luostarinen, 1979; Welch and Luostarinen, 1988). Two types of increasing involvement are often implied: an increasing involvement in any one foreign market through an orderly process of exporting, agency establishment, sales subsidiary, and finally production subsidiary with the possible intervention of a licensing or other contractual form also being included. Second, orderly stepwise penetration of different foreign markets beginning with the closest market in terms of psychic distance (Hallen and Wiedersheim-Paul, 1993) and often physical distance, gradually extending to more distant and therefore more difficult markets. The proponents of the model hypothesize that commitment to internationalization increases with each further step into the international arena. There is a feedback relationship between the level of internationalization and commitment to further internationalization. Many longitudinal, cross-sectional and case studies show that a growing international awareness in managers is a major motivating force in overcoming barriers to internationalization, and psychic barriers are perceived to be lower as internationalization proceeds. These stages are often tied to hypotheses on the learning of firms. At each stage, the firm acquires knowledge of the market, or it can transfer lessons learned in one foreign market to another (Newbould *et al.*, 1978).

It is obvious that internationalization patterns are influenced by the previous stages in the internationalization of the company. The key barriers identified in stage models are the lack of knowledge and of resources, and thus their applicability to smaller firms is likely to be stronger. As such, barriers to internationalization as seen by a small inexperienced firm will be easily overcome by a well-established transnational (Vermeulen and Barkema, 2002). This means that different firms enter a market in different ways and at different moments in time. This is acknowledged by proponents of the Uppsala model who expect jumps in the establishment chain of firms with extensive experience in other foreign markets. The stages approach finds an echo in models of foreign market servicing because such models attempt to establish the conditions under which a firm will service a foreign market by a particular method (Telesio, 1979; Contractor, 1981). The generic methods are exporting, licensing, and foreign direct investment. Each of these methods has a variety of subtypes, and the interactions between the methods are, in practice, very important.

Exporting is separated from the other two main forms of foreign market servicing by the location factor in that the bulk of the value-adding activities takes place in the home and not in the foreign market. International licensing appears to combine the best of both worlds; that is, the advantage in technology and skills of the licensing transnational plus the local knowledge of the licensee. However, the same might be said of an international joint venture. The choice between licensing and direct investment is crucial in illustrating the choice between licensing, an external market solution, and direct investment, an internal solution (Buckley and Casson, 1976, 1981). The major motives for conducting foreign direct investment are market-oriented, cost-oriented and, for control of key inputs, either low-end (for example raw materials) or high-end (for example strategic assets).

Buckley and Casson (1976) used a cost–benefit analysis to suggest an internationalization path. Their claim was that, in normal conditions, the fixed costs associated with licensing are lower than those resulting from FDI. They are, however, higher than exports because of the need to guarantee that the licensing agreements are respected by the licensees. Since the opposite happens with variable costs, market-servicing tends to follow the sequence: exporting–licensing–FDI. Buckley and Casson (1981) added that the switch in modes of market servicing is also affected by the life-cycle of the product, the firm's familiarity with the foreign market, and the firm's degree of internationalization.

Vernon and his followers at Harvard were the first to acknowledge the relevance of trade theories to help explain MNE activity. Vernon used the product life-cycle to explain the foreign activities of TNCs (Vernon 1966). His starting point was that in addition to immobile natural endowments and human resources, the propensity of countries to engage in trade also depended on their capability to upgrade these assets or to create new ones, notably technological capacity (Dunning, 1992). In order to introduce the dynamics of technological change into the Heckscher–Ohlin model, the product life-cycle theory was applied to international capital flows. It was argued that firms based in high-wage countries had a greater propensity to develop new products because of high per capita incomes and high unit labour costs in their home economy. The model suggested that when a new product was developed, a firm normally chose a domestic production location, because of the need for close contact with customers and suppliers, because of uncertainties concerning the production and because of low price elasticity of the product. As a product matures, the technology becomes more difficult to protect and as price elasticity grows, long-run production runs based on established technology become possible. The firm will begin to look for lower-cost production locations in other industrialized countries with bigger market opportunities. The decision to invest is seen as a strategy to sustain technological and managerial advantages before they become diffused in overseas markets. Vernon's original article (1966), for instance, focused on postwar US investment in Europe. When it became economic for US companies to invest abroad, Western Europe was the preferred choice of location since demand patterns were close to the USA and labour costs were relatively low at that time. When the product enters its standardized phase, the lowest-cost supply point becomes a priority, and production can be transferred to developing countries, replacing exports from the parent company or even exporting back to the country of origin (Vernon, 1966). The third stage of evolution is referred to as the standardized product stage. Both the product and the production process are now completely standardized, while there is pressure to be price competitive in the face of this increased competition. In order to decrease the product's price, production costs must be reduced, particularly if the process is labour-intensive. Because the product and the production process are standardized, the company can now relocate manufacturing operations to a low labour-cost country. The strategy is to serve both the home and developed countries' markets from these developing countries.

Although the international trade literature on FDI has developed separately from development economics, it embodies a host of implications for economic and social development. Essentially, these implications derive from the fact that international trade theory tends to assume that market forces ensure an efficient allocation of resources internationally to maximize welfare. The point of departure for arguing that FDI is welfare-enhancing is that some countries are well-endowed with conditions conducive to certain types of FDI. Roughly, developing countries will attract capital in labour-intensive or natural-resources-intensive sectors, as these are the sectors where they enjoy comparative advantages *vis-à-vis* industrialized countries. An international relocation of capital and productive resources in these sectors will enhance global welfare and facilitate the process of adjustment in both the host and the home country. The inflow of capital to developing countries will make more investment capital available and thus speed up development, and it will provide badly needed foreign exchange. Moreover, by providing a bundle of well-tried and tested managerial skills and technology, FDI will enable the host country to exploit its comparative advantages more efficiently. The most important effect on developing countries will, according to this perspective, be that FDI is trade-enhancing, in that FDI will enhance production and export capacity.

The product life-cycle theory of FDI introduced dynamics to the theory of comparative advantage, arguing that developing countries will enjoy comparative advantages with regard to mature and especially standardized products. Consequently, technology transfer through FDI will mainly take place where the products that the technologies are associated with are in the mature stages of the product cycle. This process favours developing countries in that they would get access to technologies without experiencing the mistakes and costs associated with the introduction of new products. Moreover, the product-cycle theory predicts that TNCs might assist developing countries in getting access to international markets. Mature products are subject to significant barriers to entry, especially at the marketing stage, and TNCs can help developing economies overcome these barriers. The influence of Vernon's original model goes way beyond its original application to the development of US direct investment in Europe and in the cheap labour countries, and beyond Vernon's own Mark II appraisal of its usefulness (1979) in response to critics (Giddy, 1978). The dynamics of the model lies in the interaction of the evolving forces of demand patterns and production possibilities. The twin rationales of cost imperatives and market pull are simply explained in Vernon's model. In some ways, its simple yet powerful dynamic, resting on the interaction of demand and supply over time, has never been improved (Buckley, 1993; Buckley and Casson, 1981).

A group of Vernon's doctoral students, notably Knickerbocker (1973), Graham (1978) and Flowers (1976), argued that the spatial distribution of the economic activity of firms resulted from their strategic response to locational variables and to the anticipated behaviour of their competitors. Knickerbocker (1973) argued that oligopolists would normally follow each other into new and foreign markets to safeguard their own commercial interests. This so-called bandwagon effect can be triggered not only by decisions of competitors but also of customers deciding to establish themselves in a certain market. Empirical evidence supports the follow-the-leader idea that FDI is subject to bunching. For instance, an analysis of FDI by US TNCs in European manufacturing industry in the 1960s seemed to support the hypothesis (Flowers, 1976). There has also been a stampede of Japanese TNCs in the US and European auto and consumer electronics industries (De Beule and Van Den Bulcke, 2001). Graham's (1978) tit-for-tat hypothesis is that a TNC, which found its home country invaded by a foreign TNC, would retaliate by penetrating the invader's home market.

An organizing framework – incorporating different theoretical approaches – has been put forward by Dunning in his eclectic paradigm in which he attempts to explain all forms of international investment (Dunning, 1979, 1993, 2001). The eclectic paradigm maintains that firms will engage in international production if they possess ownership advantages in a particular market to overcome the liability of foreignness; if an enterprise perceives it to be in its best interest to add value to these ownership advantages rather than to sell them to foreign firms; and if locational advantages make it more profitable to exploit these assets in a particular foreign location rather than at home.

In explaining the growth of international production, several strands of economic and business theory assert that this is dependent on the investing firms possessing some kind of unique and sustainable competitive advantage (or set of advantages) relative to that (or those) possessed by their foreign competitors. Since the 1960s, the extant literature has come to identify three main kinds of firm- or ownership-specific competitive advantages. A first set are those competitive advantages relating to the possession and exploitation of monopoly power, as initially identified by Hymer (1976) and Bain (1956) and the industrial organization scholars (Caves, 1971, 1980; Porter, 1980, 1985). These advantages stem from some kind of barrier to entry in final product markets to (potential) competitors.

A second set of ownership advantages consist of a bundle of scarce, unique and sustainable resources and capabilities, which essentially reflect the superior technical efficiency of a particular firm relative to those of its competitors. The identification and evaluation of these advantages has been one of the main contributions of the resource-based (Wernerfelt, 1984; Dierickx and Cool, 1989; Barney, 1991; Conner, 1991; Conner and Prahalad, 1996; Montgomery, 1995) and evolutionary theories of the firm (Nelson and Winter, 1984; Cantwell, 1989, 1994; Dosi *et al.*, 1988; Dosi *et al.*, 2002; Saviotti and Metcalfe, 1991; Teece *et al.*, 1997).

The basis of the resource-based view of the firm is that it is the heterogeneity, rather than the homogeneity of its resources that give each firm its unique character. As such, resource-based views of the firms tend to see differences across companies as the result of differences in efficiency, rather than differences in market power (Montgomery, 1995). In explaining these differences, resource-based theorists tend to focus on resources and capabilities that are long-lived and difficult to imitate (Conner, 1991). In the resource-based view history matters, profits are persistent, and change most often occurs slowly and incrementally (Peteraf, 1991).

The evolutionary theory of the firm has a similar focus but pays more attention to the process or path by which the specific ownership advantages of firms evolve and are accumulated over time (Dunning, 2000). In contrast, or in addition to internalization theory, it tends to regard the firm as an innovator to promote its long-term prosperity, rather than an organiser of transactions to optimize the efficiency of existing resources. Evolutionary theory is, a dynamic theory, which, seeks to explain the diversity of firms. It thereby concentrates on the firm's long-term strategy towards asset-protection and augmentation, and the implications for its routines and the development of their dynamic capabilities (Nelson and Winter, 1984; Teece *et al.*, 1997).

A third kind of firm-specific advantages are those relating to the competencies of the managers of firms to identify, evaluate and harness resources and capabilities from all over the world, and to coordinate these in a way which best advances the long-term interests of the firm. Organizational scholars have stressed that these advantages tend to be management-specific rather than firm-specific (Prahalad and Dox 1987, Bartlett and Ghoshal 1989). While the focus of interest is similar to that of the resource and evolutionary theories, the emphasis of organizational-related theories is on the capabilities of management to orchestrate and integrate the resources it can internally upgrade or innovate, or externally acquire, rather than on the resources themselves. The objective is assumed to be as much directed to the growth of assets as to optimizing the income stream from a given set of assets (Dunning, 1998).

The eclectic paradigm has also included location advantages of countries as a key determinant of the foreign investment of transnational corporations. Location advantages include the spatial distribution of natural and created resource endowments and markets, input prices, quality and productivity (for example labour, energy, materials, components, semi-finished goods), economic system and strategies of government, such as commercial, legal, educational, transport and communication provisions, as well as ideological, language, cultural, business and political differences (Dunning, 1981, 1988, 1992; Ghoshal, 1987).

While the observation that location-specific characteristics matter to firms is hardly novel (Smith, 1776; von Thünen, 1826; Marshall, 1890), for the most part neither the economics nor the business literature has given much attention to how the emergence and growth of the cross-border activities of firms might be explained by the kind of location-related theories which were initially designed to explain the location of production within a nation state; nor to how the spatial dimension of FDI might affect the competitiveness of the investing companies.

There have been numerous geographical theories of particular value-added activities of firms and of geographical distribution of FDI. They include the location component of Vernon's product-cycle theory (1966), Knickerbocker's 'follow-my-leader' theory (1973), which was one of the earliest approaches to analysing the bunching effect of FDI, and Rugman's risk-diversification theory, which suggested that TNCs normally prefer a geographical spread of FDI to having all their eggs in the same geographic basket (1975, 1979). However, researchers extended, rather than replaced standard theories of location to encompass cross-border value-added activities. In particular, they embraced new location advantages such as exchange rates, political risks and inter-country cultural differences, and placed a different value on a variety of variables common to both domestic and international location choices such as wage levels, demand patterns, policy-related variables, supply capacity and infrastructure. These add-on or re-valued variables could be easily accommodated within the existing analytical theories (Dicken, 1998).

The emergence of the knowledge-based global economy and asset-augmenting FDI is compelling scholars to take a more dynamic approach to both the logistics of the location of corporate activities, and to the competitive advantages of nations and regions (Dunning, 1998). Firms need to take account not only of the presence and cost of traditional factor endowments, of transport costs, of current demand levels and patterns, and of Marshallian types of agglomerative economies; but also of distance-related transaction costs (Storper and Scott, 1987), of dynamic externalities, knowledge accumulation, and interactive learning (Enright, 1990, 1998, 2000; Florida, 1995; Malmberg, Sölvell *et al.*, 1996), of spatially related innovation and technological standards (Antonelli, 1998; Sölvell and Zander, 1998; Frost, 1998), of the increasing dispersion of created assets, and of the need to conclude cross-border augmenting and asset-exploiting alliances (Dunning, 1995, 1998). As such, since 1990, location has been taken up in explaining the stickiness of certain locations in an increasingly slippery world (Markusen, 1994). Theories suggest that firms may be drawn to the same locations because proximity generates positive externalities or agglomeration effects. Economists have proposed agglomeration effects in the form of both static (pecuniary) and dynamic (technological) externalities to explain industry localization (Baptista, 1998). Theoretical attempts to formalize agglomeration effects have focused on three mechanisms that would yield such positive feedback loops: inter-firm technological spillovers, specialized labour, and intermediate inputs (Marshall, 1890).

A distinction should be made between two broad types of agglomeration economies. One type relates to general economies of regional and urban concentration that apply to all firms and industries in a particular location. Such external economies lead to the emergence of manufacturing belts or metropolitan regions (Porter and Sölvell, 1997). These urbanization economies do not consist of increased efficiency of the enterprises themselves but of reduced transport and search costs for the customers and, therefore, lead to more customers than the individual enterprise would have been able to attract (Pedersen, 1997). A second type of agglomeration refers to localization economies. As advances in transportation and information obliterate distance, cities and regions face a tougher time attracting and anchoring income-generating activities (Markusen, 1996). Economists, geographers and economic development planners have sought for more than a decade for alternative models of development in which activities are sustained or transformed in ways that maintain relatively high wage levels, social contributions and quality of life. They have searched for 'sticky places' in 'slippery space' (Markusen, 1996), examining the structure and operation of these geographic concentrations of interconnected companies and institutions.

One extensively researched formulation is that of the flexibly specialized industrial district. In the original formulation of the industrial district, Marshall (1890) envisioned a region where the business structure is comprised of small, locally owned firms that make investment and production decisions locally. Scale economies are relatively minimal, forestalling the rise of large firms. Within the district, substantial trade is transacted between many small firms buying and selling from each other for eventual export from the region. What makes the industrial district so special and vibrant, in Marshall's account, is the existence of a pooled market for workers with specialized skills, the provision of specialized inputs from suppliers and service-providers, and the relatively rapid flow of business-related knowledge between firms, which result in what are now called technological spillovers.

All of these factors are covered by the notion of agglomeration, which suggests that the stickiness of a place resides not in the individual location calculus of firms or workers, but in the external economies available to each firm from its spatial conjunction with other firms and suppliers of services. In Marshall's formulation, it was not necessary that any of these actors should be consciously cooperating with each other in order for the district to exist and operate as such. But in a more recent adaptation (Piore and Sabel, 1984), based on the phenomenon of successful expansion of mature industries in the so-called 'Third Italy' (Goodman and Bamford, 1989), and extended to other venues in Europe and the United States (Scott, 1988; Storper, 1989; Paniccia, 1998), researchers have argued that concerted efforts to cooperate among district members to improve district-wide competitiveness can increase the stickiness of the district. While agglomeration economies signal external economies passively obtained by enterprises located close to each other, collective efficiency (Schmitz, 1989; Pedersen, 1994) indicates advantages which enterprises may achieve through active collaboration. Localized information flows, technological spillovers and specialized pools of knowledge and skills will ensure the revitalization of these seedbeds of innovation in these clusters. Clusters are considered as networks of production of strongly interdependent firms, knowledge-producing agents and customers linked to each other in a value-adding production chain (OECD, 1999).

However, many of the faster-growing regions of the world turn out not to be formed by small, locally owned, vertically or horizontally specialized enterprises. There exist regions where a number of key firms or facilities act as anchors or hubs to the regional economy. These clusters are dominated by one or several large, locally headquartered firms, in one or more sectors, surrounded by smaller and less-powerful suppliers. These hub-and-spoke districts thrive on market power and strategy rather than on networking (Gray *et al.*, 1996; Markusen, 1996). Yet a third variant of rapidly growing industrial districts may be termed satellite platforms (Markusen, 1996), a congregation of branch plant facilities of externally based firms. Tenants of satellite platforms may range from routine assembly functions to relatively sophisticated research. They stand alone, and are detachable spatially from either up- or downstream operations within the same firm or from agglomerations of competitors and external suppliers or customers (Glasmeier, 1988).

Another way of discerning different clusters is based on the origin of the industry in a specific location: indigenous or transplanted. Some industries grew up as indigenous industries and were afterwards exposed to a globalizing economy of increasing levels of international trade and investment. In the beginning, indigenous (hub-and-spoke) clusters are characterized by tightly linked local firms and a relatively small numbers of foreign-owned subsidiaries. Over time, the number of foreign subsidiaries in indigenous industries increases because of the globalizing economy. More specifically, successful industries attract transnationals that set up or acquire local companies to have access to the available strategic assets. Other industries originate as a direct result of the increasing levels of international trade and investment between countries and regions. These transplanted (satellite platform) industries are originally characterized by a limited number of local firms and by (relatively many) foreign branch plants that are rather weakly embedded in the local economy. Transplanted industries are likely to continue to rely on their parent company or network members for key supplies or core technologies for some time, and will only slowly develop strong 'local' ties, set up R&D units, and grow to become clusters. Alternatively, the virtuous circle of economic development by embedding foreign plants in the local economy does not materialize and the agglomeration of firms remains a satellite district. One would expect to find the relatively high value-adding subsidiaries in industry cluster locations, because they are attractive locations for foreign-owned subsidiaries, both in terms of the opportunities for learning and knowledge transfer and in terms of the specialized inputs and labour they provide. They can be seen as 'tapping into' the sources of knowledge and ideas, and scientific and technical talent which are embedded in cutting-edge regional innovation complexes (Florida, 1995). There will obviously also be foreign subsidiaries in non-cluster locations, but they are more likely to be of the market-seeking or resource-seeking types (cheap factors of production), rather than the higher value-adding subsidiaries in industry clusters.

In summary, these contemporary economic events suggest that the nature and composition of a country or region's comparative advantage, which has always been based on the possession of a unique set of immobile natural resources and capabilities, is now more geared to a distinctive and nonimitable set of location-bound created assets and the presence of strong indigenous firms with which foreign TNCs can form alliances to exploit or complement their own core competencies (Dunning, 1996). Nation states are not only becoming increasingly dependent on the cross-border activities of their own and foreign-based corporations for their economic prosperity (Porter, 1996; UNCTAD, 1997; De Beule and Van Den Bulcke, 2004), but the competitiveness of these corporations is increasingly determined by the institutional framework in which they operate (Oliver, 1997). In particular, both national governments and sub-national authorities are recognizing the need to provide the appropriate factor inputs, both for their own firms to generate the ownership-specific assets consistent with the demands of world markets, and for foreign subsidiaries to engage in the kind of value-adding activities which advance both the technological efficiency and the dynamic comparative advantage of the immobile assets (Porter, 1994; Peck, 1996; Dunning, 1998).

The present

The current argument (Buckley, 2002) is that the collective international business research project has been the statement of, and then the successful engagement with, a series of big research questions. These research questions are essentially empirical issues in the world economy, which can be listed as follows:

- Explaining the flows and impact of FDI, particularly flows of FDI from USA to Europe, with a lesser concentration on flows to less-developed countries.
- The explanation of the existence, strategy and organization of transnationals. The dominant paradigms of explanation are the internalization approach, Dunning's OLI framework and resource-based theories of the firm. Incompatibilities between these approaches are not completely resolved.
- 'New' forms of operation – international joint ventures (IJVs) and alliances. The twofold division of explanation between internalization/ transaction-cost views and resource-based 'strategic' analysis have been reconciled by many authors, but difficulties in compatibility remain given the different backgrounds and hypotheses.

These three phases of successful research endeavour are neither temporarily distinct, nor fully resolved. However, they represent a distinct intellectual achievement of considerable coherence and power. Furthermore, they fed (and feed) back into other disciplines and succeeded in exporting international business concepts to other areas of social science. The concern now is that the international business research community may be an importer of concepts, techniques and results and only a minor exporter. This is a good measure of an academic discipline's worth and standing.

The future: the new big question?

There are a number of candidates for the new big empirical question to form the core of a collective research programme. They include globalization, geography and location, international mergers and acquisitions (M&A), and new international institutions (for example non-governmental organizations, NGOs).

Globalization is an obvious candidate. However, its meaning, effects and dynamic are much debated and much misunderstood, and it is in danger of becoming the cliché of our times (Kobrin, 2001). Globalization implies inter-connectedness, networks of relationships between a large number of hetero-geneous social, cultural, political and economic organizations. The spatial reach and density of global and transnational interconnectedness weave complex webs of networks of relations between communities, states, inter-national institutions, non-governmental organizations and transnational corporations (Held *et al.*, 1999).

Globalization is currently blamed for much of what goes wrong in developed as well as developing countries. Protests against globalization or, before, internationalization, and transnationals are not new. TNCs typically have been criticized for specific reasons, and while specific criticism of transnationals persists, much of the current concern is more general. Today, more and more anti-globalization and anti-multinational campaigners are treating transnationals, and the policies that supposedly give them free reign, as the root cause of political injustices around the globe (Klein, 2002). Although this wave of protest may resonate more broadly than those of the past, this widespread concern about the process of globalization and the role of TNCs is less than explicit.

The international business research community is in a good position to provide clarity and elucidation. The big problem here is achieving coherence in the absence of agreed definitions, scope, empirics and future agenda. There is also much incursion into traditional international business research space by outsiders. An overarching paradigm of the types listed above is not currently available, or, more accurately, not currently agreed upon. If con-sensus were agreed in the conversations of international business scholars, then there is much promise in this area and an opportunity to recolonize lost areas of research space.

Similarly, renewed attention to the role of economic geography holds a great deal of promise. It is paradoxical that spatial issues have receded in a subject that is centrally concerned with geography (of nations, of compa-nies, of technologies, of transactions, of people). Recent work on 'active subsidiaries' of TNCs, on the locational aspects of technology and innova-tion, on the role of states and on the neglected aspects of migration and (differential) demography point to a renaissance in this area which can rein-vigorate international business.

On a more micro strategic level, the analysis of international M&As has much promise. This also entails the restructuring of existing TNCs. It can interface with both analyses of FDI and of joint ventures and alliances as sub-stitutes or complements to M&A activity. Perhaps this field like its empirical focus moves in waves!

To date, most of the literature on the internationalization of firms has focused on the steady onward, deepening involvement of international business operations (Benito and Welch, 1997, Buckley, 1996). Admittedly, transnationals are by their very nature in a continuous state of flux. Change is endemic in such enterprises but the precise form change takes may well vary from one part of the firm (MNE) to another. At any one time, some parts may be growing rapidly, others may be stagnating, and still others may be in steep decline. Change itself may be the result of a planned strategy of adjustment to changing internal and external circumstances or the 'knee-jerk' response to a sudden crisis. Whatever its origin, however, corporate restructuring will have a specific spatial expression. The changes that occur within the TNC itself will be projected into particular kinds of impact on the localities in which the company locates, relocates, expands or contracts.

Finally, the role of new institutions in the global economy such as NGOs may be an interesting research focus (Doh and Teegan, 2003) requiring new techniques and data-sets. The intervention of NGOs in MNE/government debate is clearly increasing and this strand of research integrates well with the interest in corporate and business ethics.

In the spirit of 'place your bets', the latter two areas will probably thrive as sub areas, but are not sufficiently all-encompassing to be a 'big question' which engages the majority of the international business academic community. Concerns remain that globalization research will fragment rather than unify a research conversation in international business. The economic geography route will revitalize whole areas of our research, and in combination with an analytical examination of globalization may well provide our next 'big question' – 'How do globalization and location interact in the world economy?'.

Questioning the big-question approach

Naturally, not everyone agrees. Sullivan and Daniels (2004) feel that research in international business is evolutionary, not episodic, and that the approach expressed in the foregoing pages is unduly restrictive in its partitioning into discrete episodes. Others feel that the distinctive nature of international business research lies in its unique mix of qualitative and quantitative tools and that the way forward is to develop new research tools. There is also a view that comparative management and the analysis of cultural differences lies at the heart of international business research.

A widely held view is that international business represents a 'melting pot' and that a unique contribution lies in the ability of international business researchers to see the big picture. This comparative advantage based on connectivity is evidenced by the wide range of research methods and the scope of the subject. The research boundaries of international business research should go beyond the firm, beyond the TNC and into its impact beyond the firm – economic, political and cultural. The ethical issues of globalization and the relationship of the firm with other institutions such as NGOs should be within its purlieu.

Is this enough? The above arguments do encompass some of the key attractions of international business as a research area. To them could be added new factors, which have not, as yet, become integral parts of the melting pot, such as demography and migration. In addition there are areas which were once central to international business but which now seem to have fallen by the wayside, such as finance.

However, international business is at its most successful when it is a collective enterprise, to inspire a collective conversation, there has to be agreement as to what constitutes the core of that conversation – the big question again.

The big picture

Three key areas suggest themselves as future (and imminent) research questions around which international business scholars can engage. They are globalization and development, the strategy of TNCs in a globally integrating world, and economic geography and business.

The first question enables international business scholars to return to the centre of policy-orientated research in economic growth and development, focusing on the analysis of the direct and indirect (spillover) benefits and disadvantages of FDI, particularly its impact on poorer less-developed countries and on the distribution of income within and between countries. The second enables 'new MNE strategy' to be analysed in that formidable set of concepts which has recently been developed (and, it must be said, imported) by international business scholars to include notions of flexibility, real options, globally integrated production and distribution systems. These concepts, integrated within a systems-theory approach, allow full attention to be paid to dynamics and it is possible to envisage the reintegration of finance theory into this set of tools. Finally, the renewed attention paid to geography, location and locationally fixed factors (to include culture) can anchor the analysis in the reality of the global economy with its endowments of fixed and locationally mobile factors that determine the 'stickyness' or 'slipperyness' of the activities of TNCs.

Conclusion

The suggested research agenda is rich, flexible, empirically tractable and policy-relevant. It should enable international business research to regain its former success and saliency. The fundamentals of the analysis are familiar: institutions (and new institutions), culture, resource endowments (both fixed and mobile) and spatial issues. The recombination of these elements in a dynamic fashion represents a challenging way forward for international business researchers.

References

Anderson, E. and Gatignon, H. (1986) 'Modes of Foreign Entry: Transaction Costs and Propositions', *Journal of International Business Studies*, 17(3): 1–26.

Antonelli, C. (1998) 'The Dynamics of Localized Technological Changes. The Interaction between Factor Costs Inducement, Demand Pull and Schumpeterian Rivalry', *Economics of Innovation and New Technology*, 6(2–3): 97–120.

Bain, J.S. (1956) *Barriers to New Competition*. Cambridge, MA: Harvard University Press.

Baptista, R. (1998) 'Clusters, Innovation, and Growth', in P. Swann, M. Prevezer and D. Stout (eds), *The Dynamics of Industrial Clustering: International Comparisons in Computing and Biotechnology*. Oxford: Oxford University Press, pp. 13–51.

Barnet, R. and Müller, R. (1974) *Global Reach: The Power of the Multinational Corporations*. New York: Simon & Schuster.

Barney, J. (1991) 'Firm Resources and Sustained Competitive Advantage', *Journal of Manangement*, 17(1): 99–120.

Bartlett, C.A. and Ghoshal, S. (1989) *Managing Across Borders: The Transnational Solution*. Boston, MA: Harvard Business School Press.

Benito, G.R.G. and Welch, L.S. (1997) 'De-internationalization', *Management International Review*, 37(2): 7–25.

Blomström, M. (1991) *Host Country Benefits of Foreign Investment*. Stockholm, Stockholm School of Economics.

Blomström, M. and Kokko, A. (1996a) *The Impact of Foreign Investment on Host Countries: A Review of the Empirical Evidence*. Washington, DC: World Bank.

Blomström, M. and Kokko, A. (1996b) *Multinational Corporations and Spillovers*. London: Centre for Economic Policy Research.

Blomström, M., Kokko, A. *et al.* (1994) 'Host Country Competition, Labor Skills, and Technology Transfer by Multinationals', *Weltwirtschaftliches Archiv* 130(3): 521–33.

Blomström, M., Kokko, A. *et al.* (2000) *Foreign Direct Investment: Firm and Host Country Strategies*. Basingstoke: Palgrave Macmillan.

Blomström, M., Zejan, M. *et al.* (1992) *Host Country Competition and Technology Transfer by Multinationals*. Cambridge, MA: National Bureau of Economic Research.

Buckley, P.J. (1983) 'New Theories of International Business: Some Unresolved Issues', in Mark Casson (ed.), *The Growth of International Business*. London: George Allen & Unwin.

Buckley, P.J. (1985) 'Testing Theories of the Multinational Enterprise: A Review of the Evidence' in P.J. Buckley (ed.) *The Economic Theory of the Multinational Enterprise: Selected Papers*. London: Palgrave Macmillan, pp. 192–211.

Buckley, P.J. (1991) 'Kojima's Theory of Japanese Foreign Direct Investment Revisited', *Hitotsubashi Journal of Economics*, 32(2): 103–09.

Buckley, P.J. (1993) 'Contemporary Theories of International Direct Investment', *Revue Economique*, 44(4): 725–36.

Buckley, P.J. (1996) 'The Role of Management in International Business Theory: A Meta-Analysis and Integration of the Literature on International Business and International Management', *Management International Review*, 36(1): 7–54.

Buckley, P.J. (2002) 'Is the International Business Research Agenda Running out of Steam?' *Journal of International Business Studies*, 33 (2): 365–73.

Buckley, P.J. (2004a) *The Challenge of International Business*. London: Palgrave Macmillan.

Buckley, P.J. (ed.) (2004b) *What is International Business?* London: Palgrave Macmillan.

Buckley, P.J. and Casson, M. (1976) *The Future of the Multinational Enterprise*. London: Palgrave Macmillan.

Buckley, P.J. and Casson, M. (1981) 'The Optimal Timing of a Foreign Direct Investment', *Economic Journal*, 91(361): 75–87.

Calvet, A.L. (1981) 'A Synthesis of Foreign Direct Investment Theories and Theories of the Multinational Firm', *Journal of International Business Studies*, 12(1): 43–59.

Cantwell, J. (1989) *Technological Innovation and Multinational Corporations*. Oxford: Basil Blackwell.

Cantwell, J.A. (1991) 'A Survey of Theories of International Production', in C.N. Pitelis and R. Sugden (eds), *The Nature of the Transnational Firm*. London: Routledge.

Cantwell, J., Ed. (1994) *Transnational Corporations and Innovatory Activities*, United Nations Library on Transnational Corporations. London: Routledge.

Casson, M. (1987a) 'Transaction Costs and the Theory of the Multinational Enterprise', in P.J. Buckley and M. Casson (eds), *The Economic Theory of the Multinational Enterprise*. London: Palgrave Macmillan, pp. 113–43.

Casson, M. (1987b) *The Firm and the Market: Studies on Multinational Enterprise and the Scope of the Firm*. Oxford: Basil Blackwell.

Caves, R.E. (1971) 'International Corporations: The Industrial Economics of Foreign Investment', *Economica* 38(149): 1–27.

Coase, R. (1937) 'The nature of the firm', *Economica* 4(November): 386–405.

Conner, K.R. (1991) 'A Historical Comparison of Resource-based Theory and Five Schools of Thought within Industrial Organizational Economics', *Journal of Management* 17: 121–54.

Conner, K.R. and Prahalad, C.K. (1996) 'A Resource-based Theory of the Firm: Knowledge versus Opportunism', *Organisation Science*, 7(5): 477–501.

Contractor, F.J. (1981) *International Technology Licensing Compensation, Costs and Negotiation*. Lexington, MA: Lexington Books.

De Beule, F. and Van Den Bulcke, D. (2001) 'Industrial Clusters and Japanese Manufacturing Subsidiaries in the Belgian Small Open Economy', in D. Van Den Bulcke and A. Verbeke (eds), *Globalisation and the Small Open Economy*, New Horizons in International Business. London: Edward Elgar, pp. 159–89.

De Beule, F. and Van Den Bulcke, D. (2004) 'Multinationale ondernemingen: Hoofdacteurs van de globalisatie', *Tijdschrift voor Politieke Economie* 26(1): 90–123.

Dicken, P. (1998) *Global Shift: Transforming the World Economy*. London: Paul Chapman.

Dierickx, I. and Cool, K. (1989) 'Asset Stock Accumulation and Sustainability of Competitive Advantage', *Management Science* (35): 1504–13.

Doh, J.P. and H. Teegan (2003) *Globalization and NGOs*. Westport, Conn: Praeger.

Dosi, G., Freeman, C. *et al.* (1988) *Technical Change and Economic Theory*. London: Pinter.

Dosi, G., Nelson, R.R. *et al.* (2002) *The Nature and Dynamics of Organisational of Organizational Capabilities*. Oxford: Oxford University Press.

Dunning, J.H. (1979) 'Explaining Changing Patterns of International Production: In Defence of the Eclectic Theory,' *Oxford Bulletin of Economics and Statistics*, 41(4): 269–95.

Dunning, J.H. (1981) *International Production and the Multinational Enterprise*. London: Allen & Unwin.

Dunning, J.H. (1988) *Explaining International Production*. London: Unwin Hyman.

Dunning, J.H. (1992) 'Governments, Markets, and Multinational Enterprises: Some Emerging Issues', *International Trade Journal*, 7(1): 1–14.

Dunning, J.H. (1993) *Multinational Enterprises and the Global Economy*. Harlow, Essex: Addison-Wesley.

Dunning, J.H. (1995) 'The Role of Foreign Direct Investment in a Globalizing Economy', *Banca Nazionale del Lavoro Quarterly Review*, 48(193): 125–44.

Dunning, J.H. (1996) 'The Geographical Sources of the Competitiveness of Firms: Some Results of a New Survey', *Transnational Corporations*, 5(3): 1–29.

Dunning, J.H. and Narula, R. (1996) *Foreign Direct Investment and Governments: Catalysts for Economic Restructuring*. London and New York: Routledge.

Dunning, J.H. (1998) 'Globalization, Technological Change and the Spatial Organization of Economic Activity', in A.D. Chandler, Jr., P. Hagström and Ö. Sölvell (eds), *The Dynamic Firm: The Role of Technology, Strategy, Organisation and Regions*. Oxford: Oxford University Press.

Dunning, J.H. (2001) 'The Eclectic (OLI) Paradigm of International Production: Past, Present and Future', *International Journal of the Economics of Business*, 8(2): 173–90.

Enright, M. (1990) *Geographic Concentration and Industrial Organization*. Cambridge, MA: Harvard University Press.

Enright, M.J. (1998) Regional Clusters and Firm Strategy, in A. Chandler, P. Hagström and Ö. Sölvell (eds), *The Dynamic Firm: The Role of Technology, Strategy, Organization and Regions*. Oxford: Oxford University Press.

Enright, M.J. (2000) 'The Globalization of Competition and the Localization of Competitive Advantage: Policies towards Regional Clustering', in N. Hood and S. Young (eds), *The Globalization of Multinational Enterprise Activity and Economic Development*. London: Palgrave Macmillan.

Florida, R. (1995) 'Toward the Learning Region', *Futures*, 27(5): 527–36.

Flowers, E.B. (1976) 'Oligopolistic Reactions in European and Canadian Direct Investment in the United States', *Journal of International Business Studies* 7(2): 43–55.

Frost, T.S. (1998) 'The Geographic Sources of Innovation in the Multinational Enterprise: US Subsidiaries and Host Country Spillovers: 1980–1990', *Sloan School of Management*. Cambridge, MA: Massachusetts Institute of Technology.

Ghoshal, S. (1987) 'Global Strategy: An Organising Framework', *Strategic Management Journal*, 8: 425–40.

Giddy, I.H. (1978) 'The Demise of the Product Cycle Model in International Business Theory', *Columbia Journal of World Business*, 13(Spring): 90–7.

Glasmeier, A. (1988) 'Factors Governing the Development of High Tech Industry Agglomerations: A Tale of Three Cities', *Regional Studies*, 22(4): 287–301.

Goodman, E. and Bamford, J. (1989) *Small Firms and Industrial Districts in Italy*. London and New York: Routledge.

Graham, E.M. (1978) 'Transatlantic Investment by Multinational Firms: A Rivalistic Phenomenon', *Journal of Post Keynesian Economics*, (1): 82–99.

Gray, M., Golob, E. *et al.* (1996) 'Big Firms, Long Arms, Wide Shoulders: The "Hub-and-Spoke" Industrial District in the Seattle Region', *Regional Studies*, 30(7): 651–66.

Hallen, L. and Wiedersheim-Paul, F. (1993) 'Psychic Distance and Buyer—Seller Interaction', in P.J. Buckley and P. Ghauri (eds), *The Internationalisation of the Firm*. London: Dryden Press, pp. 244–60.

Hansen, M.W. (1998) *Transnational Corporations in Sustainable Development: An Appraisal of the Environmenal Implications of Foreign Direct Investment in Less Developed Countries*. Copenhagen: Copenhagen Business School.

Hedlund, G. and Kverneland, A. (1983) 'Are Entry Strategies for Foreign Markets Changing? The Case of Swedish Investments in Japan', in P.J. Buckley and P. Ghauri (eds), *The Internationalisation of the Firm: A Reader*. London: Dryden Press.

Held, D., McGrew, A. *et al.* (1999) *Global Transformations*. Stanford: Stanford University Press.

Hennart, J.F. (1982) *A Theory of Multinational Enterprise*. Ann Arbor, MI: Univerity of Michigan Press.

Hennart, J.F. (1991) 'The Transaction Cost Theory of the Multinational Enterprise', in C.-N. Pitelis and R. Sugden (eds), *The Nature of the Transnational Firm*. London and New York: Routledge, pp. 81–116.

Hill, C.W. and Kim, W.C. (1988) 'Searching for a Dynamic Theory of the Multinational Enterprise: A Transaction Cost Model', *Strategic Management Journal*, (9): 93–104.

Hill, C.W., Hwang, P. *et al.* (1990) 'An Eclectic Theory of the Choice of International Entry Mode', *Strategic Management Journal*, (11): 117–28.

Hymer, S. (1960) *The International Operations of National Firms: A Study of Direct Investment*. Cambridge, MA: MIT Press.

Hymer, S. (1968) 'La grande corporation multinationale: Analyse de certaines raisons qui poussent à l'intégration internationale des affaires', *Revue Economique*, 14(b): 949–73.

Hymer, S. (1970) 'The Efficiency (Contradictions) of Multinational Corporations', *American Economic Review*, 60(2): 441–8.

Hymer, S. (1976) *The International Operations of National Firms: A Study of Direct Investment*. Cambridge, MA: MIT Press.

Johanson, J. and Wiedersheim-Paul, F. (1975) 'The Internationalisation Process of the Firm: Four Swedish Cases', *Journal of Management Studies*, 12(3): 305–22.

Johanson, J. and Vahlne, J.E. (1977) 'The Internationalization Process of the Firm: A Model of Knowledge Development and Increasing Foreign Market Commitments,' *Journal of International Business Studies*, 8(1): 23–32.

Jones, G. (1996) *The Evolution of International Business*. London: Routledge.

Kindleberger, C.P. (1969) *American Business Abroad*. Cambridge, MA: MIT Press.

Klein, N. (2002) *No logo: De strijd tegen de dwang van de wereldmerken*. Rotterdam: Lemniscaat.

Knickerbocker, F.T. (1973) *Oligopolistic Reaction and the Multinational Enterprise*. Cambridge, MA: Harvard University Press.

Kobrin, S.J. (2001) 'Sovereignty@Bay: Globalization, Multinational Enterprise, and the International Political System', in A.M. Rugman and T.L Brewer (eds), *Oxford Handbook of International Business*. Oxford: Oxford University Press.

Kojima, K. (1973) 'A Macroeconomic Approach to Foreign Direct Investment', *Hitotsubashi Journal of Economics*, 14(1): 1–21.

Kojima, K. (1978) 'Direct Foreign Investment to Developing Countries: The Issue of Over-Presence', *Hitotsubashi Journal of Economics*, 19(1–2): 1–15.

Kojima, K. (1982) 'Macroeconomic versus International Business Approach to Direct Foreign Investment', *Hitotsubashi Journal of Economics, June* 23(1): 1–19.

Kojima, K. and Ozawa, T. (1984) 'Micro- and Macro-Economic Models of Direct Foreign Investment: Toward a Synthesis', *Hitotsubashi Journal of Economics*, 25(1): 1–20.

Kokko, A. (1994) 'Technology, Market Characteristics, and Spillovers,' *Journal of Development Economics*, 43(2): 279–93.

Lall, S. and Streeten, P. (1977) *Foreign Investment, Transnational and Developing Countries*. London and Basingstoke: Palgrave Macmillan.

Lipsey, R.E. (1999) *The Role of Foreign Direct Investment in International Capital Flows*. Cambridge, MA: NBER.

Luostarinen, R. (1979) *Internationalisation of the Firm*. Helsinki, Acta Acadamie Oeconomicae, Helsinki School of Economics.

Magee, S.P. (1977a) 'Information and the Multinational Corporation: An Appropriability Theory of Foreign Direct Investment', in J.N. Bhagwati (ed.), *The New International Economic Order*. Cambridge, MA: MIT Press.

Magee, S.P. (1977b) 'Multinational Corporations, the Industry Technology Cycle and Development', *Journal of World Trade Law*, 11(4): 297–321.

Malmberg, A., Sölvell, Ö. *et al.* (1996) 'Spatial Clustering, Local Accumulation of Knowledge and Firm Competitiveness', *Geografiska Annaler*, 78(2): 85–97.

Markusen, A. (1994) 'Studying Regions by Studying Firms', *The Professional Geographer*, 46: 477–90.

Markusen, A. (1996) 'Sticky Places in Slippery Space: A Typology of Industrial Districts', *Economic Geography*, 72(3): 293–313.

Marshall, A. (1890) *Principles of Economics*. London: Macmillan.

Montgomery, C.A. (1995) *Resource-Based and Evolutionary Theories of the Firm: Towards a Synthesis*. Dordrecht: Kluwer Academic Publishers.

Nelson, R. and Winter, S. (1984) *An Evolutionary Theory of Economic Change*. Cambridge, MA: Harvard University Press.

Newbould, G.D., Buckley, P.J. *et al.* (1978) *Going International: The Experience of Smaller Companies Overseas*. New York: John Wiley and Sons, Inc.

OECD (1999) *Boosting Innovation: The Cluster Approach*. Paris: OECD.

Oliver, C. (1997) 'Sustainable Competitive Advantage: Combining Institutional and Resource Based Views', *Strategic Management Journal*, 18: 697–713.

Ozawa, T. (1979) *Multinationalism: Japanese Style*. Princeton: Princeton University Press.

Paniccia, I. (1998) 'One, a Hundred, Thousands of Industrial Districts. Organizational Variety in Local Networks of Small and Medium-sized Enterprises', *Organization Studies*, 19(4): 667–700.

Peck, F.W. (1996) 'Regional Development and the Production of Space: The Role of Infrastructure in the Attraction of New Inward Investment', *Environment and Planning A*, 28(2): 327–39.

Pedersen, P.O. (1994) *Clusters of Enterprises within Systems of Production and Distribution: Collective Efficiency, Transaction Costs and the Economies of Agglomeration*. Copenhagen: Centre for Development Research.

Pedersen, P.O. (1997) 'Clusters of Enterprises Within Systems of Production and Distribution: Collective Efficiency, Transaction Costs and the Economies of Agglomeration', in M.P. Van Dijk and R. Rabellotti (eds), *Enterprise Clusters and Networks in Developing Countries*. London: CASS.

Peteraf, M.A. (1991) 'The Cornerstones of Competitive Advantage: A Resource-based View', *Strategic Management Journal*, 14: 179–91.

Piore, M.J. and Sabel, C.F. (1984) *The Second Industrial Divide*. New York: Basic Books.

Porter, M.E. (1994) 'The Role of Location in Competition', *Journal of the Economics of Business*, 1(1): 35–9.

Porter, M.E. (1996) 'Competitive Advantage, Agglomeration Economies, and Regional Policy', *International Regional Science Review*, 19(1–2): 85–94.

Porter, M.E. and Sölvell, Ö. (1997) 'The Role of Geography in the Process of Innovation and the Sustainable Competitive Advantage of Firms', in A.D. Chandler, Jr., Ö. Sölvell. and P. Hagström (eds), *The Dynamic Firm: The Role of Technology, Strategy, Organizations, and Regions*. Oxford: Oxford University Press.

Prahalad, C.K. and Doz, Y.L. (1987) *The Multinational Mission: Balancing Local Demands and Global Vision*. New York: Free Press.

Rosecrance, R. (1996) 'The Rise of the Virtual State', *Foreign Affairs* 75(4): 45–61.

Rugman, A.M. (1975) 'Motives for Foreign Investment: The Market Imperfections and Risk Diversification Hypothesis', *Journal of World Trade Law*, 9 (September–October): 567–73.

Rugman, A.M. (1979) *International Diversification and the Multinational Enterprise*. Lexington, MA: Lexington Books.

Rugman, A.M. (1980) 'Internalization as a General Theory of Foreign Direct Investment: A Re-Appraisal of the Literature', *Weltwirtschaftliches Archiv* 116(2): 365–79.

Saviotti, P.P. and Metcalfe, J.S. (1991) *Evolutionary Theories of Economic and Technological Change: Present Status and Future Prospects*. London: Harwood.

Schmitz, H. (1989) *Flexible Specialization. A New Paradigm of Small-scale Industrialization. Sussex*, Institute of Development Studies.

Scott, A.J. (1988) 'Flexible Production Systems and Regional Development: The Rise of New Industrial Space in North America and Western Europe', *International Journal of Urban and Regional Research*, 12: 171–86.

Smith, A. (1776) *An Inquiry into the Nature and Causes of the Wealth of Nations*. Oxford: Clarendon Press.

Sölvell, Ö. and Zander, I. (1998) 'International Diffusion of Knowledge: Isolating Mechanisms and the Role of the MNE', in A.D. Chandler, Jr., P. Hagström and Sölvell, Ö. (eds), *The Dynamic Firm: The Role of Technology, Strategy, Organization and Regions*. Oxford: Oxford University Press.

Storper, M. (1989) 'The Transition to Flexible Specialisation in the U.S. Film Industry: External Economies, the Division of Labour, and the Crossing of Industrial Divides', *Cambridge Journal of Economics*, 13(2): 273–305.

Storper, M. and Scott, A. (1987) 'The Wealth of Regions. Market Forces and Policy Imperatives in Local and Global Context', *Futures*, 27(5): 505–26.

Sullivan D.P. and Daniels, J.D. (2004) 'Defining International Business Through its Research', in P.J. Buckley (ed.), *What is International Business?* London: Palgrave.

Teece, D.J. (1981) 'The Multinational Enterprise: Market Failure and Market Power Considerations', *Sloan Management Review*, 22(3): 3–17.

Teece, D.J. (1982) 'Towards an Economic Theory of the Multiproduct Firm', *Journal of Economic Behavior and Organization*, March 3(1): 39–63.

Teece, D.J. (1985) 'Multinational Enterprise, Internal Governance, and Industrial Organization', *American Economic Review*, 75(2): 233–8.

Teece, D.J., Pisano, G. *et al.* (1997) 'Dynamic Capabilities and Strategic Management', *Strategic Management Journal* 18(7): 509–33.

Telesio, P. (1979) *Technology Licensing and Multinational Enterprise*. New York: Praeger.

Turnbull, P.W. (1987) 'A Challenge to the Stages Theory of the Internationalization Process', in P.J. Rosson and S.D. Reed (eds), *Managing Export Entry and Expansion*. New York: Praeger.

UNCTAD (1997) *World Investment Report, 1997: Transnational Corporations, Market structure and Competition Policy*. Geneva: United Nations.

Vermeulen, G.A.M. and Barkema, H.G. (2002) 'Pace, Rhythm and Scope: Process Dependence in Building a Profitable Multinational Corporation', *Strategic Management Journal*, 23(7): 637–53.

Vernon, R. (1966) 'International Investment and International Trade in the Product Cycle', *Quarterly Journal of Economics*, (80): 190–207.

Vernon, R. (1979) 'The Product Cycle Hypothesis in a New International Environment', *Oxford Bulletin of Economics and Statistics*, Nov. 41(4): 255–67.

von Thünen, J.H. (1826) *Der isolierte Staat in Beziehung auf Landwirtschaft und Nationalökonomie*. Jena: Fischer G.

Welch, L. and Luostarinen, R. (1988) 'Internationalization: Evolution of a Concept', *Journal of General Management*, 14(2): 34–55.

Wernerfelt, B. (1984) 'A Resource-based View of the Firm', *Strategic Management Journal*, (5): 272–80.
Williamson, O.E. (1975) *Markets and Hierarchies: Analysis and Antitrust Implications*. New York: The Free Press.
Williamson, O.E. (1979) 'Transaction Cost Economics: The Governance of Contractual Relations', *Journal of Law and Economics*, 22: 223–61.
Williamson, O.E. (1985) *The Economic Institutions of Capitalism*. New York: The Free Press.

Index